Paranormal People

The famous, the infamous and the supernatural

Paul Chambers

BLANDFORD

ACKNOWLEDGEMENTS

I am extremely grateful to the following people without whose help this manuscript would have been difficult to complete: Neil Dubé, Dr. Mark Biddis and various members of the Association for the Scientific Study of Anomalous Phenomena for their advice and discussions on matters of the paranormal. The same thanks also go to the various people, particularly the librarians, who have helped me within the Natural History Museum, Royal Astronomical Society, Society for Psychical Research, University College London, and Senate House Library. I would also like to thank Stuart Booth and Antonia Maxwell for their invaluable help and assistance in the production side of things at Cassell.

I would also like to say a big thankyou to Him Davy, Phil Dolding, Jon Finch, Colin Chifford, Clare Souter, Dawn Windley, Tim Hackwell, Emma Clowes and Ian Coles for their support and encouragement during the past few years. Thank you also to my nearest and dearest, Rachel Baxter and Sally, Martyn, Matthew and Francis Chambers, for their moral (and financial!) encouragement throughout the years.

A BLANDFORD BOOK

First published in the UK 1998 by Blandford

Cassell plc, Wellington House
125 Strand, London WC2R OBB

Text copyright ©1998 Paul Chambers

The right of Paul Chambers to be identified as the author of this work has been asserted by him under the provisions of the UK Copyright, Designs and Patents Act 1988.

Distributed in the United States by Sterling Publishing Co., Inc.,
387 Park Avenue South, New York, NY 10016-8810

A Cataloguing-in-Publication Data entry for this title is available from the British Library
ISBN 0-7137-2711-X (hardback)
      0-7137-2712-8 (paperback)

Designed by Richard Carr
Printed in Great Britain by Mackays of Chatam

CONTENTS

INTRODUCTION

F ROM OUR EARLIEST recorded history there have always been people who possess apparently paranormnal powers. The earliest evidence dates from 30,000-year-old cave paintings in northem Europe which indicate that our early ancestors used ceremonies and rituals as part of their belief systems. As with many modern animist cultures, it is likely that these ceremonies and rituals were presided over by, or even directed at, a central figure within the tribe who was credited with healing powers or the ability to commune directly with the spirits. Later, in biblical times, such people were revered as prophets, soothsayers or messiahs and were said to display a host of psychic abilities, including seeing the future, interpreting dreams, transmuting one solid object into another, healing and communicating with the spirit world. Centuries after this, people claiming or displaying such powers were persecuted, ostracized and even executed for being witches or devil-worshippers. From being seen as a spiritual threat, in more recent times certain psychic powers have become something of a mainstream form of entertainment. Attempts to turn gifted individuals into celebrities or even to base new religions around them have mostly ended in controversy and failure. Equally, the scientific community, freed in the nineteenth century from the restraints of the Church, has steadfastly ignored or campaigned against psychic individuals sometimes but not always with good reason.

Currently the range of psychic abilities and experiences being claimed by individuals are greater than ever before. New fields within the paranormal are opening up all the time and it is difficult to distinguish possibly genuine experiences from those that are caused by misunderstanding, deception or naïvety. In addition to this current diversification in paranormal phenomena, there are also thousands of cases that have been recorded by psychic researchers and other organizations over the last 150 years. The vast majority of these cases have never been properly investigated, for although the information necessary to do so often exists, the time and financial resources often do not. It is the aim of this book to introduce and analyse a wide range of the strange phenomena that have been experienced and reported by individuals. In an effort to avoid the dogmatic nature of many recent books on the subject, theories and opinions from all sides of the paranormal debate have been taken into account, thus allowing readers to make informed decisions about the plausibility of what is being described. Areas not often touched upon by conventional paranormal publications, such as unusual psychological disorders and the sensitive subject of frauds, are also included. As a result, this book provides a complete survey of the theories, observations and controversies that are associated with paranormal people and with the world of the paranormal as a whole.

PSYCHIC PHENOMENA

INTRODUCTION

M OST PEOPLE ARE familiar to varying degrees with what would be called telepathy, precognition or extrasensory perception (ESP). These experiences are normally small affairs such as thinking about a friend only moments before they telephone or dreaming about an event that occurs a few days later. Mostly, they are significant enough to be possible examples of coincidence.

The psychic powers discussed in this chapter are those associated with the human mind but not on the whole with other factors, such as discarnate entities, alien races, monsters, etc. These powers include telepathy, ESP, psychokinesis, psychometry, remote-viewing and precognition, all of which are not, as yet, recognized by science, although some psychology textbooks do now have entries related to them. Yet these are the psychic powers that some scientists find it possible to believe in over and above all other paranormal topics. Thus most of the laboratory-based research into the paranormal has concentrated on proving or disproving the existence of telepathy and ESP. Early experiments using apparently highly psychic people, such as Uri Geller and Doris Stokes, were abandoned, for despite some positive results the controversy generated did more damage than good. Instead, modern parapsychology laboratory experiments involve the repetition of simple tests, such as card-guessing, using ordinary people under strictly controlled conditions in order to try and get small but statistically significant results. This sort of painstaking work by people such as the late Charles Honorton has provided evidence in favour of the existence of ESP, although the statistical margins are still slim enough to permit scepticism.

As well as university parapsychology laboratories, the Cold War superpowers are alleged to have carried out extensive research into developing psychic powers as a potential military weapon. This research began in the Soviet Union in the mid-1950s and apparently produced a number of psychics with, among other things, strong psychokinetic powers. Film of these experiments and rumours of others prompted the CIA to begin a programme, entitled Operation Stargate, of its own. While information about these studies is classified, some of the subjects involved in Operation Stargate have come forward to give detailed descriptions of the remote-viewing aspect of the programme.

Remote-viewing subjects were trained to describe scenes they would expect to see at a given map reference. Initially, distinctive civilian locations, such as wind turbine farms, were used as targets. Success in this led the CIA to try friendly military targets and then eventually Eastern Bloc ones, although this has been officially denied. One of the most interesting conclusions from these experiments was the CIA's discovery that they could train almost anybody to become a successful remote-viewer. This runs contrary to many psychics' belief that their powers are inherited and therefore cannot be nurtured.

Operation Stargate's remote-viewing experiments were co-ordinated by Ed May and the results were evaluated by an American government committee. Their report was published in November 1995 and suggests that a statistically significant effect could be determined from the laboratory experiments. It also stated that no evidence of psychic powers having been used in espionage operations could be found – something that the remote-viewers from Operation Stargate disagree with. Other scientists have disagreed with the evaluation committee and claim not to be able to reproduce such results themselves.

Although remote viewing is rarely experienced by non-psychic people, examples of telepathy, ESP and precognition are apparently common events. Admittedly most people do not become aware of these, mostly minor, incidents unless they are looking for them, which is always an unsound way of researching such phenomena. Psychologists explain away apparent examples of precognition and telepathy (the most commonly reported psychic phenomena) as coincidence. Using precognitive dreams as an example, the theory is that the average human has between three and eight dreams a night, the subjects of which, over a long period of time, are bound to coincide with future events, such as aeroplane crashes, earthquakes, etc. Others counter this argument by producing literally thousands of examples of psychic phenomena which are so specific that the coincidence odds climb to astronomical levels.

The idea that the human mind is capable of producing and utilizing such powers does find favour among a minority of psychologists. They point out that the mind has learned to adapt to the existence of light and sound waves to produce three-dimensional sight and stereoscopic hearing, which have allowed the development of visual and oral communication between individuals. It is therefore possible that another, as yet unknown, factor has been utilized by the brain for psychic communication with each other or our surroundings.

Those who accept the existence of psychic powers have suggested that they are abilities that would have been commonly used in ancient times but are now dying out through lack of use. This is doubtful. The history of our species, *Homo sapiens*, is well known and in evolutionary time we are not that far removed from our ape ancestors. The split between our lineage and that of the chimpanzee occurred approximately 6 million years ago and we still share over 95 per cent of our genetic material with chimpanzees. If we had a common psychic ancestor one would expect to see evidence of psychic powers in modern primates, but this so far has not been the case. One of the main characteristics of our fossil lineage is the large increase in brain capacity that has occurred in the last 2.5 million years. The advancement of the brain has allowed the evolution of language, reasoned thought and artistic ability, most of which are thought to have developed in the last 40,000 years. It is doubtful that a useful tool like being able to communicate silently between people would be discarded by evolution. It is therefore perhaps more probable that psychic powers are a modern development as the result of an increased brain size and may even be the start of a new function within the human brain.

Those who still doubt the existence of hidden abilities within the brain should ask themselves whether, in a hypothetical society where everybody was blind, anybody would believe the descriptions given by a person who had developed the ability to see.

Gerard Croiset

❖

PSYCHOMETRY

GERARD CROISET WAS probably the most famous of all the psychic detectives in Europe. He is thought to have helped solve a number of important murder cases and was keen to promote the scientific study of his powers.

Born in 1909 in Holland, Croiset had an unhappy childhood. He was abandoned by his parents in 1917 and then moved from one foster home to another, until he was returned to his natural mother in 1920. He claims to have had a number of psychic experiences during childhood, including ones where he was able to tell people their life histories by simply handling their possessions. This ability is known as psychometry.

After a number of different jobs and failed enterprises, Croiset married but, through stress, suffered a nervous breakdown shortly afterwards. Not long after his recovery, he was visiting a watchmaker's workshop when he absent-mindedly picked up a ruler. Instantly a whole series of images flooded into his head concerning the watchmaker's youth. These turned out to be correct and Croiset's career as a clairvoyant took off from there. His reputation grew in Holland and, despite a number of premonitions which foretold World War II, he remained there when the Nazis invaded. Being half-Jewish, Croiset was sent to a concentration camp but was released soon after his arrival. He was later caught working for the Dutch resistance and was returned to the concentration camp, but was again released without harm. He survived the war and afterwards was present at a lecture on parapsychology given by Professor Tenhaeff of Utrecht University. Croiset befriended Tenhaeff and demonstrated his psychometric powers to him. Tenhaeff was impressed and the two began an earnest study into the phenomenon of psychometry.

The first involvement with the police occurred in March 1949, when Tenhaeff was asked to bring Croiset to a courtroom in Hertogenbosch. He was presented with two sealed boxes and asked to describe any impressions he got from them. Croiset was able to detect that one box contained a bloodstained shoe that had belonged to a girl who had been killed nine years previously. He then had a vision of two children cycling along a woodland path. In the scene a poacher deliberately knocked the children off their bicycles and strangled them. He said that tinfoil had been found nearby and that he thought the name 'Stevens' was involved. The police were astounded and confirmed that he had accurately described the murder scene and that they were currently holding a suspect whose name was Stevenson. Although Croiset had added nothing new to this crime, the police were impressed enough to use him again on other cases.

Croiset's fame gradually spread throughout Europe, so much so that in 1956 he moved to Utrecht to avoid publicity and to be closer to Professor Tenhaeff. On 11 December 1959 a Kansas professor, Walter Sandelius, contacted Tenhaeff to see if Croiset could help find his missing 24-year-old daughter, Carol. Sandelius spoke to Croiset by phone the next day. Croiset said to him, 'I see your daughter running over a large lawn and then crossing a viaduct. Now I see her at a place where there are shores, and near them a large body of water with landing stages and many small boats. I see her riding there in a lorry and a big red car.'

He confirmed that she was still alive and that the professor would hear something definite at the end of six days. On the sixth day Professor Sandelius went downstairs to phone Croiset again and was amazed to find his daughter sitting on the sofa. It turned out that she had run away from home to seek adventure but had returned when she had no more money. After quizzing her as to her whereabouts and movements, Sandelius found that Croiset's descriptions had been quite correct.

Croiset always refused payments for such cases. He would instead insist that people send a written report of what had happened to Professor Tenhaeff at Utrecht University. Despite his high profile in murder cases, he was often very reluctant to describe people he would clairvoyantly 'see' associated with a crime scene in case he accidentally implicated innocent people. In fact, Croiset claimed that it was very difficult for him to focus in on criminal suspects, whereas it was very easy for him to focus in on people who had deliberately or accidentally disappeared. To his dying day, he was never adequately able to describe the mechanisms behind his strange powers.

One of his most famous and controversial cases concerned a missing girl in Scotland. She was 17-year-old Pat McAdam, who, together with her friend Hazel Campbell, was hitchhiking from Glasgow to their home village of Annan on 19 February 1967. A lorry picked both girls up and, after a long stop in a service station during which Pat and the driver drank a number of whiskies, Hazel was dropped in Annan at 2 p.m. Hazel assumed that the driver was going to drop her friend off next, but Pat was never seen again. A nationwide hunt was launched which, three weeks later, produced the lorry driver, who claimed to have dropped Pat off on the outskirts of Dumfries. Despite a large number of sightings of the lorry, no firm evidence was ever found to implicate the driver or anybody else in the girl's disappearance. More crucially, Pat's body also remained missing.

A journalist who had followed the case from the beginning, Frank Ryan, was in Holland in early February 1970 when he decided to pay a visit to Croiset to see if he could uncover any new information concerning Pat's disappearance. After being shown a missing poster of the girl, he immediately sensed that a transport café had played a central part in the disappearance. He went on to describe a place with a river, fir trees and a bridge with grey tubular railings. On one side of the bridge was a cottage, with advertising signs and a white paling fence around it. He sketched the scene and warned Ryan not to publish any details yet.

Ryan took the description, the sketch and a photographer to a bridge that he thought matched Croiset's description. It didn't, but the photographer claimed to know of another bridge three miles away. When they arrived, Ryan stood in a state of shock. Croiset's description was identical to the scene he saw in front of him. He decided to inform the McAdam family about what he was doing and persuaded them to let him take Pat's Bible back to Holland with him.

On handling the Bible, Croiset immediately exclaimed 'She's dead!'. He went on to say that the body was trapped among some overhanging roots along the river near the site he had previously described. On a large-scale map, Croiset pinpointed a nearby cottage which would have a wrecked car in the garden with a wheelbarrow leaning against it.

On his return to Scotland, Ryan gathered together a group of witnesses and went in search of the cottage and the car. They found them exactly as Croiset had described. There was an old Ford Popular, converted into a henhouse, in the garden with a black wheelbarrow leaning against it. The police were immediately informed and, among the tree roots in the river bank, a woman's black dress, stockings and handbag were found. The discoveries made front-page news. However, further inquiries eliminated all the clothing from the case. Croiset was consulted again and this time said that although the body had been lodged in the tree roots, flood waters had swept it into the Solway Firth and that it would not be recovered. Pat McAdam's body was never found, although the lorry driver was later arrested and sentenced to 30 years' imprisonment for a different murder and a rape.

An interesting sideline to this case came in 1975, when the BBC interviewed Gerard Croiset about the case for a reconstruction they were filming. While being interviewed by the author Colin Wilson, Croiset claimed that he could see the murder and that the driver had killed Pat with a heavy spanner. He also claimed that the police had found the body. This was not true, for although a woman's body had been found in the area, it was definitely not Pat McAdam's.

One of Croiset's least successful, but very public, predictions occurred in late November 1979 when he was asked by the *Sun* newspaper for his impressions about the identity of the serial killer, the Yorkshire Ripper. The description he gave included statements that the killer lived in the centre of Sunderland and had a squashed nose and a limp. In the light of Peter Sutcliffe's arrest, all Croiset's information (and that of other psychics) was seriously wrong, but there again Croiset always claimed that he was never good at describing murderers.

This turned out to be one of his final predictions, for on 20 July 1980 Croiset died suddenly at the age of 71. Obituaries from around the world gave him credit for hundreds of solved crimes and likened him to a psychic Sherlock Holmes.

❖

Since his death, some authors have sought to question the validity of Croiset's claims. Most noticeable among these was Piet Hein Hoebens (who believes that all psychics are frauds). He has accused Croiset of stage trickery and claims to be able to reproduce many of Croiset's more mundane psychic feats, such as his stage trick of predicting the characteristics and life histories of people sitting in numbered chairs before they arrive at his public meetings. Hoebens also doubts the validity of many of Professor Tenhaeff's claims for Croiset. For example, he accuses Tenhaeff of publishing selective information and of adding details to certain cases. There does appear to be some evidence for this.

Despite these accusations, however, many of Croiset's cases were independently witnessed and some of his visions were published before any results that they confirmed came to light. Even with acknowledged successes such as the Pat McAdam case, Hoebens claims that Croiset could have paid an associate to fly over to Scotland to phone the descriptions back to him. Though possible, this is unlikely, as the first description was produced only hours after an unscheduled meeting between Croiset and Ryan.

There is no doubt that Croiset loved publicity and was very theatrical in his manner. Colin Wilson (in *The Psychic Detectives*) describes Croiset's personality like this: 'In spite of a rather dramatic manner, and his obvious love of the limelight, there was something sincere and childlike about him that made it impossible to dislike him.'

Croiset, like the majority of psychic detectives, claimed to use a psychic ability that has been dubbed psychometry. This is a clairvoyant power where a psychic claims to be able to see the past history of an object (or someone associated with it) simply by holding it. Naturally, the potential this has for aiding the police in their work is enormous and it is therefore not surprising that psychometrists have been asked to help, in an unofficial capacity, on some criminal cases. The standard procedure is to hand the psychometrist an object found at the crime scene or associated with the victim. The psychometrist then describes any impressions or visions connected with the object in the hope that they may shed light on the case.

Although there have been numerous instances of psychics volunteering information to the police about cases, the police rarely contact the psychics themselves. Psychometry has also been used in archaeology and other historical fields with great success.

As was true with Croiset, it can be very difficult to verify some of the claims made by psychometrists. Police forces will almost never confirm any accurate information given to them by psychic means for fear of ridicule, or the more serious possibility of being cross-examined on the subject in court. The latter would almost certainly lead to the collapse of a case.

In 1990, Detective Chief Superintendent Eddie Ellison discovered that there were no official reports of psychics having helped in British Metropolitan Police Special Operations Unit cases. Out of curiosity, he invited officers to volunteer any contributions to cases they had had from psychics. Despite assurances of anonymity, no one came forward. This lack of official confirmation renders the investigator almost totally reliant on the psychics' versions of events when dealing with the authorities. There are two problems associated with this. The first is that certain psychics have been known to exaggerate their contributions to solving cases. Although this is usually just embellishment, some psychics have made claims that have later turned out to be totally false. There was a video tape of a psychic allegedly predicting the assassination attempt on Ronald Reagan but it came to light only after the incident and later turned out to have been recorded hours after the shooting. There was also the case of a man who used a police band radio to get up-to-the-minute information about events and then phoned the details through to media organizations so that it looked as if he had predicted them minutes before they happened.

The second problem is that of accuracy. Some of the information given can be extremely vague and there is sometimes a tendency for psychics and their supporters to twist the predictions to fit the facts and vice versa. Croiset was more specific with his descriptions, and his psychometric readings were often witnessed by several people and subsequently turned out to be accurate. However, even the best-testified predictions would have much more weight behind them with official verification from the police.

This does not mean that psychometry cannot be proved without the authorities' help. Psychometry has not been widely studied under laboratory conditions, but it has been tested by many psychical researchers and organizations with some favourable results. The mechanisms that underpin its existence have only been guessed at so far. Madame Blavatsky (see page 127) maintained that the universe is permeated by a psychic ether that is capable of storing historical and future information. Thus accessing this ether would provide the history and future of an object. Other theories involve the use of telepathy to read a criminal's mind or Jung's theory of the collective unconscious.

The ability itself apparently comes in varying degrees. Some psychometrists seem to be capable of peeling back the layers of history associated with objects so that they can dip into its history at any point, while others can only sense the emotions associated with objects or their owners. Psychometrists like Croiset were able to receive detailed visions of actual scenes. As with many things in the psychic world, it has been noticed that psychometrists are best at picking up strong emotions, such as love, anger and sorrow, associated with objects and that recent events are stronger and easier to read than distant ones.

One final oddity is that some psychometrists have discovered their powers after a mental trauma or head injury. Croiset had a nervous breakdown in his youth and another powerful psychometrist, Peter Hurkos (on whose life Stephen King's book and film *The Dead Zone* were loosely based), fell off a ladder and hit his head.

Psychometry is a difficult concept to believe in, let alone explain, yet the evidence suggests that such a mental power does exist. Its connection with crime scenes and popular exponents such as Croiset ensure that public interest will remain considerable for some time yet.

Gef the Talking Mongoose

❖

POLTERGEIST

THE STRANGE AFFAIR of Gef the talking mongoose has caused much debate among psychic researchers. Does it represent a fraud, a genuine talking animal or a poltergeist phenomenon? Gef's antics attracted much publicity in the 1930s and helped in the gradual discrediting of psychic investigator Harry Price (see page 215). Although the case is now largely forgotten or ignored, it still makes for interesting reading.

It centres around a remote farmhouse at a place called Cashen's Gap on the west coast of the Isle of Man. The farm was owned and managed by James Irving, who, at the time of the haunting, was a 60-year-old retired commercial traveller. He was noted for his good humour and story-telling abilities. He lived with his wife, Margaret, and their 13-year-old daughter, Voirrey, who seems to have used the farm's isolation to immerse herself in extensive reading. She was particularly fascinated by wildlife and all things mechanical. The impression given by the newspaper reporters who met the family is that they seemed to be happy enough, honest and level-headed.

According to the account given by Harry Price, the haunting started in the summer of 1931 when the family heard scratching noises from behind the panelling of the farmhouse. These noises escalated to spitting sounds and the sound of an animal breathing heavily. James Irving naturally decided that an animal was responsible and laid down poison to kill it. When this had no effect, he spent a number of nights lying in wait for it with a shotgun, but this too failed. He seems to have started communicating with the elusive beast initially by making animal noises at it. When these were mimicked by the invisible guest, Voirrey tried singing nursery rhymes, only to find that these too were repeated back. Before long the animal began to show itself to the family, particularly to Mrs Irving and Voirrey. The creature was described by James Irving as being 'about the size of a three-parts-grown rat, without the tail, and able to squeeze through a one-and-a-half-inch hole. Its body was yellow like a ferret's, its long bushy tail was tinged brown and its face was shaped like that of a hedgehog.'

The strange creature began to talk normally and informed the family that it was a mongoose that had been born in Delhi on 7 June 1852. They christened it 'Gef'.

Gef would speak to the family in a shrill, high-pitched voice, often in what it claimed were different languages, including Spanish, Welsh and Russian. Gef would announce its presence by calling out the name of a member of the family and it also seemed to be capable of supernatural feats. For example, Gef could see in the dark and would describe the movements of people when the lights were out. It would often throw objects about the house and would hide things, only to make them reappear later on. It could describe people's actions that were taking place many miles away which, when checked by James Irving, would prove to be accurate. Throughout the whole affair, James Irving kept a detailed diary of events.

Gef's fame grew locally and it wasn't long before the mainland press got wind of the goings on at Cashen's Gap. In September 1931 the first journalists appeared at the farm. Despite coaxing and cajoling, Gef refused to either speak or show himself to all but one of the visiting reporters. The one reporter who did hear Gef speaking to Voirrey and Mrs Irving while he was some distance away initially described the voice thus: 'Had I heard a weasel speak? I do not know, but I do know that I've heard today a voice which I should never have imagined could issue from a human throat.'

He later followed this report up with another that seemed more doubtful about Voirrey's role in the affair, for although he could see Voirrey's lips during the whole time that Gef spoke, he does hint that Voirrey may have been subconsciously throwing her voice.

In early 1932 all the publicity drew the case to the attention of Harry Price, who, being wary of ridicule, sent a friend of his (given the pseudonym 'Captain Macdonald') to investigate the case. Macdonald arrived at the farm on 26 February and interviewed the family. Gef did not make an appearance until the investigator was about to leave for his hotel, at which point a shrill voice from inside the house shouted 'Go away! Who is that man?'. On his return the next day, Macdonald was shown some water trickling from a hole in the wall and was told by James Irving that this was Gef urinating. Later, while having tea, a needle bounced off the teapot and this was ascribed to Gef throwing things. Later still, Macdonald heard Gef talking to Voirrey and Mrs Irving while they were upstairs and he was downstairs. Macdonald tried to persuade Gef to show itself, but Gef replied, 'No, I don't mean to stay long as I don't like you!' Macdonald tried to creep up the stairs but trod on a loose floorboard, causing Gef to shout, 'He's coming!'. Gef said and did no more while Macdonald was around, so he returned to the mainland once more.

Ten days after Macdonald's departure, an old friend of the Irving family, John Northwood (another pseudonym), arrived at the farm to check that the family were surviving the onslaught of reporters. After some coaxing, Gef began talking to Northwood. The conversations would vary from strange almost idle chat to vicious accusations and threats. On hearing that Northwood's son Arthur was due to arrive at the farm, Gef became angry and shouted, 'Tell Arthur not to come. He doesn't believe. I won't speak if he does come. I'll blow his brains out with a thrupenny cartridge!'

Northwood visited a few days later with his sister-in-law and niece. Again Gef spoke, describing the contents of the sister-in-law's bag, although apparently this information was known by Voirrey. Afterwards Northwood wrote a favourable report to Price about the incidents. He seemed convinced that Gef was not a fraud by the Irvings but a genuine talking animal.

The press gradually lost interest in the case even though, according to James Irving's diaries, Gef became more active than ever. The farm was not proving very lucrative at the time and Gef apparently helped out the family by providing them with killed rabbits. This is suspect, as one of Voirrey's favourite games was to go rabbit-hunting with her pet dog. Gef would also provide other objects, such as paintbrushes and small items of clothing. In the house itself, Gef was credited with moving furniture around, singing songs and reading aloud from newspapers. Still very shy and retiring, he would demand that food be left for him on the crossbeams of the house so that he could eat at will.

Gef finally agreed to be photographed by Voirrey, but although several photographs were taken of it on a five-bar gate, none shows sufficient detail to determine whether the creature was a mongoose or even animate. In March 1935 Gef claimed to have plucked some of his own hair and left it on the mantelpiece. The photographs and the hair were forwarded to Captain Macdonald and from him to Harry Price. When Price received these objects, he dispatched Macdonald once more, who again heard Gef speak. An expert zoologist examined Gef's hairs and thought they had almost certainly come from a long-haired dog.

On 30 July 1935 Harry Price and a magazine editor, Richard Lambert, arrived at Cashen's Gap determined to see the evidence for themselves. They were to be disappointed, for on their arrival they were informed by James Irving that Gef had not been seen for several weeks. In the three days that Price and Lambert were there, Gef did not make an appearance. They returned home after having first removed some of the pet dog's hair for comparison with the ones sent earlier. They proved to be a perfect match, again placing doubt on the validity of the whole affair.

Not long after their departure from the island, Gef reappeared at the farm, leaving footprints behind. James Irving sent three casts to Price, who in turn passed them on to the Natural History Museum in London. The museum's report on them said that none of them seemed to bear any relation to the others. One was possibly made by a dog, another by a North American racoon and the third was never formally identified. None was thought to have been made by a mongoose.

The credibility of Gef and the Irvings was rapidly dissipated as more and more journalists dismissed the case as a hoax, although Richard Lambert received record libel damages after being branded an 'unstable, hysterical crackpot' by Sir Cecil Levita. Speculation did still arise in the press, but the Irvings were largely left alone, apart from one further visit by Macdonald and another by the psychic researcher Dr Nandor Fodor. Price and Lambert published a book on the affair, *The Haunting at Cashen's Gap*, in 1936.

❖

The theory that is most often advanced in this case is that Voirrey was responsible for faking the whole affair. Evidence in favour of this includes her fascination with animals, her above average intelligence, the loneliness and boredom associated with an isolated farmhouse existence and the fact that Gef seemed to appear only when she was around. She could have made Gef's shrill voice and the stunts, such as killing rabbits, throwing things and moving objects, were all within her capabilities. The final attempts to convince people of the truth of the matter by providing photographs, footprints and hair could have been stunts she arranged, probably unaware of how easily such things could be proved fake.

If this is the case, then to a certain extent the family must have either helped or turned a blind eye to the hoaxing. In the four years during which the affair was investigated, both the parents, although more particularly Mrs Irving, claimed to have seen Gef and heard him speak. Both parents and visitors to the farm witnessed Gef talking while Voirrey was in full view. Mrs Irving was witnessed having long conversations with Gef while Voirrey was sitting only feet away. The more extraordinary events they describe, such as Gef bouncing a ball in time to music and moving furniture about cannot be attributed to Voirrey unless her parents were lying too. Yet the overall impression given by the Irvings to everyone who came into contact with them was that they were genuinely honest. They seem to have gained nothing financially from the affair. In fact, with the amount of visitors they received and had to entertain, they were probably put to an awful lot of trouble. It should also be borne in mind that it was James Irving who first 'discovered' Gef and taught the mongoose to talk.

The one serious doubt that parapsychologists have about this case being a complete hoax is its similarity to known poltergeist cases. The sequence of events and conditions at Cashen's Gap exactly match those of other classic poltergeist cases (see the Enfield Poltergeist, page 38 and the Fox Sisters, page 122). The haunting began with scratching noises and rapidly escalated to encompass objects being thrown, apports and speaking. The focus, Voirrey, follows tradition by being a girl between the ages of 12 and 20. Gef's mood swings, insults, boastfulness, lies, clairvoyance and exaggerated human voice are all common features in those rare cases where poltergeists speak.

Poltergeists are also notorious for producing an abundance of phenomena to everybody except those investigating them. They seem to be unwilling to provide concrete evidence of their existence and are fond of practical jokes. Some people say this could be why the dog hairs were placed on the mantelpiece.

A further possibility is that the affair started off as poltergeist activity but, as commonly happens in such cases, the phenomena ceased after a few months. In the absence of real activity, Voirrey perhaps continued to fake the phenomena herself in order to keep attention on herself and the farm. This hypothesis, generally laughed at by sceptics, seems to be quite commonly put forward in poltergeist cases in which apparently genuine phenomena degenerate into forgery. This vastly decreases the value of those cases for research purposes, for once forgery is suspected, one can never fully rely on any other evidence again. Sadly, despite the close correlation between Gef and other poltergeist cases, the dog hairs, photographs and footprints do lessen the credibility of the case. It is unlikely that the truth will ever be known.

Kenneth Odhar

❖

SEER

K ENNETH ODHAR (Cainneach Odhar in his native Gaelic) was an extraordinary seer whose prophecies seemingly came true many centuries later.

It is thought that he was born around the year 1600 in the parish of Vig on the Isle of Lewis. His prophetic powers reputedly started soon after adolescence, when he was given a white fairy stone through which he could see the future. He gained a local reputation as a seer, making numerous correct predictions. Stories of his powers soon spread and before long he was invited to live on the feudal estate of Kenneth Mackenzie near Brahan Castle on the Cromarty Firth. In 1623 Mackenzie died and was replaced by the first Earl of Seaforth whose grandson, also called Kenneth, befriended Kenneth Odhar. He removed him from his simple peasant lifestyle and began introducing him to local nobles and scholars.

It was from this time that the first accurate reports of his predictions begin to appear. An old man, Duncan Macrae, asked of Odhar how he would die. With apparently typical tactlessness, Odhar replied that the old man would die by the sword. This seemed very unlikely, bearing in mind the man's old age and the relative peace between the Scottish clans at the time. However, in 1654 Duncan Macrae was indeed slain after making an unintentional threatening gesture to a troop of parliamentary soldiers while out walking.

In 1630 the Earl of Seaforth allowed Odhar to stay with an Inverness man who took the trouble to record his predictions. This was fortunate, because although Odhar was remarkable at predicting events in the near future, it is his recorded long-range prophecies that are regarded as truly remarkable. Many of these concern minor events that are of little political or physical consequence, but others do seem to refer to important events or achievements within the Seaforth dynasty and Scotland itself.

Examples of seemingly unimportant predictions include his prophecy that a woman called Annabella Mackenzie would die of measles within the village of Baile Mhuilinn. A 95-year-old woman of that name did not come to the village until 1860 and the odds suggested that she would die of old age rather than anything else. However, within two years of her arrival, she did indeed die of measles. Similarly, he predicted that a famous eight-ton boundary stone, called the Pretty Stone, would be uprooted from dry land and end up in the centre of the bay below. This happened on 20 February 1799 in a violent storm.

These may sound like rather trivial predictions that could perhaps be written off as coincidence. However, some of his other predictions concerned more momentous events and are specific enough not to be written off as mere chance.

While staying in Inverness, Odhar was walking across a bleak patch of moorland when he stopped and said to his companion, 'Thy bleak moor shall, ere many generations have passed away, be stained with the best blood of the Highlands. Heads will be lopped off by the score, and no mercy shall be shown.' It was that exact piece of moorland where, in 1746, the bloody battle of Culloden took place.

It seems that he may also have predicted a twentieth-century event after decreeing that a great flood from a loch above the village of Beauly would destroy a village nearby. This seemed to be sheer lunacy at the time, as there was no loch anywhere near Beauly. However, in the first half of this century a dam was built across the River Conon at Torrachilty, creating an artificial lake a few miles away from Beauly. In 1966, unusually heavy rain caused the dam to overflow and, in turn, the river to burst its banks. The flood waters poured into the small village of Conon Bridge, causing havoc by destroying property and farms there.

It is unfortunate for Odhar that he did not use his abilities for his own well-being, for, thanks largely to his lack of common sense, he met an unexpected and rather unpleasant death. By the 1660s Odhar's original friend, Kenneth Mackenzie, had become the third Earl of Seaforth and was called away to Paris on the king's business. His wife, Isabella, became anxious after not hearing from him for several months and Odhar was summoned to the castle. When asked by Isabella what her husband was doing, Odhar replied with some pride that the earl was in a sumptuous room, happy and not ready to return home yet. When asked why, Odhar stated that the earl was 'on his knees before a fair lady'.'

Isabella was outraged at this news and ordered that Odhar should be boiled alive in tar. Despite his protests, he was taken up to Chanonry Point, in Fortrose, and prepared for execution. He begged the Scottish ministers present to take down his final predictions, all of which concerned the future of the Seaforth dynasty.

He said that the final Seaforth chief would be both deaf and mute and would have four sons, all of whom would die, one of them on the water. He also predicted that this earl would have two daughters, the white-hooded one of whom would return from overseas and eventually kill her sister, thus terminating the Seaforth bloodline. He then predicted that the timing of these events would be known by the presence of four lairds, whom he named as Gairloch, Chisholm, Grant and Ramsay. He said that one of the lairds would be hare-lipped and the others buck-toothed, half-witted and a stammerer. There was also to be another laird, who would kill four wives but marry a fifth who would outlive him.

After these predictions had been written down, Kenneth Odhar was executed. A stone with a simple inscription now marks the place of his death.

As regards this last set of predictions, there seemed to be no sign of them materializing and during the early eighteenth century the Seaforths became increasingly rich and powerful. Then in 1754 Francis Humberstone Mackenzie was born and, aged 12, had an attack of scarlet fever that rendered him deaf. He unexpectedly inherited the chieftainship of the clan in 1781 and led a distinguished political, diplomatic and military career. He married and had four sons and six daughters. Of the sons, two died in infancy, one died (as predicted) at sea in a naval battle and the other died of natural causes in his early twenties. In his later years Francis's speech degenerated considerably until he could communicate only with hand movements. He died in 1815 and it was remarked at the time that among his neighbours and peers were indeed the buck-toothed Sir Hector Mackenzie of Gairloch, the retarded Laird Grant, the stammering Macleod of Ramsay and the hair-lipped Chisholm of Chisholm. There lived also at that time the laird of Tulloch (Duncan Davidson), who, some years *after* the death of the last Seaforth, had four wives who died in childbirth and a fifth who outlived him.

As for the remaining predictions, after the death of her husband and some years after the death of her father, the eldest daughter, Mary, returned to take control of the estate. She kept on her widow's weeds, which included a white hood, and before long was known as Lady Hood. Tragically, Odhar was accurate to the last and one day Lady Hood was driving her younger sister through some local woods when the horses bolted and the carriage overturned. Lady Hood survived the crash, but her sister was killed.

❖

The nature and style of Kenneth Odhar's prophecies are similar to those of other more famous seers, such as Nostradamus and Mother Shipton. These people all made a long series of recorded prophecies that were apparently not to come true until years or even centuries after their death. On the face of it, they appear to offer *prima facie* evidence as to the existence of precognition as their predictions were recorded and in circulation for many years before the events they concerned actually occurred.

Nostradamus has been praised for his quatrains (four-line verses) concerning the second Antichrist, whom he calls 'Hister', a name not that dissimilar to Hitler. Similarly, Mother Shipton has been credited with predicting twentieth-century inventions such as the submarine and the telephone. Much study, both historical and astrological, has been made of both these prophets' writings, the results of which provide a good summary of the arguments for and against the existence of such long-range predictions.

Mother Shipton is reputed to have been born Ursula Southiel in 1488 near Knaresborough in Yorkshire. During her life she was revered first as a witch and then as a soothsayer. When she died, in 1561, she was famous throughout England and was known as 'The Northern Prophet'. The many prophecies that she made were recorded in a series of books published in the seventeenth, eighteenth and nineteenth centuries. She was credited with predicting the Great Fire of London, which occurred 105 years after her death, with the verse: '...in the City of London as master shall cry and weep, what a City this was when I left...but now scarce a house is stood to entertain us.' Another famous prophecy concerns satellite communications: 'Around the world words shall fly, in the twinkling of an eye.' Her prediction of the end of the world states: 'When women dress like men and trousers wear and cut off all their locks of hair. When pictures look alive with movement free. When ships like fishes swim beneath the sea. When men outstripping birds can soar the sky. Then half the world, deep drenched in blood, shall die.' This would appear to be an uncannily accurate description of twentieth-century inventions and fashions and would therefore place the end of the world firmly within our reach.

Historical research into Mother Shipton has, unfortunately, found little evidence to confirm her existence. The first reference to her is not until 1641 and it is uncertain how many of the verses attributed to her are genuine; some were undoubtedly made up. It has also been argued that many of her prophecies are too vague to be tied to any one particular historical event. For example, the Great Fire of London prophecy could equally well apply to the state of the City after German bombing runs in World War II.

Many of these criticisms do not apply to the most famous of all prophets, Nostradamus, or Michel de Nostradame, who lived in Provence between 1503 and 1566. In his lifetime he wrote an entire volume containing hundreds of quatrains, many of which have been interpreted as prophecies of the future. Nostradamus is credited with predicting virtually every major historical event to have occurred in Europe, as well as in other countries that weren't even discovered or colonized in his lifetime, such as America, Australia and South America. Nostradamus is also credited with predicting the Great Fire of London in the following verse:

The blood of the good shall be wanting in London,
Burnt by the fire of twenty and three the sixes,
The old lady shall fall from her high place,
Of the same sect many shall be killed.

The references to the fire comes from the three sixes (1666), the mention of fire and the nickname for St Paul's Cathedral (the old lady) which was destroyed in the fire. Other verses are seemingly just as accurate, such as those that have been taken to refer to Napoleon (named as the first of three Antichrists) and Hitler (the second Antichrist).

Critics of Nostradamus point out that much of the detail in his verses comes from rather liberal translations of the original Languedoc tongue in which they were written. For example, the word 'fire' in the verse quoted can be better translated as 'thunderbolt' and 'old lady' as 'the eccentric woman'. Modern historians also believe that Nostradamus was a closet Protestant and that his verses are merely a hidden commentary on the Catholic Inquisition that was occurring around him at the time. It is difficult to know who to believe in the war of words that has been exchanged over Nostradamus's quatrains.

One theme that holds for most of the well-known prophets is their predictions for the end of the world. Mother Shipton would appear to set it in our times, while Nostradamus gave the date as 9 August 1999. Kenneth Odhar chose instead to predict the end of the lineage that had him put to death. The Buddhists believe that the earth will survive only 2,500 years beyond the death of the Buddha (who was born around 2,500 years ago) and the Christian tradition has the Book of Revelation. This obscure and almost fantastic New Testament book, written by St John of Patmos in the first century AD, deals with a series of visions he had about the events that would lead to Armageddon and the second coming of Christ. The most enigmatic and often quoted verse from the Book of Revelation (13:18) states that all followers of the Antichrist would bear the number of the beast, 666, on their right hand or forehead.

More than any other, this one phrase illustrates a major problem with the interpretation of prophecies. Many Christian groups are eager to see the end of the world (so that they can be saved and meet their Saviour) and have been looking for the signs mentioned in the Book of Revelation. The number 666, with its sinister implications, has been seen as a key means of identifying the end times. This number has been attributed to everything from credit cards to bar codes, from Mikhail Gorbachov (also seen as the third Antichrist by Nostradamians) to Saddam Hussein. Much twisting and turning goes on to make historical events fit the prophecies that some people have attributed to them.

Odhar's prophecies, on the other hand, are reasonably specific and while it is easy to be sceptical about the translation of the word 'fire', it is less easy to dismiss the deaf and dumb earl, his offspring and the four lairds. When put next to his other prophecies, such as those concerning the battle of Culloden and the loch at Beauly, it is hard not to be impressed.

As regards the mechanism behind Odhar's apparent ability, this is harder to explain or to link to more conventional types of precognition. There is a theory that precognition can occur only if the event prophesied, or at least news of it, such as a newspaper headline, is witnessed later on by the prophet. Many of Odhar's took place years after his death, so there was no way for him to witness them. There seems to be no obvious pattern to his prophecies. Many predict completely trivial events or describe changes in the local scenery, some of which he himself did not understand: for example, his description of a train was 'strings of black carriages, horseless and brideless...led by a fiery chariot'. He did seem to be able to use his power at will (as the incident leading to his death revealed) – something that few modern psychics can do.

Ted Serios

❖

THOUGHTOGRAPHY

THE PARANORMAL SEEMS to specialize in producing eccentric figures with apparently amazing claims. Ted Serios fits this description perfectly, but were his thoughtographs genuine or clever fakes?

In 1967 Dr Jule Eisenbud published a book entitled *The World of Ted Serios*. Serios had come to Eisenbud's attention through an article written in the American popular paranormal magazine *Fate*, which described the ability of a chain-smoking and alcoholic bellhop to produce images on a film using telepathy. Eisenbud's curiosity was stimulated, particularly as it appeared that Serios had been tested and vindicated by a number of professional photographers and scientists. After much trouble, a meeting between Eisenbud and Serios was arranged in Chicago in April 1964.

Before Eisenbud arrived on the scene Serios had had very little interest from the press and the public. He discovered his talent when a workmate found that under hypnosis Serios became an excellent remote-viewer. A syndicate was formed to try and find buried treasure using these powers – with only moderate success. In order to try and better pinpoint the locations of buried treasure, one of the syndicate members handed Serios a camera and told him to project an image of the location on to the film. The results were so amazing that Serios at first thought it was all a practical joke. Eventually he gave up the treasure-hunting and returned to Chicago to become a bellhop once more.

At his first meeting with Eisenbud, Serios turned up slightly drunk and, after some persuading, stared intently into the lens of a Polaroid camera and pressed the shutter. A completely black photograph emerged. He did this a further six times, producing blank photographs on each occasion. However, on the eighth attempt the photograph came out displaying a vague misty image of an oblong object. A person present recognized it as the Chicago Water Tower. After a rest, Serios tried again and this time produced an equally blurred photograph of a local hotel that had burned down seven years previously.

Eisenbud was impressed enough to find the money to get Serios to Denver in order to assess him more scientifically. In front of a scientific panel, Serios managed to produce a discernible image of the clock in London's Westminster

Abbey. A second demonstration was arranged, but Serios panicked at all the attention and disappeared back to Chicago. He was persuaded to return for another demonstration, but disgraced himself by arriving blind drunk. He irritated the panel to the point that they were about to leave when he grabbed the camera, stared into it and produced a photograph of a double-decker bus. The scientists present testified to their belief that he had not been visibly fraudulent.

For the next three years Eisenbud was to witness and receive hundreds of 'thoughtographs' from Serios. Some of them were very strange indeed. In 1965 Serios produced 11 photographs of a glass-fronted shop. In two of them the name 'The Old Gold Store' was visible on a sign outside. It was to be two years before someone recognized the photographs as being of a tourist shop in Central City, Colorado. The strange thing was that the shop had been renamed 'The Old Wells Fargo Office' at least seven years previously. The photograph showed the modern-day shop front, but with the old name on the sign.

Such alterations within his thoughtographs were common. For example, a photograph that showed an aircraft hangar had the name 'Royal Cainadain Mounted Police' in place of the correct spelling, 'Canadian'. Also, when asked to produce a photograph of the Denver Hilton, he instead produced a photograph of the Chicago Hilton.

Serios found that his greatest success was when he used a 'gismo' (his term) to help concentrate his mind. The gismo would be a cardboard or plastic tube, sometimes with cellophane on either end, which Serios would hold against the camera and then press the trigger. The use of this gismo immediately led to charges of fraud against Serios. The magician James Randi alleged that the gismo could contain a lens at one end and a transparency at the other, which would focus the slide on to the film. Despite these allegations, though, no such lenses or slides were ever found on Serios during any of his hundreds of demonstrations. Neither was an explanation provided for the photographs he produced of requested objects or for the ones produced by simply staring into the camera. Serios could produce a photograph while blindfolded, with no lens in the camera, and could sometimes reproduce photographs of postcards sealed in an envelope. He was also never caught cheating, despite occasionally being blind drunk during his performances.

Serios's powers were always coming and going in strength, but in May 1967 they started seriously to wane and he began producing hundreds of blanks (completely black or white photographs). Shortly before his final photograph in June 1967, Serios described losing his power as being like a curtain coming down. His final photograph was of a curtain!

❖

Ted Serios is an example of one of those cases where the majority of para-psychologists believe in the phenomenon, or the possibility of it, while most sceptics feel that they have proved a fraud.

The use of Serios's gismo is pivotal to this controversy, with famous debunkers suggesting various methods by which transparencies, microfilms and lenses could be used to project an image on to the film. None of the people who have proposed these methods have ever practically demonstrated how it was done, or explained the many successful photographs produced without the gismo.

Eisenbud states that he took many precautions to minimize the possibility of fraud. This included buying sealed film from different shops, using two cameras at once and placing Serios up to 20 yards from the camera. Successful photographs were produced under all these conditions, although sceptics always explain away the case because of the gismo.

Serios's thoughtography has been classified as a form of psychokinesis (the ability to affect objects with the mind). The control that Serios had over this abil-ity suggests that it was not merely a spontaneous phenomenon and that it was most likely his brain that was responsible. His ability to produce photographs of items sealed in envelopes suggests that he had clairvoyant ability as well.

The photographs themselves are blurred and always seem to be taken from the point of view of a person looking at a scene. The perspective of the scene portrayed, resembling what would be expected from a normal photograph, does lend weight to the theory that Serios used hidden transparencies to fake the photographs. It has also been noticed that his photographs were normally of localities that he had visited or had an interest in. However, the misspelling of words and the merging of old and new features within the same photograph were difficult to do convincingly in those days, although it is much easier these days with computers. This perhaps suggests that some form of clairvoyant ability is again at work, although what mechanism would be capable of altering the film's chemistry to replicate the effect of light on it can only be guessed at. The release of the shutter at Serios's command suggests that light may be necessary in the process, although the shutter pressing may simply have been a specific point in time for Serios to focus on.

Most of Serios's photographs were of static objects or buildings, and he only rarely produced photographs of people or personal possessions. This may be a function of his remote-viewing capabilities, for although remote-viewers can sometimes 'see' the same view as a person standing in a location, they can rarely focus on the actual individual.

Other examples of thoughtography are extremely rare but may possibly include some of the more plausible photographs of ghosts. An example of this comes from J. Traill Taylor, who in 1893 persuaded medium David Duguid to 'place' images of ghosts on to the plate of a camera which was capable of producing a three-dimensional result. When viewed in three dimensions, the 'ghosts' were found to be flat, with no depth of field, suggesting that they had been imposed upon the scene and therefore did not exist as a three-dimensional object before the camera.

Other phenomena that apparently involve the projection of mental powers on to recording apparatus include so-called Electronic Voice Phenomena (EVP). Here questions are asked in front of a tape recorder that is recording only white-noise static. When played back, discarnate voices can be heard above the static, some of which have reportedly answered the questions given to them. EVP voices have been explained as a form of telepathy, where the mind projects the voices on to the audio tape. It is interesting to note that despite the large number of home video cameras in circulation, there have been almost no reports of ghosts or other similar spontaneous phenomena occurring on the tapes.

Emilie Sagée

❖

BILOCATION

ACCORDING TO RESEARCH done by Robert Dale Owen, Emilie Sagée is thought to have been born in Dijon, France, on 3 January 1813. An orphan, she was educated at a convent and began a teaching career when she was 16.

In 1845, aged 32, she was taken on as a French teacher in an exclusive girls' school, the Pensionat von Neuwelcke, which was some four miles from the port of Wolmar in the Russian Baltic province of Livonia. It seems that she had a sweet and gentle nature and was liked immensely by both the pupils and staff at the school. However, before long strange stories started to circulate about Mademoiselle Sagée.

Both pupils and staff at the school had apparently noticed that Emilie had been seen in two places at once on a number of occasions. These reports were treated as rumours until, a few weeks after her arrival at the school, her double appeared alongside her physical body in front of a number of witnesses.

The first time this happened was in front of 13 pupils, while Emilie was giving a lesson. Apparently she had her back to the children and was writing on the blackboard when her double appeared beside her. It mimicked her every action perfectly although apparently the double did not have any chalk in her hand. Following this confirmed sighting, the double appeared a number of times in the ensuing weeks.

During preparations for a festival, Emilie was helping to fasten up the dress of one of the pupils, Antonie von Wrangel. There was a mirror hanging behind them in which Antonie spied not one but two Emilies buttoning her dress. The small girl promptly fainted. Antonie was again to witness the double while helping to nurse Emilie when she had been taken to bed ill. She saw the colour drain from Emilie's face and then spotted the double walking about the room, apparently in full health.

Perhaps the most famous sighting of Emilie's double was when it appeared in front of the entire school of 42 pupils. The girls were in the school hall doing embroidery when their supervising teacher got up and left them alone to visit the headmistress. Soon after this, Emilie's double appeared in the vacant teacher's chair at the front of the class. The hall overlooked the school garden and the girls were amazed to see the original Emilie in the garden collecting flowers, while her double sat in front of them. It was noticed that after the appearance of her double, the original Emilie's movements slowed down considerably. Two of the bravest girls went up to the double and tried to touch it. They described feeling a faint resistance, like going through muslin, when doing so. One of the girls walked right through the legs of the double without any ill effect, or getting any reaction from the double or Emilie herself. Eventually the double faded away and Emilie started gardening again at a more normal pace. When questioned later Emilie said that while gardening, she had noticed that the teacher had left the pupils unattended and was annoyed at this, wishing that she could look after them instead.

Emilie and her double continued to make regular appearances over the next year. It was reported that Emilie eventually learned to know when her double had materialized, because she felt sluggish and weak until it disappeared again. However, despite her popularity, a number of parents withdrew their girls from the school and in 1846 the school directors reluctantly sacked her. It was the nineteenth school she had had to leave in 16 years because of her double.

One of her pupils, Julie von Guldenstubbe, kept in contact with Emilie for a few years while she was privately teaching several children nearby. Her double was still making appearances, as the children apparently told Julie that they had two Aunt Emilies. All contact was lost with Emilie when she moved to Russia in the 1850s.

It was a chance meeting between Robert Dale Owen and Julie von Guldenstubbe (then a baroness) in London in 1853 that led to Owen researching the case and eventually writing it up in his book *Footfalls on the Boundary of Another World*, published in 1860.

❖

Emilie Sagée's case falls into a category of psychic phenomena known as *doppelgängers* (German for 'double walker') or fetches. A *doppelgänger* or fetch is the spiritual double of somebody that is either seen by the person themselves or, as with Emilie, by others. Seeing your own *doppelgänger* is supposed to be an omen of death.

In 1886 the Society for Psychical Research (SPR) published a monumental book entitled *Phantasms of the Living*. This contains literally hundreds of cases involving people witnessing apparitions of living people, including themselves. To anybody who has the patience to read through this work, it will soon become apparent that *doppelgängers* are not that uncommon as a reported phenomenon. Indeed, it is rumoured that the poet Goethe encountered his own *doppelgänger* when out riding one day, although it didn't bring about his imminent death.

Assuming all the stories about Emilie Sagée are true, it would appear that there is a direct connection between Emilie herself and her *doppelgänger*, as evidenced by her change in colour and behaviour when her double had materialized. This suggests that the effort of making a *doppelgänger* involves the taking of 'something' from the physical body. What this something actually is remains a matter of speculation. Is it merely the effort of being in control of two 'bodies' at once or is it something more sinister connected with the psychic mind? What seems clear from the reports is that Emilie did not have any control over either the appearance of the *doppelgänger* or its movements. This differentiates bilocation from an out-of-body experience (see Robert Monroe, page 87), where the person transfers their consciousness to a separate spiritual body that remains invisible to normal people. Out-of-body experiences usually remain under the full control of the astral traveller and usually occur when the perceiver is in a relaxed, almost hypnotic state. It does not fit into the category of bilocation, where a person can project a conscious visible image of themselves to another location. There would seem to be more of a connection between Emilie Sagée's case and those of ghosts of the living.

An example of ghosts of the living, taken from the records of the SPR, was related by Lieutenant Larkin of the RAF. Shortly after the finish of World War I, he was at an airbase writing letters when he heard somebody walking along the corridor outside. The door opened and a friend of his, David McConnel, came in and briefly greeted him before leaving again. Lieutenant Larkin later learned that his friend had died in a plane crash at the exact time as his sighting. It appeared that when he died McConnel had been able to project an image of himself to his close friend Larkin.

In cases where the ghost of a living person is seen, the living person is usually undergoing some form of strong emotion at the time and cases such as Larkin's are often collectively called crisis apparitions. It is thought to be these that cause the projection of the 'ghost' in the first place, usually to a close relative or friend. In Emilie's case, if it can be associated with crisis apparitions, it appears that the mechanism may have been more sensitive than in most apparitions. Emilie's desire to be in the classroom covering for her colleague may have triggered the appearance of the *doppelgänger* in the classroom. Her illness may also have triggered the *doppelgänger's* appearance for it has also been noticed that out-of-body experiences are more commonly reported in people who are ill or even dying.

There is, of course, a rather more mundane explanation for the case of Emilie Sagée. The story as we know it came from one of Emilie's pupils, Julie von Guldenstubbe, who related it to Robert Dale Owen. When Owen came to try and track down Sagée, he could find no record of her birth in Dijon (although he did find a very similar name) and could not find the location of the school around which the story was based. The facts of the case are therefore totally reliant upon von Guldenstubbe's version of events, as related to Owen some 15 years after they occurred. As the chapter on frauds (see pages 170–93) illustrates, people's versions of events cannot always be relied upon to be either accurate or truthful. The Sagée story could have been a school rumour that became exaggerated over time.

Every school in the world would seem to have areas that are said to be haunted by its pupils and there is always a constant stream of stories, rumours and specu-lation about teachers. Maybe an unusual incident, such as pupils being convinced that they had seen Sagée in two places simultaneously, started a rumour of bilo-cation. Although Julie von Guldenstubbe was at school with Sagée, it is not recorded whether she actually witnessed the *doppelgänger* herself. We also know nothing about von Guldenstubbe's personality and whether she was of an honest disposition or not. However, many of the details of the case fit in well with research done decades later on ghosts of the living and other related psychic phenomena.

John Godley

❖

PRECOGNITION

T HERE IS A WIDESPREAD belief among psychics and mediums that the gift they have been given cannot be used to help them gain money or status. This is said to explain why even the most gifted psychics have not been able to produce, say, winning lottery numbers. However, even the psychic world seems to have its exception to this rule, in the form of John Godley.

In 1946 John Godley (who was later to become Lord Kilbracken) was an undergraduate at Oxford University. On the night of 8 March he had a dream that he was looking at the next day's racing results, complete with winners and prices written out in full. Being a keen racegoer, he noticed two horses that he had previously, and unsuccessfully, backed and was surprised to see that they had won their respective races. The horses were called Bindal and Juladin and both had odds of 7–1.

He awoke remembering the dream and the two horses, but thought no more about it until he was scanning the racing pages and saw that both horses were running that afternoon. Fortunately for research purposes, Godley had the foresight to mention the dream to some of his friends, all of whom advised him to back the horses. He grudgingly placed some money on Bindal (the first to run) and was shocked when it did indeed come in first. Godley promptly placed all his winnings on Juladin and spent a tense couple of hours waiting for the result. Sure enough, the horse came in first. Godley and his friends won over £30 between them. As for the odds, the horses ran at 5–4 and 5–2 respectively, so the combined odds were 7⅞–1, very close to the dream's 7–1. This may seem like coincidence, and as the event was not repeated in the following couple of weeks, Godley wrote it off as such himself. However, on the night of 3 April 1946 (two days before the Grand National) Godley had another dream. The format was the same as the previous one, with him reading the race results in a newspaper. Unfortunately, he could remember the name of only one winner, a horse called Tubermore. There was no Tubermore running the next day, but the day afterwards, in the first Aintree race, there was a horse called Tuberose. This was sufficiently close to persuade Godley, and his brother and sister, to place an each-way bet on the horse. It came in at odds of 100–6, giving a return of £60 to the gamblers. Godley comments that he had never heard of the unconsidered outsider, before that day and that it never won a race afterwards.

There followed a succession of eight dreams after this, six of which produced winners. They all involved reading the results in a newspaper, except for the final dream, which occurred on 28 July 1946. Godley dreamed that he went into an Oxford hotel to ring up his bookmaker to ask for some racing results. This was most unusual, as Godley claims to have always got his results from the evening papers. He remembers himself smoking a cigarette and also the phone booth being stuffy. When he got through he asked for the result of the previous race, to which the reply was, 'Certainly, sir. Monumentor at 5–4.'

On looking through the paper the next day, he found a horse called Mentores running. Although this was not identical to his dream, he backed it anyway. To be on the safe side, Godley deliberately reproduced the conditions of his dream by going into the hotel and ringing up his bookmaker. When he asked for the result of the previous race, a voice replied, 'Certainly, sir. Mentores at 6–4.'

Although that was the end of his run of precognitive dreams, he did have one further isolated dream in 1947 and another in 1958. Luckily for us, Godley had chosen to impart his dreams to his friends and family, many of whom have testified to the Society for Psychical Research (SPR) as to the validity of his claims, helping us to accept that the events occurred as described. Godley also had the kindness to send the details of two further dreams to the SPR as soon as they happened, although unfortunately neither of them came true.

❖

The evidence for this being a true case of premonition seems to be quite impressive. The events were witnessed in advance, occurred on a number of occasions and also formed a pattern that could allow them to be recognized as premonitions. The horses that won all had long odds and were not favourites. None was an animal that Godley had a vested interest in winning. The premonitions themselves were also only of personal relevance to Godley, rather than involving national or international disasters. These are the conditions that parapsychologists look for when declaring a case of premonition valid.

Reports of premonitions of this kind are not that unusual and most people have had similar experiences in their lives at some point. However, it is unusual for people to win money and to do so consistently. John Godley's precognition experiences fit into a recognized pattern whereby the central event of the premonition is not actually witnessed by the person concerned. In these cases, the voyeur will often dream of reading a newspaper headline describing the event or will have a vision of watching it on television. Some people even report hearing media-style commentaries in the background of their visions. This was so with the October 1966 Aberfan disaster, in which a coal slag heap slid down on to a village school, killing 144. Many people reported having had premonitions of this event, a large number of them claiming to have seen newspaper headlines as opposed to witnessing the actual events. This might suggest that premonitions are centred on individuals and their reactions to an event rather than the event itself. The strong emotion that people feel when learning of disasters (for example, the Kennedy assassinations) has also been linked to the precognitive mechanism.

However, Danah Zohar (in *Through the Time Barrier*) points out that John Godley was clearly quite a gambler and that possibly his subconscious was picking horses for him and conveying the information in the form of dreams. On balance, though, coincidence would be unlikely to produce such a number of dreamed winners in that space of time even if, by the laws of probability, it is bound to happen to somebody at some time. Other precognitive experiences about events such as car and plane crashes are now looked upon critically due to the increasing frequency of these events. For example, there is now on average a commercial plane crash every two weeks, something related to the increase in plane travel over recent years.

Many tests have been done on the nature of premonitions, including the setting up of a premonition registry in the 1980s. Those who have studied them have noticed that the people most liable to experience precognition are women in their mid-forties and that 85 per cent of their premonitions involve death or disaster. Other studies have noted, perhaps unkindly, that many of these people are also neurotic and have an inflated idea of their success rates. One particularly interesting study by C. Tart in 1993 found that 32 per cent of marijuana users reported precognitive experiences and that they were also liable to score higher in laboratory tests. In fact, attempts to study precognition in the laboratory have so far had a low success rate. Sceptics use this as evidence of its non-existence; others point out that its spontaneous nature makes it difficult to know when it will occur next. Various authors suggest that the careful recording of nightly dreams eventually produces a recognizable pattern of precognition within them, but this again runs into the criticism that the majority of the events predicted are common everyday experiences, such as meeting old friends unexpectedly.

The Enfield Poltergeist

❖

POLTERGEIST

THE ENFIELD POLTERGEIST was the basis of a well-publicized, long-running case that was investigated by two Society for Psychical Research (SPR) members from 1977 to 1978. It seems to present strong evidence in favour of the existence of the phenomenon and the paranormal activity witnessed at this north-London home is typical of poltergeist hauntings. The case still causes considerable controversy among some of the people who were involved with it, although it is particularly remarkable for the amount of access that the investigators were given and the detailed recording of events that occurred.

In the summer of 1977 the Harper family were living in a semidetached council house in the north London borough of Enfield. The family consisted of Mrs Harper (then a mid-forties divorcée) and her children Rose (aged 13), Janet (aged 11), Pete (aged 10) and Jimmy (aged 7). At approximately 9.30 p.m. on 31 August Mrs Harper had just put Janet and Pete to bed in their shared room when they called out to her, complaining that they could hear a shuffling noise. By the time she had gone upstairs the noise had stopped and she told them to stop playing games. Not long after this the shuffling started again and Mrs Harper returned to see a heavy chest of drawers, well out of the children's reach, move several inches across the floor. She pushed it back into place but it started to move again and this time, when she tried pushing, it refused to budge. At that moment four clear knocks sounded from the wall. Terrified and aware that something strange was occurring, Mrs Harper got her family up and moved them next door into the house of Vic and Peggy Nottingham. Vic Nottingham and his son went into the house and were greeted by more knocking coming from the walls. They searched the house and gardens but could find no obvious explanation for the events and so the police were called in.

It was late at night when the police arrived. They too heard the knocking and witnessed a chair slide a few feet across the kitchen floor when nobody was near it. Extremely puzzled, they left, unable to do anything, and the Harper family slept the night in the sitting room.

The next evening, and for the following three days, the phenomenon continued, with marbles and Lego bricks being flung through the air at lightning speed. Some were found to be hot when picked up. In the first week of September Mrs Harper had a vicar and a local medium to the house, but things got no better. In desperation she permitted a neighbour to call the *Daily Mirror* newspaper, in the hope that they might be able to solve the problem in return for some publicity.

Reporter George Fallows and photographer Graham Morris duly arrived and spent an evening waiting for the poltergeist to show itself. It never did and in the early hours they decided to leave. No sooner had the front door shut than the things began again, causing the two journalists to run back into the house. They were greeted with a hail of flying objects, one of which hit Morris hard above his eye, leaving a bruise for some time afterwards. Seeing the obvious terror of the family, Fallows contacted the SPR to see if they had anybody who could help in the matter. The SPR assigned a newcomer to its ranks, Maurice Grosse, to investigate the case. Grosse, a middle-aged businessman and industrial inventor, quickly witnessed a wealth of spontaneous phenomena, including the flying marbles, a shirt hopping off a table and a door opening and closing by itself. After only a few hours he knew he needed help and on 9 September 1977 he requested assistance at a SPR meeting. A rather unenthusiastic and overcommitted Guy Lyon Playfair, an experienced parapsychologist who had witnessed poltergeist activity when working in Brazil, told Grosse to contact him if things got bad. The next day the case was headline news in the *Daily Mirror* and subsequently led to Mrs Harper, Mrs Nottingham and Grosse being interviewed on LBC Radio and Radio 4. Playfair heard both interviews and cancelled a Portuguese holiday to get involved himself.

Playfair arrived at the house on 11 September and, together with the photographer Graham Morris, soon witnessed a marble drop dead at his feet while standing outside Janet's open bedroom door. The marble did not roll when it landed on the hard surface – something that Playfair and Grosse could not repeat afterwards. This was to be the first of an estimated 2,000 or more separate examples of usual phenomena to be recorded over the next 13 months.

Grosse and Playfair noticed that much of the activity was associated with the presence of Janet, and a special eye was kept on her by the investigators and Mrs Harper. Playfair tried tying the leg of a chair to Janet's bedside with wire to stop it moving. The chair fell over and the wire was found to be snapped. Again the chair was bound, and this time the wire was wrapped several times around it, but still the chair fell over and the wire snapped. The same evening they witnessed an armchair overturn and a bed move on their own and a book fly through the air at right angles to its point of origin. Many attempts were made to photograph the phenomena and record them on tape, but, as Playfair says, the poltergeist seemed to be a bit camera-shy. Things would either occur outside the range of the equipment or the equipment would mysteriously malfunction at crucial times. Morris found that his camera flashes would drain themselves, even after being recharged, and both Grosse and Playfair had numerous problems with their audio tape recorders, including parts of the machinery bending themselves while inside the casing.

In early October Playfair bought in the medium Annie Shaw, hoping that the poltergeist might want to communicate through her. Inside the house Mrs Shaw went into a trance and the 'entity' apparently took over her body. Afterwards she declared that there were several entities in the house feeding off a leakage in Janet's and Mrs Harper's auras. She then 'fixed' the leaks and left. Things died down considerably until late October, but then the paranormal activity resumed with a vengeance as furniture and other items were thrown around the house. It seemed to be getting more violent and threatening as well, including an incident where the iron grille from the bottom of a fireplace flew through the air and landed only inches from Jimmy's head while he was asleep. A gas fireplace was also physically ripped from the wall. Accompanying this were barrages of knocks that would sometimes continue for hours on end, keeping the weary family awake at night.

Following examples from other poltergeist cases, Playfair and Grosse tried to communicate with 'it' by getting it to knock once for yes and twice for no in reply to their questions. Playfair's first attempt got the required response until he asked, 'Do you realize that you are dead?' After that all hell broke loose in the house, with one upstairs room being totally ransacked. No further communications were made in this manner between Playfair and the poltergeist. Grosse, however, had more success and through the rapping code managed to establish that the entity had lived in the house for 30 years but had left 53 years before. Eventually the knocking became nonsensical and Grosse asked, 'Are you having a game with me?' A couple of seconds later he was struck on the head by a box full of cushions.

There was an escalation in activity throughout the autumn and early winter and the poltergeist seemed to be attempting to communicate with the investigators. They invited it to write out a message, leaving a pen and pencil unattended for a few minutes. When they returned, they found a message written out that said, 'I will stay in this house. Do not show this to anybody else or I will retaliate.' This was followed soon after by the odd message, 'Can I have a tea-bag?' When a tea-bag was placed on the table, another one appeared near it.

Shortly after this, Jimmy saw an apparition of an old man's face and was badly scared. Janet, who was continually being thrown out of bed, was showing what Playfair deemed to be classic signs of spiritual possession. She would twitch and convulse at night, sometimes violently, and would go into trance-like states, repeating threatening phrases over and over again. The SPR conducted a brief investigation, which apparently set out with the idea that the children were faking the phenomenon. All their experiments were therefore conducted with the aim of catching the children out rather than objectively studying events.

It was at the beginning of December that the most interesting phase of the haunting started. For a number of days a strange growling male voice over which she claimed to have no control was heard coming from Janet's throat. Grosse persuaded it to call out his name by leaving the room, and this seemed to establish formal vocal communication with the poltergeist. The voice would not perform in public but would answer questions if the others were out of the room. In between obscenities, the voice divulged that its name was Joe Watson and then later claimed to be Bill Haycock, a 72-year-old man who had lived in nearby Durant's Park and had come to see his family but found the Harpers there instead.

The physics department at London University's Birkbeck College had lent the investigation one of its research assistants, Richard Robertson, for two weeks and he turned out to be very useful. He was present on the day that appeared to mark a peak in the poltergeist's activity, 15 December 1977. This was also the day that Janet started menstruating – something that the investigators considered significant given the suggested connection between adolescence and poltergeist activity. Robertson began talking to 'the voice' through Janet's bedroom door. At first it just wanted to talk about women's periods, but he eventually persuaded it to levitate Janet. There followed the sound of Janet bouncing up and down on the bed and then silence. He tried to open the door but found that it was jammed shut by the bed. When he did get in he found that a red line had been drawn around the light and that Janet was claiming to have walked through the wall into the next-door house. The next-door neighbour, Mrs Nottingham, refused to believe this and went to her house to check. In the corresponding room to Janet's, Mrs Nottingham found one of her books, *Fun and Games for Children*, that had definitely been in Janet's bookcase when it had been tidied minutes before. Robertson then persuaded Janet, or at least her mysterious voice, to make a cushion disappear from the room. At the same time a salesman was walking towards the Harpers' house and he saw the cushion suddenly appear on the roof. Another neighbour also witnessed this and added that she had seen Janet floating horizontally in the middle of the room surrounded by floating cushions. It was later calculated that Janet must have been at least 28 inches above the bed's hard, firm mattress.

After these incidents the haunting went through a phase of destructiveness in which Janet was attacked by having objects thrown at her, causing bruising in some cases. She even had a cushion stuffed into her mouth in an apparent attempted suffocation. Fires were started, two goldfish were allegedly 'electrocuted' by the entity, rotting smells appeared and obscene messages were scrawled on the walls. Another medium, Gerry Sherrick, managed to calm the haunting down for several weeks by again mending the family's 'leaking auras'.

The worst of the haunting was over by the spring of 1978 although several apparitions were witnessed by the family and Grosse's *doppelgänger* was seen on the stairs by a neighbour checking on the house. The strain on the family was still acute and Janet was admitted to hospital to allow her to recuperate. Activity continued on a lesser scale in her absence and Jimmy began to exhibit trance-like symptoms. Janet returned a few weeks later in much better physical and mental health.

Although the case was, in common with most poltergeist activity, beginning to wind itself down, it seems to have finally been laid to rest by a visit from the Dutch psychic Dono Gmelig-Meyling. The psychic found possible links between the case and the death of Grosse's daughter two years previously and Grosse became convinced that his daughter's spirit had got him involved in the case to distract him from his grief. The last phenomenon associated with the case was recorded in October 1978.

This high-profile case had attracted journalists and mediums from a number of countries. Thanks to the efforts of Grosse and Playfair, it had been extensively studied and all the phenomena had been logged in detail. They had also helped the family cope with the associated stresses and strains and had prevented the investigation from turning into a media circus.

One interesting sideline comes from Professor J. Hasted of Birkbeck College's physics department. In 1982 he tested Janet to see if she could 'paranormally' lose weight. She was seated on an electronic weighing machine which should have remained constant as long as she kept still. Instead there was a drop of nearly a kilogram over a 30-second period. Professor Hasted could not explain this scientifically, although he did speculate that it might have been caused by Janet slightly levitating or possibly using psychokinesis to affect the machine's recording mechanism. Playfair's account of the investigation became a best-selling book, *This house is haunted!*, which was published in 1980.

❖

The paranormal activity witnessed at the Harpers' house is a typical, if somewhat extreme example of a poltergeist haunting. Poltergeists derive their name from the German *poltern*, 'to knock', and *Geist*, 'spirit', and have been recognized as a separate psychic phenomenon since the late 1890s. Their historical record, however, goes back much further than this, with the first documented case coming from 858 BC, when a Rhine farmhouse was plagued by a demon that threw stones, shook the walls, moved objects and created loud banging noises. Other cases have come from ancient Rome, China and Wales, with an increasing number being recorded from the Middle Ages onward until, with the advent of nineteenth-century Spiritualism, their documentation became very common and thorough indeed.

To psychic investigators, poltergeist phenomena offer an ideal chance to try and make sense of the seemingly random happenings of the psychic world. Poltergeist cases frequently last long enough and are active enough for investigators to be able to witness and document the phenomena themselves, instead of having to gather second- or third-hand statements from witnesses, as is so often the case with UFO, ghost and other spontaneous phenomena. Poltergeists are generally not shy (although they are somewhat camera-shy) and many of the events, as in the Enfield case, can be witnessed by several people at once, including credible witnesses such as the police, vicars, council officials and, hopefully, psychic investigators. The range of phenomena exhibited by the poltergeist can be large, often overlapping into other areas of psychic activity such as telepathy, ghosts, stigmata, etc., and, best of all, some poltergeists have even been prepared to communicate with people, including investigators, thus giving a greater understanding into the nature and psychology of the force behind the poltergeist phenomenon.

A typical poltergeist episode will follow a quite strict set of codes. Most hauntings begin with the onset of small thumping or scratching noises on the walls or ceiling of the house. The Enfield case began with a shuffling noise associated with the furniture. Soon after the thumps and bangs small objects may be moved (usually unwitnessed at first) or disappear altogether. Stones are often thrown, to be followed soon after by the movement of larger objects and furniture, sometimes in front of many witnesses. The time taken for the phenomena to progress from noises to object movement can be as little as a few hours or as long as a few weeks. Most poltergeist cases do not progress beyond this stage and may continue at this level for a number of days or weeks before suddenly stopping. Some, however, can escalate enormously.

As a poltergeist haunting continues, the phenomena usually grow in their unusualness and violence, as if the poltergeist itself is gaining an increased strength. Large items of furniture can be floated across the room, kitchen appliances ripped from their sockets and objects appear and disappear at will, even from locked cupboards and chests. Strange smells and noises can emanate from nowhere. People can be levitated and are commonly thrown out of bed at night. Objects can be thrown at people and miss them by inches or strike them but without causing injury. In the most extreme cases the poltergeist can bite, scratch, punch or kick people, leaving bruises and weal marks. Only very rarely will a poltergeist actually speak or manifest itself to its public. In most cases the activity lasts for less than a year and stops as suddenly as it started. Sometimes the poltergeist will give a final burst of outrageous energy before disappearing for good. However, aside from the bizarreness of the phenomenon itself, one of the most fascinating aspects of the poltergeist is that it usually centres itself around a single individual, usually an adolescent girl, whom it may torment and even physically hurt. This individual, traditionally called a 'focus', is statistically likely to be a girl between the ages of 12 and 20, although people of every type and age are documented as having being the focus of activity. Poltergeist focuses are normally unaware that they are causing or are the focus of the phenomenon and the majority of them do not relish the honour as they can suffer ridicule, harassment and prejudice. In the Harper household the focus was Janet Harper, who was aged 11 at the start, with most of the phenomena occurring only when she was in the house and many of them centred specifically around her.

The focus is often found to have been angry, frustrated or depressed at the time of the outbreak of activity, suggesting that the poltergeist itself may be a manifestation of subconscious anxiety and that the movement of objects and other phenomena is a hidden faculty of the mind. The ability of the mind to subconsciously influence matter in poltergeist cases has been given the term Recurrent Spontaneous Psychokinesis (RSPK) and most parapsychologists divide into two separate camps over the degree to which the human mind and RSPK influence poltergeist hauntings. One camp says that RSPK, and therefore the human mind alone, is solely responsible for the phenomenon, while the other camp believes that a disembodied spirit is at work, utilizing the subconscious energy of the focus. The arguments for both theories are strong.

A study of poltergeist cases by W. G. Roll in 1977 revealed that the majority of poltergeist focuses were unhappy, angry or suffering from another form of personal anxiety. Adolescents are particularly prone to anxieties and depression, which could explain the high proportion of poltergeist cases associated with them. Roll also found that many poltergeist focuses had other psychological problems, such as eating disorders, seizures and epilepsy, and that they had above-average scores when tested for other psychic powers such as telepathy and clairvoyance. It is thus argued that the frustrations and pent-up emotions associated with adolescence are capable of being expressed by the subconscious mind in the form of poltergeist activity. In this way individuals can express their anger without fear of punishment, and some researchers actually claim to have witnessed feelings of pleasure and relief within the focuses after a burst of poltergeist activity.

Evidence in favour of the poltergeist having a subconscious origin can be gained from the fact that many of the paranormal phenomena associated with poltergeists have, at some point, been associated with other psychic people. For example, the nineteenth-century Spiritualist craze brought forward many so-called physical mediums who held seances during which objects would spontaneously move, appear and disappear (see Daniel Dunglas Home, page 81).

Home himself fitted the ideal model of a poltergeist focus. Shy and lonely as a child, physically weak and prone to illness throughout his life, he was 17 when his powers began. He claimed that his powers came from the spirits, but he was clearly in full control of them himself and the similarity between his phenomena and those of poltergeists is unmistakable. Many other mediums and psychics, including the healer Matthew Manning, have been associated with RSPK or poltergeist activity at some time during their careers.

Other phenomena that poltergeists share with living psychics include extrasensory perception and clairvoyance.

In April 1974 a council house in southern England was plagued by rappings associated with a 12-year-old girl who was given the pseudonym Susan Black. Two trained and highly sceptical investigators, Barrie Colvin and Reinhart Schiffauer, were asked to investigate. They discovered that they could persuade the rapping noises to emanate from various walls in the house and from household objects, including a notebook being held by one of the investigators. An attempt at communicating was made using a rapping code, where one rap meant yes and two meant no. In this manner they determined that the poltergeist was a spirit called Eric Waters, who had been murdered nearby about 50 years previously. In the course of these communications Colvin and Schiffauer became convinced that Susan and her mother were responsible through their unconscious for creating the noises, as there definitely seemed to be evidence of telepathy between them and the poltergeist. To test whether there was any ESP at work, a series of tests using numbered cards was performed. In the first test the target cards were seen by everybody in the room and the poltergeist managed to identify the number on the card correctly six times out of six. In the second test only one of the investigators saw the cards and even so the poltergeist managed to get 16 out of 18 right - a significant score. In the third test nobody saw the cards and the poltergeist managed to get four out of six right before refusing to continue with the experiment. Other significant factors about the case were the bland, inconsistent and childlike conversations with the poltergeist and the fact that all rapping ceased completely once Susan was asleep. Susan was also noted to be a shy, anxious girl who looked on the poltergeist as a playmate.

Although not as violent and mischievous as some examples, Susan Black's poltergeist was obviously displaying clairvoyant powers, particularly when correctly identifying the cards that nobody had seen. Another classic case of clairvoyance occurred in the still hotly debated case of Gef the Talking Mongoose (see page 16). As well as ESP and physical mediumship, the bite marks and scratches that poltergeists produce on the focused individual are strangely reminiscent of the stigmata seen on the devoutly religious.

Those who believe in the human origin for poltergeists will always mention the following experiment carried out by Kenneth Batcheldor in the early 1960s. Batcheldor and a group of friends deliberately set out to create a poltergeist and spent many nights sitting in a circle with their hands flat on a table trying to induce some activity. Eventually the table started to levitate (confirmed by electrical switches on each of the legs) and before long the group was successfully levitating tables weighing over 46 pounds at chest height for periods of over 20 seconds with their hands still flat on the table. In addition to this, the group experienced a drop in temperature in the room, rapping noises from the walls and table, and a stone and a box of matches which were thrown at the group – all common poltergeist phenomena.

So if it is possible to deliberately create a poltergeist, then surely they must be a product of the mind? Not necessarily so. People who believe in a spiritual cause would argue that all the above phenomena can be explained by a spirit acting in conjunction with the frustrated energy of a human mind. As well as this, there is evidence for the presence of spirits in poltergeist activity, most notably in those rare cases where a focus is not present.

One such case occurred in a small family engineering workshop in Cardiff. The disturbances started soon after the boss, Jim, and his staff occupied the bottom half of a building in 1987. They initially took the form of small stones, bolts and coins being thrown around the workshop, ricocheting off the walls and shelving. Objects soon started to disappear and reappear in strange places. In one case, a paint scraper that had appeared from nowhere was found to be red hot to the touch – a common finding in poltergeist cases.

Soon the workmen found that the poltergeist would listen to and obey the men's commands. It began when Jim suggested they should record the events and a pen and paper promptly appeared beside him. When money was requested, several pennies and old coins fell to the floor. Similarly tools and parts would drop from the air when requested. It was later found that all these objects had been in the workshop or the solicitor's office above the workshop. In typical fashion the events escalated to lights exploding, large objects moving and people constantly being locked in the toilet. Refusing to believe that supernatural powers were at work, Jim called in the police on a number of occasions to try and find evidence of an intruder or trickery. Before leaving one day, he placed a carburettor float on the workshop gas fire and challenged it to be moved by the morning. On the way home he stopped to buy some cigarettes and was horrified to find that the change he had been handed back contained the carburettor float. He returned to the workshop to find it had gone from the gas fire. Soon the telephones in the workshop and the workmen's homes were plagued with line faults that British Telecom were unable to explain. Worse still, carburettor floats started to appear everywhere. They would be found in people's clothes, cars and often embedded in the ceiling of the workmen's houses.

In 1989 Professor Fontana, a psychologist from the University of Wales, was called in by the workshop's insurance company to investigate. He discovered that there was a corner of the workshop where, if objects were thrown, they would be returned immediately, sometimes from a completely different direction. Fontana tested this phenomenon when different people were present and even when the workshop was completely deserted, still obtaining the same effect, suggesting that there was no individual focus in this case. For a period of a year the poltergeist was quiet, but then it came back with a vengeance, becoming violent and unpleasant. It destroyed equipment and scattered tools, dishes and other objects. A fertilizer sack hovered above a customer before emptying itself on him. Carburettor floats bombarded people from every direction and in every conceivable location, including a supermarket car park. When again requested for money, £5 notes started to appear around the workshop until a total of £70 was recovered. The source of the money was never identified. The activity ceased with three sightings of an apparition of a small boy dressed in an old-fashioned school uniform. The last time he was seen he was waving goodbye, after which the activity died down until it stopped apart from a continual thumping coming from the ceiling. When the ceiling tiles were removed, a child's teddy bear and a rubber ball, which had disappeared some time previously, were found hidden in the ceiling space.

The Cardiff poltergeist case did not have a focus, making the subconscious theory hard to prove and suggesting that a discarnate entity was responsible. Cases where the poltergeist communicates directly with people have also added weight to the disembodied-spirit theory.

Poltergeists generally communicate in one of three ways: using raps or knocks, writing messages or speaking directly. The rapping-poltergeist phenomenon is covered in the discussion of the Fox Sisters (see page 122) and is relatively common. It is, however, the rarer speaking poltergeist, as exemplified by the Enfield case, that has excited parapsychologists.

Poltergeists normally speak only towards the end of a haunting, when the activity is at its peak. Before speech occurs, the poltergeist will usually make a variety of strange sounds, particularly animal noises, followed by strange gargling or rasping sounds, before finally forming words. Some researchers have conjectured that the poltergeist has to go through a process of learning how to speak.

When they do speak, most poltergeists are rude, aggressive, abusive and immature. The case of Gef the Talking Mongoose has already been mentioned. Gef could speak and was continually swearing and threatening both the family and visitors to the farm, accusing them of being cheats and liars. Talking poltergeists, including the Enfield Poltergeist, normally claim to be spirits of people who have died in mysterious circumstances, although historical research does not usually provide any evidence for the claims. The voices themselves are normally exaggerated versions of human ones, being either abnormally high- or low-pitched. It is certain that some poltergeist voices have emanated from the throat of their focus, but whether this is done consciously or subconsciously is a matter of debate.

Researchers have noted a similarity between poltergeist conversations and the psychological phenomenon multiple personality disorder (see page 63). Somebody who has this disorder will have developed, usually as the result of a trauma, two or more separate personalities within the same body. These will show a remarkable similarity to those displayed by talking poltergeists. They are often extremely rude, fond of swearing and making threats, immature and claim to be dead spirits or demons possessing the patient.

The association of poltergeists with known psychological problems again seems to indicate that the poltergeist is merely a manifestation of an aspect of the human mind, although there is still an argument that multiple personality disorder and poltergeists are cases of spiritual or demonic possession.

Although the case outlined here would appear to suggest that there is ample evidence for the existence of poltergeists as a phenomenon, there are alternative explanations for some cases, including the Enfield one.

Apart from cases where a physical explanation is found, such as an air lock in a water pipe causing a knocking noise, the only common explanation for poltergeists is that the focus is deliberately faking the phenomenon to gain attention. This has undoubtedly happened. For example, in 1984 a TV crew caught a 14-year-old girl in Columbus, Ohio, throwing objects when people's attention was diverted. Another investigator, Anita Gregory, who witnessed the later stages of the Enfield Poltergeist, has suggested that this could be the explanation here too. She complained that everybody was excluded from the children's bedrooms when some phenomena, including the speaking and levitation, were taking place and that Janet Harper would giggle and laugh while phenomena were occurring. She also felt that the two original investigators, particularly Maurice Grosse, had become too friendly with the children, who might have been faking the phenom-ena in order to keep them around the house. Her conclusion was that, while the case might have started off as real, it probably ended as a fake. This degeneration from genuine poltergeist activity into faking by a focus is an extremely common theory used when fraudulent behaviour is suspected. It is suggested that once the original phenomena die down, the focus will continue them in order to please investigators or to perpetuate the interest that is being shown in them. It is usually very obvious when a poltergeist phenomenon is being faked and it is not long before a cheat is caught out. However, once faking has been found to occur in a case, this casts doubt on all the other phenomena, genuine or otherwise, that have been recorded so far.

As can be gathered from this example, the poltergeist is a controversial area of the paranormal where a satisfactory explanation cannot be found by either psychic investigators or sceptics. Perhaps this too is an aspect of the poltergeist itself. It is, whether faked or not, a mischievous and malevolent phenomenon that takes great delight in causing confusion, panic and terror whenever it can. In common with many areas of the occult, poltergeists offer enough evidence to keep people's interest, but not enough to provide any absolute proof.

PSYCHOLOGICAL PHENOMENA

INTRODUCTION

DESPITE SOME OUTSTANDING advances in neural science in the last 50 years, many of the functions and workings of the human brain are still largely unknown. Psychology (the study of the human mind and its function) is still a young and controversial science, with few definite conclusions reached about the nature of human personality or its capabilities.

It is the aim of this chapter to present to the reader a number of psychological or psychiatric conditions that, although they appear to be paranormal in nature, are in fact acknowledged by professional psychological bodies to be functions of the human brain. The various conditions discussed, including multiple personality disorder, mass hysteria and autism, all last long enough in the patient to allow for their study by science and their existence has therefore been recognized by those who might otherwise have dismissed them. Although the symptoms are accepted, this does not mean to say that the condition is too. Many psychologists regard some of the conditions discussed in this chapter as being the wilful creation of a hysterical mind and therefore not independent psychiatric states of mind.

A particular problem is the use of hypnosis as a means of diagnosing psychiatric conditions. Hypnosis, first discovered by Franz Mesmer in the 1770s, has been used by psychologists as far back as the middle of the last century. Freud used it to explore the memories of hysterical patients in order to find their hidden neuroses and it is central to the diagnosis of past-life regression, multiple personality syndrome, alien abductions and, in part, hysteria and false memory syndrome. This, combined with the fact that it is generally only those psychiatrists who are interested in such phenomena who report it, has led to doubt over the existence of some of these conditions as independent psychological disorders.

To many researchers the causes of the phenomena are academic. Whether somebody has seven personalities within one brain is due to a childhood trauma or post-hypnotic suggestion is of no consequence. The human mind, whether by natural means or inducement, is still capable of producing such phenomena.

As new psychiatric conditions are recognized and studied, some parapsychologists have noticed an overlap between these phenomena and those currently classified as paranormal: for example, in multiple personality disorder, where the apparently separate personalities coexisting within the same brain bear a resemblance to the separate personalities exhibited by the control spirit that many mediums use to chair their seances. Other hypnotic, autosuggestion and false memory methods possibly underlie many cases of reported alien abduction, satanic abuse and past-life regression. More conventional human emotions, such as paranoia, greed, curiosity and a desire for attention may also lie behind some fraudulent or exaggerated claims.

Perhaps more interesting than this are the psychological disorders that are accepted by scientists but for which no full explanation can be found, such as the ability of apparently mentally disabled people to perform complex sums. These abilities imply that there are mechanisms at work within the brain which we know almost nothing about. It is this relative ignorance of the human brain and of the origins/causes of many psychological problems which may allow for the possibility of the existence of more random mind phenomena, such as ESP.

Advances in technology, such the CAT scan, medical isotope markers and genetics, have allowed the closer study of the reactions within the brain that cause personality and personality disorders. This is bringing closer together the more theory-based psychologists and the practical-based neural scientists. All this is of benefit to parapsychologists as well.

In recent years the temporal lobe region of the brain has been found to produce hallucinatory experiences involving feelings of floating, leaving the body, suffocation and oppression when it is stimulated by strong magnetic fields. Some of these induced sensations are similar to those reported in cases of out-of-body-experiences, near-death experiences, alien abductions and poltergeists. It has therefore been suggested by some scientists that strong magnetic fields (possibly associated with geological faults) could stimulate the temporal lobe into making people believe that they are experiencing a paranormal phenomenon. Some work has been done on trying to link the location of certain types of paranormal phenomena with geological features, but these have had mixed results. Perhaps by using theories such as this to explain away paranormal behaviour, the rationalists begin to sound more unconventional than the occultists.

The Salem Witch Trials

❖

MASS HYSTERIA

D ESPITE THE RECENT upsurge of interest in occultist matters, it is hard to imagine what it must have been like to live in a highly religious and superstitious
society where the slightest misfortune could be interpreted as a curse from a
neighbour. It was in such a New World society that some innocent fortune-telling
led to the deaths of 21 people on suspicion of witchcraft.

The village of Salem in Essex county lay about 15 miles north of Boston,
Massachusetts. Up until the time of the witch trials, Salem had been a remarkably
tolerant and prosperous place which had many intellectuals in its midst, including
Reverend Increase Mather, a founder of nearby Harvard University. In common
with much of the region, the village was under the influence of the Puritan Church
and it was in the house of one of its ministers, the Reverend Samuel Parris, that the
events which would lead to the now infamous witch trials began.

In February 1692 a group of local girls, including Parris's nine-year-old daughter, Elizabeth, and 11-year-old niece, Abigail Williams, had been fortune-telling
using an egg broken into a glass as a crystal ball. The aim was to try and find out
the identities of their future husbands, but instead the yolk apparently formed
into the shape of a coffin, badly scaring the girls. A few days after this the
Reverend Parris observed that his daughter and niece were acting peculiarly,
creeping around on all fours and weaving in and out of the legs of chairs and
tables like cats. More alarmingly, they began to go into convulsions, throwing
themselves into supposedly impossible shapes and uttering curses and oaths at
those around them. Within a week this behaviour had spread to five other girls in
the village, Ann Putnam (aged 12), Mary Walcott (aged 16), Elizabeth Hubbard
(aged 17), Mercy Lewis (aged 19) and Mary Warren (aged 20). At the time, the
Reverend Deodat Lawson described the convulsions as being 'so strange as a well
person could not screw their body into and...much beyond the force of the same
person when they are in their right mind'.

In the following months the convulsions began to spread to other women in
the village. The Reverend Parris, who suspected witchcraft was at work in the

village, had the foresight to move both Elizabeth and Abigail away from Salem to another settlement nearby.

As the talk of witches and devils grew in the village, one of tormented girls' aunt, Mary Sibley, persuaded the Reverend Parris's Caribbean slaves, Tituba and John, to make a special cake which, when fed to their dog, would remove the spell from the girls and transfer it to the animal. This was done on 25 February. The dog died and at last the girls were freed from their spell. When asked to say who had bewitched the girls, they replied that it was Tituba and two locally suspected white witches named Sarah Good and Sarah Osborne. The three women were arrested on 29 February and within the day were brought before two local magistrates on the charge of witchcraft and sorcery.

The two magistrates, John Hathorne and Jonathan Corwin, seemed to have conducted their cross-examination of the women on the assumption that they were guilty and that they knew the names of more witches within the village. On top of this, Sarah Good's husband, William, testified that his wife was a witch, saying that he had seen a strange wart on her body which he felt sure was used for suckling her familiars. Similarly, her four-year-old daughter, Dorcas, testified to actually seeing birds suckling from her mother. Mrs Good's fate was sealed when the five 'bewitched' girls were brought into the courtroom. On seeing her they immediately began convulsing again and started complaining that her spectre had been pinching and biting them.

Things went as badly for Sarah Osborne. Tituba was called to the witness box and testified to seeing a thing 'with wings and two legs and a head like a woman' suckling from Mrs Osborne, who, Tituba said, had signed her name in a book belonging to the devil. The five girls again convulsed in front of her.

There was some legal debate as to whether the evidence of the convulsing girls was acceptable in court. The Reverend Cotton Mather and a magistrate from a nearby village pointed out that it would be stupid for a person accused of witchcraft to use sorcery within a courtroom and argued that the names the girls had given could just be innocent misunderstandings. Neither Hathorne nor Corwin listened to these arguments and the trial continued with more damning evidence from Tituba, who claimed to have met the devil and to have seen the names of nine other people (not all of them local) involved in a coven. All three women were placed in jail to await further action.

On 11 March the situation worsened when three of the convulsing girls named two more local women, Martha Cory and Rebecca Nurse, as also being witches. Martha Cory was a highly devout Christian and a respected member of the community who had annoyed Hathorne by being openly sceptical about the whole trial. Although she did not believe in witchcraft, she now found herself on trial for it.

Her trial followed much the same pattern as the others, with the girls convuls-ing at her very sight. At one point in the trial Mrs Cory bit her lip. This immedi-ately led one of the convulsing girls to complain that her lip too had been bitten. The girl was examined and teethmarks were indeed found on her lip. It was thus for 'biting her lip' that Mrs Cory was eventually charged. The Reverend Nicholas Noyes added, 'I believe that it is apparent that she practiseth witchcraft in the congregation.'

By this time another member of the clergy, the Reverend Deodat Lawson, was urging caution over the trials. His words went unheeded. More direct action was taken by John Proctor, the employer of Mary Warren, one of the convulsing girls. He rode into town and kidnapped Mary back to his farm, where he gave her a sound thrashing to try and bring her back to her senses. This seemed to work and it later turned out that Mary Warren was the only girl out of the five accusers to return to full sanity after the episode was over.

Meanwhile, the trial of Rebecca Nurse had followed the usual course. She too was a devout churchgoer, but the Reverend Parris argued that if Judas could remain among the disciples, so could a witch like Rebecca remain within the church so as to damage it from within. On hearing of Rebecca's conviction, her sister (Sarah Cloyse) stormed out of the courtroom. On 4 April she was named, along with Elizabeth and John Proctor (the man who had saved Mary Warren), by the girls as being a witch. A whole series of people were arrested, including Giles Cory, the husband of Martha, a young mischievous girl named Abigail Hobbes and two long-suspected witches called Bridget Bishop and Candy, a negro slave. On 20 April Ann Putnam had a vision in which she witnessed the figure of an ex-minister, George Burroughs, living in a local village. She claimed that he had used sorcery to kill his first two wives and so he too was arrested, on 4 May. After the usual testimonies and after giving a rather confused defence, in which he did himself more harm than good, Burroughs was also convicted and put in jail. A few days after this, on 10 May, Sarah Osborne died in jail of natural causes.

The escalation of events within Salem had begun to seriously worry some of the more rational local ministers. The Reverend Cotton Mather used his influence to persuade the Governor of Massachusetts, Sir William Phips, to convene a special inquiry, called a Court of Oyer and Terminer, to examine the matter more closely. To be on the safe side, Governor Phips ordered all the suspects to be placed in irons and then put the commission under the charge of Chief-Justice William Stoughton. Unfortunately for the witches, John Hathorne was also on the commission. Cotton Mather tried to influence the judges by saying, 'It is better that ten witches go free than one innocent person be convicted.' However, this fell on deaf ears, as the commission gave the go-ahead for the first execution.

On 10 June Bridget Bishop was hanged. During the next month other cases were evaluated by the commission. When examining the case of Rebecca Nurse, the commission, including Hathorne, decided that she was innocent and should go free. This so enraged Ann Putnam that she returned to court with stories about how Rebecca's ghost had tried to strangle her. A retrial was ordered and the very confused and timid Rebecca was reconvicted on the evidence of Ann Putnam and her rather hysterical mother. A further petition to the court was made on behalf of Rebecca but to no avail. On 19 July Rebecca Nurse, Sarah Good, Susannah Martin, Elizabeth Howe and Sarah Wildes were all hanged.

When asked by the Reverend Noyes to confess to her crime, Sarah Good replied, 'You are a liar! I am no more a witch than you are a wizard and if you take away my life, God will give you blood to drink!' These words turned out to be prophetic, for some 25 years later the Reverend Noyes died of a massive lung haemorrhage, having choked on his own blood.

On 5 August a further six people were put on trial. Five of them were convicted immediately and the sixth, Elizabeth Proctor, was released on the advice of Cotton Mather, as she was pregnant. The other five, John Proctor, the Reverend George Burroughs, John Willard, Martha Carrier and George Jacobs, were all hanged on 19 August.

On the gallows Burroughs recited the Lord's Prayer perfectly to the crowd. As no witch is supposed to be able to do this, people started to plead for his release. In contrast to his other pleas for clemency, Cotton Mather assured the crowd that the devil was quite capable of assuming the form of a minister and reciting prayers. Burroughs was hanged.

In mid-September, Giles Cory refused to issue a plea when tried. This was probably because offering a plea of either guilty or not guilty would have enabled the county to claim his land, should he be convicted. He thus remained silent and was tortured by having heavy weights placed on his chest so that he had to fight for every breath. He died at noon on 19 September. In his diary Samuel Sewall wrote, 'About noon at Salem, Giles Cory was pressed to death for standing mute. Much pains was used with him...but all in vain.'

In the meantime, another 16 people had been found guilty of witchcraft. Of these five pleaded guilty and were allowed to live provided they repent, one escaped from jail, another was allowed to live because she was pregnant and a further woman was delayed from being punished until an illness she had cleared up. On 22 September the remaining eight convicted people, including Martha Cory, were hanged.

As if things were not bad enough, the girls continued to name literally hundreds of people as witches. Over 50 people were named in the nearby village of Andover alone. A total of 250 people were now being called to trial, including three magistrates, a Boston merchant (who was released after suing his accusers) and a man who was arrested for 'firing a mare's fart'. Matters were well and truly out of hand.

Cotton Mather and his father, Increase, pleaded to the General Court of Massachusetts to disband the commission and on 29 October this happened, bringing an end to the witch trials. A total of 21 people had died as a result of the affair.

In the aftermath of the trials, the Reverend Parris was banned from the village for starting things off in the first place. Some of the hanged people, including Rebecca Nurse, received posthumous pardons and many of the survivors were paid compensation. On 19 August 1703, 11 years after the hangings, all but seven of the accused people were pardoned. The remaining seven received a semi-pardon in 1957. Perhaps wary of its dubious past, the town of Salem changed its name to Danvers in the early twentieth century.

❖

Salem society was undoubtedly highly puritanical and superstitious, and belief in the devil and the supernatural would have been strong. Suspected witches had been previously brought before the authorities, including Bridget Bishop, but had always either been found innocent or at worst been placed in the stocks. The village boasted a number of 'wise women' and these seemed to be tolerated before the onset of convulsions in the girls.

The description of the initial symptoms displayed by the girls (convulsions, writhing, senseless talking, etc.) corresponds closely to modern descriptions of hysteria, as well as to those of the Convulsionnaires in St Médard churchyard (see page 75). The girls were of the right age to experience hysterical symptoms, although whether it was the fear that prompted their fortune-telling that triggered it cannot be certain. Perhaps the Reverend Parris was, in this respect, correct to link his daughter's and niece's behaviour to the egg-gazing incident. He was, however, wrong to put it down to witchcraft. A diagnosis of hysteria is further reinforced by the fact that John Proctor was able to remove the symptoms from Mary Warren by giving her a whipping.

Hysteria is psychologically contagious and seems to have spread from Parris's family to some of the other girls associated with the egg-gazing incident. Once the firm connection between witchcraft and the convulsing girls had been made, the need to find the source of the evil became apparent. After the cake incident, the girls seemed to have begun naming people whom they disliked or distrusted in the community. Among those who were first accused, Tituba was a slave who held superstitious beliefs and knew of pagan rituals and as such was a prime target for suspicion. Sarah Good was noted as being a particularly unpleasant character who was bad-tempered and was said to have cursed people under her breath. It is likely that the girls (along with many other people in the community) had had dealings with her and disliked her. She too was therefore a natural choice. Sarah Osborne, along with Sarah Good, was a local wise woman, making her suspicious to the girls as well.

Once the initial victims had been chosen by the girls, the superstitious people of Salem kept the momentum going themselves. The next few people to be charged all seem to have been chosen more by the adult population than by the girls, although the girls were willing to go along with their choices. Martha Cory was accused for being sceptical about the trials, Sarah Cloyse for storming out of the courtroom, and John and Elizabeth Proctor for kidnapping and whipping Mary Warren. Abigail Hobbes, who was a local prankster and troublemaker, was also victimized, as were Bridget Bishop and Candy the slave for being witches and also George Burroughs for being suspected of killing his previous two wives. However, the choice of Rebecca Nurse is perplexing. All reports of her are complimentary and it seems that even the commission was prepared to let her off. It may have been that Rebecca Nurse had upset Ann Putnam's mother, for she seems to have done everything in her power to get her reconvicted. After this, the floodgates opened and anyone and everyone was put on the suspect list. Everyone, that is, apart from the convulsing girls, their relatives and the magistrates, whose behaviour was the strangest of all.

Viewed like this, the Salem witch trials do seem to be an escalation of a rather trivial incident into religious genocide. In medieval Europe and America, and in modern Africa, witchcraft cases are usually centred around personal misfortunes, such as cattle dying or family illness. The evidence connecting such misfortunes to those accused of witchcraft is normally quite circumstantial. In Salem, perhaps it was the psychical evidence of the convulsing girls that convinced them of the accused's guilt.

When looking at the case of the Salem witches, it is hard to think of such things occurring in modern society. Yet suspected witches are still regularly killed by mobs in South African townships. There are also modern religious comparisons in some small American towns, where belief in the devil and evil spirits remains strong among fundamentalist Christians. False memory syndrome (a technique for implanting non-existent memories usually into impressionable people) has been used by over-zealous priests to get members of their congregation (usually adolescent girls) to remember being abused by their parents or prominent opposers of the Church. In 1992 in Edenton, North Carolina, Robert

Fulton Kelly was convicted on 99 counts of child sex abuse that supposedly took place in his day-care centre. The trial was extremely controversial, with many witnesses', therapists' and children's testimonies being excluded. The case is thought to have started as a falling-out between Kelly and the local church. Rumours of child abuse started to circulate in the town and the police were called in. Many parents consulted therapists in order to interview their children about being abused by Kelly. A number of highly dubious techniques were employed to get the children to give the desired statements, including denying them after-dinner desserts and using suggestive interviewing techniques. In 1989 Kelly was arrested and accused of 100 counts of rape, sodomy and child sexual abuse. In addition to the stories of sexual abuse, Kelly was also accused (but not charged) of hanging children, tossing them into shark tanks, shooting babies and placing children in a microwave oven. He was also accused of abusing children who were not even living in the town at the same time as him. One child even said that Kelly had flown him into space in a hot air balloon. Doctors found no physical evidence of sexual abuse and there were no adult witnesses to any abuse. Despite this, Kelly was found guilty and sentenced to twelve life terms.

In Britain in the 1980s and 1990s there was a string of cases (in the Orkney Islands, Cleveland, Nottingham and Rochdale) in which large numbers of children were taken into care after psychologists deemed they had been used in satanic rituals. Later inquiries returned the children to their parents (some after spending years in care), after finding that the psychologists had been asking leading questions during interviews. Many of these questions were not dissimilar to those asked during the Salem trials. A 1995 independent inquiry by the British government into child abuse concluded that there was no evidence for the existence of satanic ritual abuse in the United Kingdom.

On a wider scale, the McCarthy Communist witch-hunts in 1950s America resulted in widespread hysteria about friends, family and neighbours being 'Commies' in disguise. This led to the political persecution of many individuals, including film stars such as Charlie Chaplin. Society and governments often use controlled hysteria to justify their means and to gain public backing. One has only to think of the propaganda put about by all sides during times of conflict or during the run-up to elections to realize that, to some degree, we are all victims of somebody else's hysteria.

'Philip'

❖

AN ARTIFICIAL GHOST

'PHILIP' WAS NOT a living personality or even a spiritual entity but the creation of a group of experimental parapsychologists. The results of the so-called 'Philip' experiments may offer a serious contribution to the understanding of ghosts and other related phenomena.

In 1972 the Toronto Society for Psychical Research, under the direction of Dr George Owen and his wife, Iris, decided to try and create an artificial ghost which they hoped to be able to materialize at a seance. Their experiment had been inspired by the work of clinical psychologist Kenneth Batcheldor, who, in the early 1960s, had managed to produce a series of mild poltergeist-type phenomena using an ordinary group of people sitting round a table.

In order to perform their experiment, the Toronto group created a fictitious historical character called Philip Aylesford, who was given a complete historical background. Philip was said to have been an aristocrat born in England in 1624, at around the time of the English civil war. He went into the army at an early age and fought for the Royalists, being knighted for his services at the tender age of 16. He later worked as a secret agent, passing information from the Parliamentary soldiers to those of the Crown. During this time he met and was friendly with Charles II and Oliver Cromwell. He married a girl called Dorothea. Later on he had an affair with a gypsy girl called Margo, who, when Dorothea found out about her, was burnt as a witch. Distraught at his inability to intervene to save her, Philip committed suicide at the age of 30 by throwing himself off the battlements of his house.

In order to 'create' Philip, the group of eight people would meet regularly and hold seances. They would meditate on Philip and concentrate on trying to get him to materialize or communicate through them. After several months they had failed to produce any significant results, although people did report the feeling of a presence on occasions. In the summer of 1974, the Owens decided a change of tactic was needed and more physical techniques were tried instead.

The first of these was the Spiritualist practice of table-turning (see Daniel Dunglas Home, page 81, and the Fox Sisters, page 122). The first few sessions produced nothing, but eventually the table began to vibrate and distinct knocking sounds were heard. Using the familiar code of one knock for yes, two for no, somebody asked whether Philip was responsible. One knock resounded. Using the rapping code, Philip then proceeded to retell the life story that had been created for him by the group. In further sessions he apparently caused the table to walk around the room and once, in front of a public audience, it was seen to walk up a set of stairs. Philip also showed himself to have a sense of humour by shuffling the table towards those who arrived late at the seances and by occasionally using the table to trap people into a corner.

Philip was also prepared to answer questions on events in his life that had not been created by the group. On one occasion he was telling the group about his time in Bohemia. When asked whether he knew the Bohemian queen Elizabeth, he replied that he had. George Owen, thinking he had caught Philip out, commented that Philip had earlier denied knowing the queen's brother-in-law, Prince Rupert. Philip replied that Prince Rupert was not, and never had been, Queen Elizabeth's brother-in-law. This turned out to be factually correct.

Rare incidents like this caused some of the group to wonder whether Philip was indeed a real person who had had a similar life to their creation or that they themselves could have possibly picked up psychometric information about a real person's life when creating Philip. However, historical investigation showed that there was no evidence for the existence of Philip or anybody like him in the seventeenth century.

It was noticed by the group that the results improved as the belief they had in Philip's existence increased and that when they were having fun (singing, joking, etc.) Philip would respond better and would sometimes rap in time to the tunes.

In 1974 the experiments were filmed by Toronto City Television. The table being used was seen not only to move, but actually to rise a short distance off the floor. A method of persuading 'spirits' to record their voices on tape, Electronic Voice Phenomena, was also tried by Kent State University, but the results were largely inconclusive, although some discernible answers were given by Philip to questions put by Iris Owen.

It was around this time that a telling incident occurred within the group. At one of the seances, a member of the group (for reasons unknown) announced to Philip, 'We only made you up, you know!' The communications stopped dead and it was some time before the group could gain the correct frame of mind to allow Philip to come through once more.

The fame of the Philip phenomenon led to a number of similar experiments, some equally successful, being set up worldwide. The Philip group itself tried to take their experiment a step further by attempting to persuade Philip to materialize or to produce poltergeist-type activity. They achieved neither aim and the group's interest in the experiment waned until, in 1977, they disbanded alto-gether. The initial results of the experiments were written up by Iris Owen in a book entitled *Conjuring Up Philip*. Apparently George and Iris Owen still occa-sionally hold seances, although whether Philip still makes appearances is not known.

❖

The Philip experiments were innovative and produced results that grabbed the interest of both the public and scientists. It is certain that Philip Aylesford was not a real historical figure and that his rather improbable life history was indeed the invention of the Toronto Society for Psychic Research. Given this, who or what was Philip?

The most familiar explanation is that Philip was indeed exactly what the Toronto group intended him to be, a mental poltergeist. This would make him a psychic manifestation of the Toronto group's collective consciousness. Evidence for this comes from the fact that, by and large, he was able to provide only infor-mation about himself that had been designated by other members of the group. Additional information tended to be only in the form of 'yes' or 'no' answers to what could be called leading questions. Someone asking, 'Did you meet with Queen Elizabeth while in Bohemia?' and being answered with a 'Yes' is not as convincing as Philip saying, 'I met with Queen Elizabeth while in Bohemia.' Also convincing is Philip's disappearance after one of the group broke the team spirit by declaring that Philip was non-existent.

The other explanation put forward is that Philip was indeed a spirit, but a rogue spirit that used the group's created information to disguise itself as Philip before contacting the group through their seances. Many people who have been involved in methods of spirit communication (seances, Ouija boards, automatic writing, etc.) have come to the conclusion that the entities they contact are dishonest, deceitful and, in some cases, threatening.

More difficult to explain is why only the one 'entity' (Philip) was ever contacted by the group. Spirit communication usually involves several different entities coming through at any one sitting, sometimes even jostling with each other to control the seance. It seems odd that only one entity should be in constant contact and masquerading as Philip for months on end.

Philip was only ever contacted through rather basic seance techniques, such as table-turning, and the group was never able to materialize him or produce poltergeist-type effects. Most people are capable of producing results from table-turning, Ouija boards and automatic writing, regardless of whether they believe in an afterlife. It is, however, very rare for people to be able to produce more advanced phenomena such as poltergeists or physical mediumship or the manifestation of spirits. Dr Owen has declared that none of the Toronto group was psychic when they started and that none developed any such skills afterwards. Trying to conjure up the physical manifestation of Philip was a disaster and small-scale effects were achieved only when using the more popular spiritualist techniques such as table-turning and rapping. This tells us that there were considerable restrictions to Philip's capabilities.

From personal experience with Ouija boards and table-turning, I am convinced that there is a link between the sitters' minds and the phenomena these devices produce. Research has shown that the greater the concentration of the group and the more they believe in what they are trying to do, the better the effects. This being so, it is not surprising that a team hoping to contact a mentally produced 'entity' should be able to do so only via more mentally associated techniques such as table-turning.

The Philip experiments have been used by sceptics as evidence for the non-existence of an afterlife and by parapsychologists as evidence for, at the very least, the existence of a psychological phenomenon that is in need of research.

Christine Beauchamp et al.

❖

MULTIPLE PERSONALITY DISORDER

MANY PARAPSYCHOLOGISTS HAVE noticed similarities between cases of multiple personality disorder (MPD) and some types of paranormal phenomenon, including mediumship, spirit possession, past-life regression and poltergeist activity. However, MPD remains a highly controversial subject among psychologists and psychiatrists, with many people still refusing to recognize its existence.

MPD is a psychological condition in which a person appears to possess two or more separate and distinctive personalities. Each may have its own self-awareness, characteristics, memories and experiences. Each can have its own name, may be of either sex and may or may not be aware of other personalities residing in the same body. The best way to describe this phenomenon is to use the example of one of the very first cases of MPD to be studied by a psychologist. The psychologist concerned was Dr Walter Franklin Prince of the Tufts Medical School in Boston, Massachusetts and his patient has always gone under the pseudonym of Miss Christine Beauchamp (her real name was Clara Fowler).

Christine Beauchamp was a 23-year-old student at Dr Prince's college when she came to his attention in 1898. He described her as being quite neurotic and highly strung, with an obsessional lifestyle that was causing problems with her studies. In an attempt to help, Dr Prince hypnotized Christine.

Under hypnosis Dr Prince discovered that Christine had two further 'personalities' that appeared to be completely separate from her own. To avoid confusion, he labelled Christine's everyday personality as BI and the subsequent two personalities BII and BIII.

BII was described as the state which everyday Christine (BI) went into after being hypnotized, but BIII was different altogether and appeared to be a separate personality. On investigation, Dr Prince discovered a complex relationship between the three personalities. Christine was apparently unaware of the existence of either of the other personalities, while BIII was aware of the thoughts and actions of both Christine and BII. The so-called BII personality, being essentially trance-like, appeared to be unaware of anything other than Dr Prince.

BIII grew in confidence and complexity and was 'born' (could exist without hypnosis) after being allowed to open her eyes during a hypnotic session. She was then able to come and go at will by taking over Christine's body at any time she pleased. BIII adopted the name Sally and would be in existence for anything from a few minutes to several days at a time. Dr Prince describes the differences between Christine and Sally as follows:

> In character she [Sally] differs very remarkedly from BI [Christine]. I would say here that Christine is a very serious-minded person, fond of books and study, of a religious turn of mind, and possesses a very morbid conscientiousness...Sally, on the other hand, is full of fun, does not worry about anything; all life is one great joke to her; she hates books, loves fun and amusement, does not like serious things, hates church – in fact is thoroughly childlike in every way.

Sally seems to have been the exact opposite of Christine and also seems to have taken a great dislike to her, playing a large number of childish pranks on her other personality.

Sally used her awareness of Christine's personality to exploit all her fears and weaknesses. For example, Christine had a mortal fear of snakes and spiders and so Sally, while in control of the body, gathered a box full of insects, wrapped it up and posted it to herself. Christine was in charge of the body when the package arrived and was severely shocked when the insects escaped around her house. Another favourite trick was for Sally to hitch lifts into the countryside and get out many miles from home. She would then 'leave', forcing Christine, who was weak in nature, to walk or hitch her way home. Sally also enjoyed destroying Christine's possessions, spreading rumours about her and writing her rude letters.

When questioned by Dr Prince, it appeared that while Sally was in control Christine was 'dead' and that Sally, as well as being aware of all the other personalities, had been in existence since Christine's birth. Dr Prince eventually decided that Sally probably represented Christine's subliminal consciousness (her subconscious).

A fourth personality emerged in 1899 which appeared to be related to an incident that had occurred six years previously. In 1893 Christine had been working as a nurse in a hospital and had received a great shock after accidentally meeting up with an old friend who had then tried to kiss her. The incident shocked her greatly and on 7 June 1899 she received a letter from this friend, who jovially referred it again. The memories this revived threw Christine into hysteria and Dr Prince was sent for. When he arrived, Christine was still having a fit but suddenly calmed down and became rational and lucid. Further questioning by Dr Prince revealed that a new personality was in control of Christine's body. The new personality was labelled BIV by Dr Prince.

Later investigation revealed that BIV had been 'born' as a result of the 1893 incident and was unaware of anything that had occurred since. Dr Prince describes BIV as follows: 'Unlike the others, she is irritable and quick-tempered, and resented as an impertinence any inquiry into her private thoughts and affairs.'

Colin Wilson (in *Mysteries*) describes BIV's character as being like that of a schoolmistress, which is a good analogy to Dr Prince's description of her. In the hierarchy of personalities, Sally (BIII) was aware of BIV's actions but not her thoughts and so started to hate her more than she hated Christine.

The emergence of BIV gave Dr Prince the clue he thought he needed in order to solve the nature of this strange case. He decided that none of the personalities represented the complete Christine Beauchamp but that Christine (BI) and the schoolmistress (BIV) represented the two fragments of her true personality and that Sally (BIII) represented her subconscious. His theory was that the incident in 1893 had so shocked Christine that her personality had reacted by splintering, with different aspects of it ending up in BI and BIV. Since that day BIV had remained dormant until being awoken in 1899.

Having decided this, Dr Prince began a course of therapy to resolve the situation. He used BII (the hypnotic state) to make BI and BIV aware of each other and before too long the personalities merged to form a much better balanced personality who was to become the new Christine Beauchamp. Sally (BIII) still remained in existence, but was unaware of the thoughts and actions of the new Christine. After much bullying, Sally was persuaded to leave Christine alone altogether and the problem appeared to have been resolved. Christine Beauchamp regained her place in college and later married one of Dr Prince's assistants.

Dr Prince's experiences and diagnosis of MPD caused much debate at the time, particularly when he encountered another example in 1910. After this, MPD remained largely a psychological curiosity until the early 1980s in North America, when renewed interest in the subject caused an explosion in the number of reported cases. These differed from Christine Beauchamp's, for instead of having a small number of personalities, psychiatrists were reporting cases where tens and even hundreds of personalities (both male and female) were coexisting in the same body.

MPD was accepted as a formal psychological phenomenon (classified as Dissociative Disorder DSM-III-R and ICD-10) in North America in the late 1980s. This caused the controversy to escalate, with proponents and opponents of MPD becoming increasingly vocal and hostile towards each other. The number of cases continues to increase as psychiatrists and the public become more aware of the syndrome. It is worth quoting two further cases to show some of the problems MPD is currently creating.

In November 1990 in Oshkosh, Wisconsin, Mark Peterson, aged 29, was convicted of raping a 27-year-old waitress known only as Sarah. This was to be no ordinary trial.

Sarah was an MPD patient who, at the time of the incident, had been diagnosed as having 18 separate personalities. Peterson met Sarah on 9 June 1990 and got on well with a personality called Franny, who was then in control of her body. He met her again two days later at a restaurant, where he was introduced to some of her other personalities, including a 'fun-loving 20-year-old' called Jennifer. Jennifer agreed to Peterson's sexual advances and intercourse took place in her car. Later in the evening Franny returned and was horrified to find out what had been going on in her absence. She telephoned the police and Peterson was arrested.

In the witness box six of Sarah's personalities had to be sworn in separately and each gave a separate testimony of what had happened. During the trial her MPD was revealed to have started with seeing her father crushed to death in a car, although, in common with most modern cases, childhood parental abuse was also cited. The jury decided that Peterson had made a sexual assault on someone he knew to be mentally ill and he was convicted of rape. After the trial Sarah was reported to have 46 personalities. Eventually, Peterson's conviction was overturned on appeal.

The final case is one where the cover of MPD was used to try and pervert the course of justice.

The case concerns Kenneth Bianchi, who was aged 27 when he was arrested for the rape and murder of ten women in the Los Angeles area. Bianchi's morbid habit of displaying his victims' naked bodies on hillsides earned him the nickname 'The Hillside Strangler'.

After his arrest, a psychological assessment was ordered. This was performed by John Watkins, who was a specialist in MPD. Watkins placed Bianchi into a deep hypnotic trance only to discover that he had a second personality called Steve. Steve professed to hate Bianchi and it was he (Steve) who had committed the murders while in control of Bianchi's body; he had set up Bianchi to take the blame. After being awoken, Bianchi denied any knowledge of Steve, although he did say that he had had black-outs when the murders were supposed to have been committed. Watkins called in other psychologists to perform a whole series of psychological tests on both Bianchi and Steve.

These tests suggested that Bianchi's personality was timid and relatively normal, while Steve's was aggressive and psychopathic. Watkins was convinced that he had found a classic case of MPD and declared that Bianchi may not have been aware that he was a murderer. Others severely disagreed with him, particularly the psychologist Martin Orne, who also tested Bianchi.

Orne assessed both personalities for a range of known psychiatric conditions and came to the conclusion that he was dealing with only one personality. Further tests involving simple word games and conundrums led Orne to the conclusion that Bianchi was faking the MPD and that he was fully aware of the crimes he had committed. Orne's scepticism was vindicated when Bianchi confessed to murdering seven of the girls and also implicated his cousin.

Despite this confession, Watkins stuck to his MPD diagnosis, claiming that Bianchi had been brainwashed into giving his confession. It later emerged that Bianchi had a long-standing obsession with psychology and psychiatry and that he had forged a psychology degree certificate in the name of Steve Walker. The case for MPD was dismissed and Bianchi was eventually judged to be criminally insane and was convicted of the murders.

❖

Modern psychologists have taken Dr Prince's initial traumatized split-personality theory and furthered it. As the number of reported cases increased, it was noticed that a large percentage of MPD-diagnosed sufferers claimed to have been mentally or physically abused in childhood. The trauma of the abuse is thought to be so stressful that the victim's personality splinters in order to hide the memories of these events. Each 'splinter' then goes on to subconsciously develop into a number of separate personalities, which may emerge when triggered by a later event (such as hypnosis) that causes the recall of the abusive episodes.

Before entering into the arguments associated with the existence of MPD as a valid phenomenon, it is worth pointing out why it has attracted so much interest from the parapsychology fraternity. Many areas of parapsychology deal with the existence of disembodied personalities apparently living within a normal human being. The chief examples of this include spirit and demonic possession, mediumship (or channelling), automatic writing, past-life regression, Ouija boards and 'talking' poltergeists. The acceptance by the American psychiatric profession of a phenomenon that acknowledges that there may be tens of separate personalities living within a single human brain seemed to offer an acceptable answer to many examples of the above-mentioned phenomena.

The parallels between many of these phenomena and MPD are indeed close. Take, for example, spirit or demonic possession. In these cases the possessed person will often suddenly change personality completely and exhibit mannerisms, traits, voices and knowledge not usually associated or out of character with their 'normal' selves. In cases of demonic possession the 'demon' will often be blasphemous, violent and abusive to those around it. It will answer to a different name and claim to be a separate entity in its own right. It will also frequently be abusive and unpleasant to or about the original personality. Although this behaviour is more extreme than the examples given above, such antagonism has been regularly reported in cases of MPD and does exhibit many of the features associated with Christine Beauchamp's third personality, Sally. Indeed, some authors have suggested that Christine Beauchamp, and other MPD cases, are examples of spirit possession.

Other similarities have been noticed between the control spirits associated with mediums which act as an interface between the medium and the spirit world. Usually childlike and mischievous, they act like a chairperson at seances, announcing the arrival of individual spirits, keeping them in order and removing undesirable ones. This type of dissociative personality again exhibits some of the characteristics that are seen in MPD and it has been suggested that the spirit control is a secondary personality, with all subsequent 'spirits' contacted during the course of a seance further examples of multiple personalities. Once one starts making comparisons between MPD and psychic phenomena, it is possible to provide an explanation for almost anything paranormal. It would therefore seem that MPD is capable of explaining some psychological phenomena in a way that would appease both parapsychologists and sceptics alike.

In common with the psychic phenomena it has been used to explain, MPD itself is still a highly controversial subject. The only place where it has been accepted as a genuine phenomenon by the psychiatric community is North America and even here it is still very controversial. For example, in a 1994 survey, 27.1 per cent of American psychiatrists doubted its existence.

Those in favour of MPD point out that each separate personality is capable of being psychologically quantified in its own right. So, for example, one personality may score a higher IQ than another, or be phobic about something that does not affect another personality. They point out that there do appear to be genuine black-outs for some personalities while others are in control and that the majority of personalities are capable of existing on their own.

Opponents of MPD offer two main arguments. The first is that the majority of cases seem to be diagnosed only by those psychiatrists who believe in it. As with alien abductions, false memory syndrome, etc., many MPD victims do not become aware of what they are suffering from until it is diagnosed, often under hypnotism, by their psychiatrist. The implication of this is that it is the psychiatrists themselves who are creating, either inadvertently or deliberately, their own cases of MPD in suggestible patients. The second argument is that the disorder is a hysterical one that, thanks to publicity over recent years, is causing people to come forward with their own self-induced symptoms.

It must be said that the dramatic increase in the number of MPD cases reported in North America does appear to put MPD into the hysterical bracket. It is hard for proponents of the disorder to explain why it is so common in North America but virtually unheard of in other countries and why modern cases seem to be increasing in severity. Pre-1980 it was common for MPD cases to exhibit from two to seven personalities in the same body. It is now not unusual to see cases involving 30 or more. It has, however, been suggested that this increase can be related to the growth in traumatic crimes such as muggings, child abuse, rape, kidnapping, etc.

Some authors draw a comparison between MPD and other historical bouts of hysterical phenomena, such as demonic possession and witchcraft in the sixteenth and seventeenth centuries (see the Salem Witch Trials, page 52), which balloon in popularity for a short time, only to be never heard of again once the subject is out of vogue. Perhaps, as with much in modern society, it is a genuine and rare phenomenon that has grabbed the American imagination and has subsequently been mimicked by hysterically disposed people or falsely induced by their overly eager psychiatrists.

Special Talents

❖

AUTISM AND MENTAL ABILITIES

IN 1849 AN Alabama slave girl gave birth to a blind and mentally impaired boy whom she named Tom Wiggins. As the boy grew, he showed little awareness of his surroundings and was apt to stand still for hours on end in the mansion house where he and his mother lived. Shortly after his sixth birthday, Tom was present at a party in the mansion where the chief entertainment was the performance of two piano concertos by a visiting musician. After retiring to bed, some of the household heard the sound of a piano coming from downstairs and, on investigation, found Tom sitting at the instrument playing a slow but note-perfect rendition of one of the concertos. The second time he played it the tempo had been corrected and the piece was declared perfect. Although it was not a diagnosed condition in Tom Wiggins's time, he was suffering from the mental condition of autism. His piano recital, although apparently paranormal, was a function of this little-understood mental condition.

Autism has long perplexed the doctors and psychologists who have studied or diagnosed the condition. It is a permanent mental condition where the individual shows signs of a reduced ability to respond to or communicate with the outside world. The degree to which autism affects sufferers varies between individuals. Some people are able to live virtually unaffected lives with the condition while others need round-the-clock attention. One of the most noted aspects of autism (as highlighted in the 1991 film *Rainman*) is the ordered and obsessional way that these people lead their lives. Many autistics are capable of extraordinary feats of concentration or single-mindedness that would reduce the average person to tears. This obsessional behaviour has also apparently created a feature of autism that, on the surface, would appear to be almost paranormal in origin.

In centuries past it was noticed that some so-called 'village idiots' were capable of outperforming even the most intelligent or gifted members of the community in certain areas. These people were often able to do rapid mental calculations, play musical instruments or draw beautifully and as such were given the name idiot savant ('the skilful or knowledgeable idiot'). With the recognition of autism as a mental condition came the realization that a large number of these idiots savants were in fact autistic. This phenomenon has produced some extraordinary abilities among people who, in every other way, seem to be extremely mentally disabled.

Stephen Wiltshire came to the British public's attention in the 1980s when, as a 12-year-old autistic, his obsession with drawing buildings gained him praise and recognition from artists and architects alike. In order to do his drawings, Stephen would be placed in front of the building for up to 15 minutes, during which time he would mentally study and observe every detail before him. Then, often hours later, he would pick up his pen and paper and do the drawing itself. The pictures that he produces using this method are extraordinary, not just because the quality of drawing is so good but because every detail from the original scene is reproduced faithfully from memory. This includes features such as individual gargoyles, windows, the time on clocks, etc. Even more intriguing are the facts that his drawings are always 'mirror-imaged' (back-to-front) and perspective-perfect (the view as seen by the human eye is reproduced exactly). Stephen's drawings have attracted the attention of many respected individuals and organizations, including London's Royal Academy of Arts.

Another autistic, Gottfried Mind, was noted throughout Europe in the early 1800s for his animal drawings, one of which was purchased by Britain's King George IV. Similarly, over 100,000 people turned up to watch the celebrated Japanese autistic artist Kyoshi Yamashita open an exhibition of his paintings in 1957.

Other autistic people have shown a remarkable ability to master musical instruments. Some have picked up (or sat down at) and played instruments they have never seen before. The piano seems to be especially popular among those who have displayed this ability. Again, musical autistics seem to be able to memorize and play long passages of music after hearing them only once. Many of them are 'pitch-perfect' (able to name and reproduce a note on hearing it). A girl known only as 'Lucy' was apparently capable of humming perfectly impossibly long passages of Tchaikovsky having heard them played to her by her mother.

Some of the most amazing skills exhibited not only by autistic but also by apparently unaffected people is the ability to perform staggeringly complicated mental calculations in a matter of seconds. Such people, sometimes called 'lightning calculators', have so impressed witnesses over the years that historical cases have been well documented and some of them even toured with circuses, being billed as having paranormal abilities.

In 1780 in America William Hartshorne and Samuel Coates examined a 70-year-old African slave named Tom Fuller. Despite being completely illiterate, it took him two minutes to tell them how many seconds there were in a year and a half, and he was even quicker when asked how many seconds a man 70 years, 17 days and 12 hours old had lived. When Hartshorne and Coates told Fuller that his last calculation was wrong, Fuller replied that they had not taken into account the leap years! In 1725 another illiterate, Jedediah Buxton, took a month to mentally calculate how many barley corns, vetches, peas, beans and lentils would fill a space of 202,680,000,360 cubic miles.

An autistic who had this ability was the German Zacharias Dase, who was considered to be an idiot and could not be taught even the basic theories of mathematics at school. Despite this he was capable of some amazing mental feats, including being able to multiply figures of over 100 digits by each together. From 1847 until his death in 1861 his ability was used by Hamburg mathematicians to create a book of logarithms for all the numbers up to 1,005,000 and he was also concerned with trying to create tables of factors and prime numbers for numbers of 7 million and upwards. Modern-day examples include a severely autistic anonymous man (featured on the BBC television programme *QED*) who is capable of calculating the day for any given date and year faster than either scientists using tables or a computer.

As well as these accepted 'special talents' displayed by autistics, some mentally disabled people have also shown evidence of what would be classified as examples of paranormal ability.

In 1937 Raleigh Drake, Professor of Psychology at the Wesleyan College in Georgia, studied the case of a severely brain-damaged boy called Bo, who was 11 years old and had a measured IQ of 55. After a series of standard tests, Professor Drake began to notice that the boy was able to repeat sentences and words from books that his mother was reading. At the next session Drake wrote down 12 numbers on a sheet of paper and asked the mother to concentrate on them. Bo was able to get nine out of the 12 right – considerably above the statistical average. Later on, under more controlled conditions, Bo managed to get 66 guesses right out of a run of 90 Zener cards (special cards developed to test ESP ability) – an average of 73.3 per cent. A chance score would be expected to be 20 per cent. Another run of 595 cards produced a correct score of 373, an average of 62.6 per cent. Later runs were performed with the child blindfolded and the mother, who was in another room, allowed only to call out the word 'ready'. This precluded the possibility of visual and verbal clues. Under these conditions two runs of 675 cards produced results of 55.2 per cent and a staggering 84 per cent correct calls by Bo. A further precaution, where the mother did not signal at all, produced a result of 40 per cent.

Performing laboratory tests of any type on autistic or mentally impaired subjects is a sensitive and controversial subject. Some parapsychologists have dared to suggest links between mental disability or illness and certain types of psychic phenomenon. This includes W.G. Roll, who noted that 25 per cent of poltergeist cases could be linked to seizures or epilepsy in the focus of the activity. It is, however, possible that these attacks could be the result of the stress induced as a result of being involved in a poltergeist case in the first place.

❖

Special talents are included within this book not because they are a paranormal phenomenon (with the exception of Professor Drake's case) but because they illustrate the hugely complicated nature of the human brain. The abilities described are not understood by either science or the people who possess them. The lightning-calculator autistics are quite incapable of explaining the mathematical laws they follow in order to get their results. In the case of autism, it would appear that these abilities are related to autistic people's obsessional nature, which leads them to memorize the minute details of buildings or the sequential nature of mathematical calculations. However, this topic was not really included to enter the considerable debate that exists on the mechanisms behind autism but to issue notes of both optimism and caution when evaluating some aspects of the paranormal.

Unexplained phenomena linked to the human mind, such as telepathy, ESP, clairvoyance and precognition, have long been dismissed by psychology and other areas of science as coincidence, fraud or self-delusion. The reasons for such dismissals are often not based on research results (for next to no university research exists on these topics) but on the gut instincts of people who will not accept their possibility. Some parapsychology research has produced results that might indicate the existence of these phenomena or at least the need to explain reported cases of it. Most scientists do not accept positive results for ESP, yet they are forced to accept the reality of the phenomenon displayed by the so-called idiot savant, despite its apparent contradiction to other mental handicaps.

Science is fond of stating how little understood the human brain is and how it is probably the most complex organ to have existed in the history of the earth. It has been estimated that only 10 per cent of the human brain's capacity is used by the average person. Even allowing for error in this figure (one wonders how it was arrived at in the first place) and the amount of room devoted to controlling the body's life-support systems, there is a large proportion of the human brain that is under-used and certainly not understood. It is therefore possible that just as the special talents of autistics give us an insight into some of the workings and complexities of the higher functions of the brain, so features such as ESP and clairvoyance also lurk deep within ourselves.

It should, however, be pointed out that the comparison between autism and ESP is clearly not a good one. The features of autistic special abilities are merely unusual when they are seen in people who otherwise appear mentally disabled or they are an extreme version of known human functions, such as mental arithmetic. In comparison, the whole area of psychic powers is both unproven satisfactorily and unpredictable and clearly not related to normal conscious brain functions.

Similarly, if one accepts that the human brain is as complex and unexplored as we are given to believe, then one also has to wonder if there is scope for psychic phenomena produced by the brain to simply be products of the complex inner workings of the mind rather than independent psychological phenomena. For example, ESP (and other phenomena) might turn out to be merely the subconscious mind quickly calculating the likely odds on an event happening and then prompting the conscious brain, so that it would appear that precognition, telepathy or clairvoyance had taken place.

Les Convulsionnaires

❖

HYSTERIA/AUTOSUGGESTION

FRANÇOIS DE PARIS was the Deacon of Paris when he died at the age of 37 in May 1727. Although an established member of the Jesuit order, he was reputed to have healing powers and had built up quite a following among Parisian worshippers. At his funeral, within the church of St Médard, a young crippled boy went into convulsions for several minutes. After he had recovered, he got up and started to sing and dance around the church. It appeared that his previously useless and withered right leg had been miraculously cured. News spread fast and before the end of the day deformed, crippled and ill people living in the Parisian slums descended on St Médard. Over the next few months many more stories of impossible cures in St Médard came filtering up from the Parisian lower classes to the more wealthy aristocrats, most of whom treated the stories as evidence of nothing more than hysteria. The Church said that the miracles were either false or the work of the devil. None the less, a number of noted writers, members of the clergy and scientists did visit the church and came back with incredible stories. Many of these were based around a group dubbed the Convulsionnaires. One aristocratic witness, Louis Adrien de Paige, managed to persuade his magistrate friend Louis-Basile Carré de Montgeron to visit the church on the morning of 7 September 1731. Before his arrival, de Montgeron was a complete sceptic and had subjected de Paige to some ridicule in the previous weeks for believing in what he considered were no more than fairground conjuring tricks. Within minutes of his arrival at St Médard churchyard, though, he had changed his mind and was to devote the rest of his life to the study of the phenomenon he witnessed.

His first sight was that of the Convulsionnaires themselves. He wrote afterwards of seeing this group of women writhing and twisting themselves into impossible shapes so that their feet were resting on the backs of their heads. Other members of the Convulsionnaires were being savagely beaten by onlookers without any sign of feeling pain or suffering injury.

De Montgeron witnessed a 16-year-old girl named Gabrielle Moler being skewered through the stomach with sharpened iron rods by four men without either bleeding or evidence of injury. She then got two men to trap one of her breasts between two shovels and told them to push against each other. The breast should have been sliced off, but instead it remained intact and did not even show signs of bruising. She was then pummelled with iron weights and mallets and subjected to further assaults with the shovels - all without any visible effect. She then stuck her head in a blazing fire and emerged unsinged.

Worse was yet to come. A number of the Convulsionnaires displayed the ability to heal wounds by sucking out infected pus from gangrenous sores and boils, leaving a clean wound behind. This was the final evidence needed by de Montgeron, who set about collecting testimonies from people who had witnessed the phenomenon or had been cured within the church's confines. By the end of 1731 he had collected enough evidence to write a volume about St Médard. By now, however, the Jesuit authorities were advising King Louis XV to shut the place down. In an effort to change his mind, de Montgeron personally presented a copy of his St Médard volume to the King. Louis XV was enraged and threw de Montgeron into the Bastille. He was later released and exiled to the south of France. Here he spent much time collecting more eyewitness accounts of the St Médard miracles and subsequently wrote a further two volumes about the affair.

The churchyard was closed to the public in 1732, but the Convulsionnaires continued to perform around Paris. In 1733 Marie Souet, dubbed 'la salamandre', demonstrated that she was incapable of being burnt by lying in a ferocious fire for a full half-hour. Pockets of activity continued to occur around Paris and in France generally for the remainder of the century, but the affair seems to have been laid to rest after the turmoil of the French Revolution.

❖

The apparently impossible events of St Médard churchyard have attracted little interest, most people believing that what occurred there was too fantastic to be taken seriously.

Those who have discussed the case rightly point out that the known version of events comes almost entirely from the volumes of de Montgeron, which give only his point of view. However, de Montgeron did put himself in danger by insisting on publishing his work and he also went out of his way to collect testimonies other than his own during his research. This suggests that a phenomenon of some kind did occur in St Médard churchyard and the nature of the events that occurred there shows strong parallels with modern cases of mass hysteria.

The psychological phenomenon of mass hysteria is poorly researched and understood. It is essentially a form of contagious mental disorder that can sweep through a large crowd of people in a matter of seconds. A good example can be seen in footage of teenage girls attending Beatles concerts in the 1960s. Their uncontrollable screaming and crying took over whole crowds in a matter of seconds. The rallies of Adolf Hitler have also been used as examples of induced mass hysteria within the attending crowds.

At the 1980 village show in Kirkby-in-Ashfield, Nottinghamshire, England, 300 children collapsed with convulsions, headaches and vomiting. All were taken to hospital and tests were performed for food and chemical poisoning, asthma and epilepsy, all of which were negative. The children recovered after a short while and no satisfactory explanation was ever found, with a diagnosis of mass hysteria being finally made. Many parents were angry at this, claiming that the children displayed real medical symptoms (fainting, headaches, etc.) not imaginary ones. Psychologists argued back that the symptoms were the physical manifestation of the hysterical ones.

Other cases of mass hysteria are more relevant to the case of St Médard churchyard. In the late 1970s the American cult leader Jimmy Jones planted stooges in his audience to suggest to other people that he was performing miracles, such as walking on water. Once the initial suggestion had been made, the entire crowd would become hysterical and believe that they were witnessing a miracle. Similarly, Evangelical Christian Churches rely on hysterical phenomena such as talking in tongues, the seeing of auras and feeling the power of God as part of their services. In other hysterical situations people can become oblivious to pain, as in religious ceremonies where body-piercing occurs or on the battlefield where soldiers carry on fighting while severely injured. In short, in a crowd situation people can be made to feel, see or believe in things that patently do not exist.

Here we see the link to the phenomena at St Médard churchyard. Were the people in the churchyard merely being swept along on a tide of hysteria, interpreting abnormal events, such as convulsions and body-piercing, as being paranormal? In truth, we shall never know what really occurred, but it is felt that the analogies between mass hysteria and the events at St Médard are close enough to provide an adequate explanation for the affair.

As an interesting side note on mass hysteria, there was a phenomenon in the 1970s and 1980s where entire buildings full of office workers would be struck by the same symptoms of headaches, nausea and tiredness. The phenomenon became known as Sick Building Syndrome. Psychologists pronounced this a classic example of mass hysteria in the workplace. Further investigation traced the illness to viruses that were breeding in and being spread by the air-conditioning system!

LINKS BETWEEN WORLDS

INTRODUCTION

B ELIEF IN AN AFTERLIFE and other planes of existence has been around for as long as recorded history. Every religion, whether organized, animist or otherwise, is based on or incorporates into its belief system the existence of a supernatural world in which live mystical beings whose will can effect the everyday lives of humans. As well as worshipping these beings, there have always been people within each society who claim to be able to utilize or communicate with these other worlds. In tribal situations this person would be the tribal elder or shaman. In ancient times they were prophets, while in modern Western society they are mediums, psychics, alien contactees and religious visionaries.

Over the past 150 years an increasing number of people have claimed to have experienced or travelled in a plane or world beyond our own. These experiences have taken a number of forms including out-of-body experiences, near-death experiences, reincarnation and mediumship. Spiritualists and mediums claim contact with deceased humans, spirits and other entities that inhabit the afterlife. A few mediums, such as Emanuel Swedenborg (see page 99), claimed to have physically visited this world, while others, such as Daniel Dunglas Home (see page 81), claimed to draw their power from it. Many ordinary people have had near-death experiences in which they claim to have travelled from this world into one where they encountered dead relatives and friends. Similarly, people who have had out-of-body experiences claim to have left their bodies elsewhere to explore different 'astral planes', some of which are similar to our own world and others which are more surreal. There are variations in which people have had experiences relating to the existence of an afterlife or to reincarnation, purposeful ghosts, automatic writing and religious visionaries.

Some of the environments described from people's experiences of other worlds show a similarity to each other. For example, the sensation of floating above one's body and being able to move freely in an astral form is reported from both near-death and out-of-body experiences. Robert Monroe's description of his Locale III, an out-of-body world he visited (see page 87), also bears some resemblance to Swedenborg's description of his 'other world'. However, very few descriptions, least of all those communicated through mediums, correspond well to the impressions of an afterlife portrayed by the Christian Church. Although specific descriptions of an afterlife are not provided in the Bible, over the centuries the Church has used the concepts of heaven and hell to provide their answer to the question of what an afterlife is like. Also not specifically mentioned in the Bible, Hell was probably a concept invented by the early Christian Church to help extract obedience and money from the public. There have been near-death experiences reported in which the protagonist has seen a hell-like locality, but they are rare and tend to occur to the devoutly religious. Unfortunately, it is very difficult to persuade 'spirits' (or whatever they are) that are contactable through mediums, Ouija boards, automatic writing, etc. to give an accurate description of their surroundings. The best description of an afterlife that I have ever managed to get through the Ouija board was that the 'entity' was 'stuck in eternal chaos'. This, like most of the transcripts obtained through paranormal means, I assumed to be either a lie or a tongue-in-cheek comment by whatever it was that produced the communication. The 'spirit' of Frederick Myers once communicated that he was not allowed to reveal any of the mechanisms at work in the afterlife. His spirit described communicating through a medium as being like 'standing behind a sheet of frosted glass which blurs sight and deadens sound – dictating feebly to a reluctant and somewhat obtuse secretary'.

Little if any scientific research time has been devoted to the concept of an afterlife and where it may be located. The ancient Greeks believed that their Gods lived on top of Mount Olympus. Animist religions believe that spirits live in everyday objects, while Jewish and Christian traditions believe that heaven is beyond the sky (remember that Jesus rose upwards on Ascension Day). The advent of quantum physics has led to some speculation that other worlds, including parallel universes, the afterlife and astral planes, could exist on different levels of molecular vibration or be in different dimensions. However, most of these theories have not been put forward by physicists, but by people who merely compare the more accessible areas of quantum mechanics with their theories.

Particularly popular with religions and occultists is the so-called Copenhagen

Theory. This asserts that matter doesn't exist in any particular state unless it is observed (measured) and that until it is observed matter remains in all its different possible states. Some proponents have taken this to an extreme, suggesting that as consciousness is a necessary factor in the existence of matter, then surely the universe as a whole could not exist unless there was someone observing it from the outside. There are many alternatives to the Copenhagen Theory in quantum mechanics, some of which rely on stranger mechanisms than consciousness to work.

Other scientists favour the idea that many of the communications with other worlds are mere products of the brain. They have linked these experiences to instability in the temporal lobe region of the brain, or to hypnagogic dreams, autosuggestion, hysteria or multiple personality disorder.

Whether the truth behind unseen worlds lies within the brain or within the fabric of space-time, it is unlikely that satisfactory evidence will be found either way and belief becomes a matter of personal faith.

Daniel Dunglas Home

❖

PHYSICAL MEDIUM

O F ALL THE mediums thrown up by the nineteenth-century spiritualist move-ment, the most amazing of all was Daniel Dunglas Home (pronounced Hume), whose power and strong personality were the talking point of the middle classes for a generation.

Daniel Dunglas Home was born on 20 March 1833 in Edinburgh, Scotland. His father was a carpenter, while his mother claimed to be a clairvoyant who was related to the Brahan seer, Kenneth Odhar (see page 21). He was nursed as a baby by an aunt who is said to have reported that his cradle would rock on its own, as if moved by invisible hands. When aged four, Home allegedly predicted the death of a relative.

In 1842 the whole of Home's family moved to Connecticut, America. Here Home was said to have been a pallid and sickly child who was obsessed with reading the Bible. In 1850 his mother died and he went to live with Mary Cook, an aunt who lived nearby. Soon after his arrival, poltergeist activity broke out in the household. Furniture moved and raps and knocks were to be heard all over the house, with many of the phenomena concentrating themselves around Home. His aunt immediately called in ministers to try and exorcize the evil spir-its from him. When they arrived, the ministers did the reverse and instead of performing an exorcism they told Home that he had a gift from heaven. Soon after this his dead mother appeared to him and told him to take his gift to the world outside. This was the final straw for his aunt, who threw her 17-year-old nephew out of her house for being a blasphemer.

Luckily for Home, the Fox Sisters' activities a few years previously (see page 122) had made Spiritualism and seances the latest darling of the middle and upper classes. He started holding his own seances and was soon being invited to stay in the houses of rich society folk. Right from the start, Home had a dislike of other spiritualist mediums, feeling that they were frauds or inferiors from whom he had nothing to learn. Indeed, his seances were very different from those of the day. For a start they were held in full daylight and involved phenomena that were deemed to be completely impossible to fake by scores of witnesses, including members of the scientific community.

A typical Home seance would commence with discarnate rapping and knocking noises and then the main seance table would begin to vibrate, tilt or lift into the air. From then on any number of amazing things could occur, including the levitation of people and furniture and the materialization of musical instruments that would play themselves. Hands would appear and write messages on pieces of paper and sometimes Home himself would become possessed and play unfamiliar musical instruments with legendary vigour. He was apparently also able to gain or lose several inches in height, even with people holding his feet to the floor.

Word of his feats reached two experienced spiritualist investigators, William Bryant and Professor David Wells of Harvard University. After witnessing a daylight seance held by Home they reported, 'We are constrained to admit that there was an almost constant manifestation of some intelligence that seemed, at least, to be independent of the circle...We know that we were not imposed upon or deceived.'

In 1852 Home first levitated himself, something that he was to become famous for. He was in the house of a rich silk manufacturer at the time and apparently started to rise towards the ceiling without warning. Some of the people present tried to pull him down again, but they too were lifted into the air. About a year after this Home had an out-of-body experience in which he was conducted around the spirit world by his guardian angel. After an unsuccessful attempt to study at college, Home was diagnosed as a consumptive and advised to leave America. In 1855 he sailed from New York to England, where he had been invited to stay with some followers of the eighteenth-century psychic Emanuel Swedenborg.

It did not take long for Home to find fame in England, particularly after a very complementary article written in the *New York Tribune* by their London correspondent Dr Garth Wilkinson. In it he states that while at a Home seance 'a bell was brought to me by a disembodied hand. I tried to hold it but I had no sooner grasped it momentarily than it melted away, leaving my hand void, with the bell only in it.'

Home also performed for the poet Robert Browning and his wife, Elizabeth. Initially Browning reported that the phenomena he had witnessed, which included a table being tilted so high in the air that he was able to move around and under it, checking for any hidden wires or other devices, was genuine and could only be supernatural in origin. However, one month later Browning renounced his earlier conclusions, saying that what he had seen was too good to be true and therefore must be the product of fraud. His wife, however, continued to be in awe of Home, which enraged Browning all the more. He eventually wrote a long poem entitled 'Mr. Sludge the Medium', which was a thinly disguised attack on Home. Many more eminent people were to witness Home's daylight seances, some admitting that what they saw ran against the laws of nature and others dismissing them as fraud but without explaining how such trickery was performed. Some of those who expressed initial belief in Home later recanted under pressure and ridicule from the scientific community and the press.

In February 1856 Home announced that his vanity and boastfulness were to be punished by the spirits and that he was to lose his powers for a period of one year. This duly happened, and he decided to travel around Italy for a while. While in the Vatican, he converted to Catholicism. Exactly a year to the day from the loss of his powers, they returned, enabling him to tour France, where he performed in front of Napoleon III and Prince Murat.

During his travels, Home met and married Alexandrina, the sister-in-law of a Russian nobleman, on 1 August 1858. Their only son, Grégoire, was born a year later and soon afterwards Home returned to England, to find that his marriage and his new acquaintances in European high society had once again elevated his standing. He performed weekly seances at the house of a Mrs Milner-Gibson which were attended by many celebrities of the day, including Tolstoy, Robert Chambers and Robert Bell, as well as political figures and minor royalty. Press coverage, which had always been hostile, softened considerably as celebrities testified to his powers.

In 1862 Home's wife died, leaving a disputed will, and he was again forced to rely on people's hospitality to survive. It was just such a situation that led Home into a serious financial scandal in 1868. A year before, Home had met a rich old woman called Mrs Lyon, whose husband had been dead for seven years. Before his own death, the husband had predicted that she would die exactly seven years after himself, fear of which caused her to seek out Home for reassurance that the prophecy was false. The dead Mr Lyon communicated through Home using a series of raps and not only renounced his prediction but also suggested that Mrs Lyon should adopt Home and give him an allowance of £700 a year! On 10 June 1867 Mrs Lyon (despite being 75 years old) allegedly made sexual advances towards Home, who refused her point blank. The result was a trial in which Mrs Lyon tried to claim back £60,000 that had been given to Home in cash and benefits. She ranted and raved in the witness box until the judge was forced to caution her for giving inaccurate and contradictory evidence. Although the judge was certain that Home had not conned the money deliberately, he found in favour of Mrs Lyon on the grounds that Spiritualism could not exist and that she had therefore been duped overall.

In the course of the trial many of Home's high-society friends deserted him, although ironically his powers seemed to be increasing dramatically. The event for which Home is most famous occurred at the house of Lord Adare shortly after the trial in 1868. Here, in front of several witnesses, Home entered a trance and floated out of a third-floor window, travelled around the side of the building and then came in through another open window on the same floor. That year he was also seen to put his head into a blazing coal fire and emerge with not a hair out of place. He then carried the hot coals around the room with his bare hands and, while holding on to their arm, allowed somebody else to carry the burning coals as well. Despite these amazing feats, Home was now exceedingly short of money and declined seances in favour of journalism and touring Europe to read poetry. During an 1871 tour of Russia he met and married Julle de Gloueline. Her considerable financial status freed Home from his part-time jobs, allowing him once again to resume his seance work.

He returned to London and agreed to be tested under laboratory conditions by the noted scientist Sir William Crookes. After a series of rigorous tests, Crookes wrote a report that ended with a statement of his absolute belief in Home's possession of mediumistic powers.

Home retired from seance work in 1873 and commenced travelling with his family. His health, never good at the best of times, suffered more and more until on 21 June 1886 he died of tuberculosis in Auteuil, France. In his lifetime Home wrote two books, *Incidents in My Life* (vol. 1, 1863, vol. 2, 1872) and *Lights and Shadows of Spiritualism* (1877). The latter is thought to have been written by his lawyer, M. W. Wilkinson.

❖

In the opinion of many parapsychologists, spiritualists and occultists, Daniel Dunglas Home was the greatest physical medium ever to have lived. Others believe him to have been nothing more than a first-class conjuror and charlatan who performed his tricks to an audience only too willing to believe him.

One of his most remarkable achievements was never to be formally found faking his paranormal feats. In an age when people were making a living from debunking famous mediums, he managed to be observed by hundreds of people (some of them eminent scientists) in well-lit conditions and yet was still never caught cheating. Many of those who did accuse him of cheating only did so some time after having been at one of his seances. These accusations occasionally followed the ridiculing of an individual who had initially testified to the validity of some phenomenon or other.

Many explanations have been put forward as to how Home could have faked his phenomena, but most are so complicated as to be impossible when it is borne in mind that Home often performed in lighted conditions in houses where he had never previously been. Even Harry Houdini (see page 210), the self-styled arch enemy of the medium, could not replicate any of Home's more spectacular feats. This did not stop him (among others) from repeatedly promising to replicate Home's feats on stage. Despite much public prompting, though, he never did. Scientific studies of Home seem only to have re-enforced the validity of his claims to supernatural powers.

James Randi maintains that Home was caught cheating on a number of occasions, but he does not list his sources. He has, however, put forward some plausible theories concerning some of Home's paranormal feats. For example, he says that when Home was seen playing an accordion inside a steel cage with one or no hands, in fact he really had a miniature mouth-organ hidden inside his mouth. This has been further supported by the fact that Home's accordion never played more than nine notes (the same as one octave from a mouth organ) and by the discovery of a set of miniature mouth organs in Home's possession after his death. Despite strong evidence like this, it must be said that practical explanations (ones not involving any mass hysteria) of Home's public demonstrations are thin on the ground.

If Home's mediumistic powers were genuine, then what exactly were they? When looked at closely, many of the phenomena that Home produced have an uncanny similarity to those associated with poltergeist hauntings. The fact that his mediumistic powers first manifested themselves as a series of rapping noises and moving furniture when he was a teenager fits in with observations that poltergeist activity usually focuses itself on an unhappy adolescent (see Gef the Talking Mongoose, page 16 and the Enfield Poltergeist, page 38). At the onset of the activity, Home had just lost his mother and had had to move in with an aunt with whom he clearly did not get on.

Although it is acknowledged that poltergeists are focused on an individual, it is very rare for that individual to be able to control the activity produced. Home would appear to have had a great deal of control over the phenomena he produced, to the extent that he could use them as a means of entertainment. Whether this ability was a product of his unconscious or the result of activity in the 'spirit world' is unknown. Home believed that his powers came from spirits and as such he was also able to do more conventional mediumistic things, such as contacting people's dead relatives, and he even claimed to have visited the spirit world personally. This does not necessarily mean that there were spirits at work, merely that his unconscious acted as if there were.

On a more sceptical front, Home's loss of power for one year does sound like a convenient excuse for an unhindered sabbatical. The dead Mr Lyon's generous bequest of £700 to Home is suspicious and mimics the methods of fraudulent mediums of the day. Despite this, Home doesn't seem to have used his seances for direct financial gain, although he was reliant upon people's hospitality for long periods of his life and would resort to working, rather than charging for seances, when the hospitality ran out.

Although the supernatural powers of Daniel Dunglas Home do indeed seem amazing, there were many other mediums of the time who could produce similar phenomena. Unfortunately, the large amount of debunking that occurred in the latter half of the nineteenth century led to much ridicule of such mediums and so they tended (as they do now) to perform to more specialized audiences, such as spiritualist churches, rather than the public at large. Home's continued insistence on working with the general public in lighted conditions has drawn admiration from all sides, although depending on your point of view he was either the greatest psychic of them all or the greatest stage magician whose performances even Houdini couldn't match.

Robert Monroe

❖

OUT-OF-BODY EXPERIENCES

PERHAPS MORE OF a psychic explorer than a psychic researcher, Robert Monroe tried to experiment and fully describe the feelings he had after discovering that he could leave his earthly body at will and travel around in astral form.

In 1958 Robert Monroe was a normal family man and businessman in his early forties who was living in Virginia, America. He had been experimenting for some time with trying to learn subliminally in his sleep, and this may or may not be connected with the experiences he was to describe. One Sunday afternoon, while the family were out, he was lying on his bed relaxing when he was suddenly struck on the head by a beam of warm light. His body began to vibrate and he experienced a short period of paralysis, which disappeared when he forced himself to move. This was to happen another nine times in the following few weeks and eventually caused him to consult his doctor, who dismissed the experiences.

Shortly after this the sensation occurred again while he was lying in bed trying to sleep. His arm was outside the bed, with his hand resting on a rug. During his experience he found that he could push his hand through the rug, then through the floorboards, and was able to feel the top of the underneath ceiling. Shocked, he immediately withdrew his arm and the sensation faded once more.

A month later, Monroe was again lying down when the vibrating sensations returned once more. This time he felt a surge within his head and experienced a floating sensation. When he opened his eyes he found himself floating only inches from the ceiling. He turned over to find that he had a perfect view of his body, which was still lying in bed next to his wife. Worried that he had died, he returned to his body immediately, thoroughly frightened by the whole experience. After consulting a friendly psychologist, Monroe decided that instead of fighting his strange feelings, he would go along with them and experiment instead. He quickly learned that he was not the only one to have experienced leaving his body, that the feelings had been dubbed out-of-body experiences (OBEs) and that they were his astral body trying to separate from his physical body.

His first few ventures outside his body were cautious and playful, mostly visiting old friends or places that he knew well. He experimented by visiting friends and then ringing them up to describe their movements, clothes and conversations at a time when his physical body was miles away at home. He claims that this was extremely successful and that he had even caught people out when they were not where they said they would be. For example, a friend of his said he was ill in bed when Monroe saw him walking outside with his wife.

After coming to terms with the notion that he could leave his body and travel anywhere at will, he started to explore this hidden realm more fully and found that he could distinguish three different 'levels' to his astral travelling: these he called Locale I, II and III.

He describes Locale I as being our current physical world and he thinks that his astral body was not designed to be there at all. He claims that both movement and navigation were difficult within Locale I and that there were small differences within what he actually saw in Locale I and true reality. For example, when describing somebody's clothes, he may have got the styles and items right but the colours wrong. Small differences between reality and what is seen during an OBE are very commonly reported by other astral travellers. Monroe also described being taken by the arm, wrist or some other part of his body and being led by an invisible entity to wherever it was that he had set out to go to.

Monroe says that in Locale II 'thought is the well-spring of existence...as you think so you are'. He describes it as being the true world of the astral body and seems to think of it as a world whose existence interpenetrates our own physical world. He tries to quantify this by describing it as possibly existing on a different vibration wavelength to our own world. It apparently shares some features drawn from the physical world but is timeless in the sense that future, present and past events do not necessarily run sequentially. He describes unpleasant areas, which are nearer to the physical world (inhabited by insane beings), and pleasant areas, which are further away.

Monroe encountered 'entities' that lived in Locale II. These were described as people who were astral travellers, asleep, recently dead or so-called higher entities. Monroe describes a variety of unusual encounters with these entities which ranged from fighting to having sex with them. He describes in detail an encounter that he had with a ten-year-old boy who was visiting Locale II while his physical body lay dying in hospital. After returning to the physical world and reading of the boy's death in a local newspaper, Monroe tried to think of ways of contacting the parents, but in the end decided not to. One is left with the impression that Locale II is a kind of dreamworld where all your fantasies, good and bad, can come true.

The final level, Locale III, Monroe discovered after turning his astral body through 180 degrees in bed so that it was face downwards. Here he saw a type of infinite wall with a dark hole in it. After a few practice attempts, he managed to travel through the hole in the wall and on the other side discovered a strange version of our own physical world. There was much in common with our world, including cities, landscapes and people, but there was no electricity or oil-powered machines. Instead people used unfamiliar pedal or steam-powered vehicles. He was invisible to the people there, but was able to communicate by merging with (possessing?) his *alter ego* in Locale III.

Monroe wrote up his experiences in a book entitled *Journeys Out of the Body*, which was published in 1971. As well as describing the above adventures, he also discusses a number of his theories about the nature of OBEs and the astral body itself. He conjectures that the astral body may be the reversal of the physical body, suggesting that it is perhaps like antimatter. He claims that astral bodies have mass and can be seen under the right conditions. He says that one astral body can communicate with another living person's astral body without either of the physical bodies being aware of it.

The book was a best-seller but it inevitably brought accusations that he was suffering from hallucinations, fantasies or vivid dreams. The parapsychologist D. Scott Rogo even suggested that Monroe had been tripping after inadvertently inhaling solvents. Following the book's publication, Monroe set up a pseudo-scientific centre for the study of OBEs. Hundreds of people volunteered to try and leave their bodies and before long Monroe and his fellow travellers had contacted and were conversing with a group of weird entities living on the astral plane. They were given a series of messages by these entities which Monroe spent years trying to decipher. The results of all this were published in the book *Far Journeys* in 1986.

This book was generally badly received for relying too much on the transcripts of the conversations with his entities and for lacking the enthusiasm of his first book. After the publication of *Far Journeys*, Monroe continued to lecture about OBEs and claimed to have visited a number of planets in the solar system, but he refused to give detailed descriptions of them, saying that no one would believe him unless he could bring rocks back.

Monroe's popularity faded somewhat in the 1980s and 1990s as more sensationalist occult subjects, such as UFOs and government conspiracies, grabbed the public interest. He died in 1995 and is still largely recognized as the person who first drew OBEs to the public's attention.

❖

To the average person Monroe's claims of leaving the body and moving freely through our own and other worlds might seem to be unbelievable. According to Monroe and others, anybody is capable of having an OBE and there are a number of ways of inducing them. I have tried most of these methods and have had no success so far.

With cases like Monroe's, there is a danger with describing experiences that occur at the edge of or during sleep, as they can so easily be confused with lucid dreams or hypnagogic experiences. It is also very difficult to prove or disprove stories of travelling to other wavelengths when the only proof is the word of the story-teller.

Based on dowsing with a pendulum, Tom Lethbridge (see page 206) speculates that there is another world that interpenetrates our own somehow in which there is no time and to which the astral body is capable of travelling during sleep. Colin Wilson (in *Mysteries*) notes similarities between Tom Lethbridge's world beyond his pendulum and Locale II. There are also some similarities between Locale II and Emanuel Swedenborg's description of the other world which he would frequently visit (see page 99).

It has been suggested that the first reported OBE was in the Bible, when St Paul (2 Corinthians, 12:2–4) wrote, 'For I know of a man who fourteen years ago was taken up as far as the third heaven. I know not whether he was inside his body or out.' Even with such a long recorded history, there is as yet little firm scientific evidence for OBEs, although it does appear to be a more common experience than was once thought. Theories range from the astral body being the part of the human consciousness that survives death (the soul) to the commonly held psychological notion that OBEs are nothing more than complex lucid dreams thrown up by the subconscious. Susan Blackmore (in *Beyond the Body*) offers strong evidence for the experience being an altered state of consciousness within the brain. Similarly, when in 1995 the psychologist J. Persinger interviewed 128 people who had regular OBEs, he found that those who experienced the greatest feeling of detachment also had symptoms of partial epilepsy, suggesting that OBEs may be no more relevant to the mind-soul problem than dreams. OBEs have also been reported as a side-effect of crack cocaine addiction, and a link has been made between high periods of geomagnetic activity (caused by earthquakes and other tectonic processes) and an area in the brain known as the temporal lobe. When the temporal lobe is stimulated with artificial magnetism it induces altered states of consciousness that include feelings associated with OBEs.

José Arigo

❖

PSYCHIC SURGERY

FAITH-HEALERS HAVE always come in for a certain amount of abuse for the very fact that their practice relies so much on patient testimony and there is little solid evidence of their works. Psychic surgery is a different matter. Here the healer actually cuts the skin and removes tumours and suchlike without the aid of anaesthetic or any disinfectant. Possibly the greatest psychic surgeon of them all was José Arigo.

José Arigo was born as José Pedro de Freitas in Congonhas do Campo in Brazil in 1918. He first realized that he had the power to perform psychic surgery after being present by the bed of a dying woman relative in his home town. As the priest was about to give the last rites, Arigo suddenly ran out to the kitchen, grabbed a knife and plunged it into the woman's vagina. After a couple of seconds he pulled out a huge bloody tumour which, together with the knife, he dumped into a sink. The shocked relatives called a doctor, who confirmed that the tumour had been removed without haemorrhaging or discomfort to the woman. The woman subsequently recovered to full health and Arigo started down the path to stardom as a psychic surgeon.

Word of this miracle spread quickly and before long Arigo was treating sometimes hundreds of people every day using psychic surgery. His format usually involved what would appear to be quite rough and violent cutting and digging at the skin with an ordinary knife. There would be no pain, little blood and wounds were said to heal unnaturally fast. During surgery Arigo claimed that he was possessed by a German doctor called Adolphus Fritz who had died in 1918 (some time in the 1800s according to some reports). Despite considerable searching, no historical evidence has been found for the existence of Dr Fritz. To add to the enigma that surrounded him, Arigo would always refuse payments for his services.

The popularity of Arigo's surgeries (he was estimated to have treated half a million people in five years) drew him enormously favourable reports in the Brazilian media. This in turn alerted him to the authorities, who frowned upon his activities. He was eventually arrested in 1956 for illegally practising medicine. Despite pleas from former patients, Arigo was given an eight-month sentence and a fine. His influence had clearly reached high places, for after his sentence was announced the Brazilian president gave him a pardon. He was not quite so lucky in 1964, when he served nine months of a 16-month custodial sentence. His jailers permitted him to continue treating people while in jail.

The appeal that freed Arigo from his 16-month sentence was presided over by Judge Filippe Immesi, who refused to make a decision without first having seen the surgeon in action. Although he arrived incognito, the judge was instantly recognized by Arigo and was invited to see the psychic surgeon close up. In his report Judge Immesi wrote:

> I saw him pick up...a pair of nail scissors. He wiped them on his shirt and used no disinfectant. I saw him then cut straight into the cornea of the patient's eye. She did not flinch, although perfectly conscious. The cataract was out in seconds...Arigo said a prayer and a few drops of liquid appeared on the cotton in his hand. He wiped the woman's eye with it and she was cured.

The judge was convinced of Arigo's powers but saw that he was breaking the law and so sent him back to prison for a further two months. Very favourable reports were also written about Arigo's surgery by a specialist surgeon (Dr Amy Lex) and the psychic researcher Dr Andrija Puharich, who actually had a cyst removed from his arm by Arigo.

As well as apparently performing impossible surgery, Arigo was famous for writing prescriptions for high doses of dangerous or even obsolete medicines. Despite serious objections from registered doctors, these prescriptions are reported to have worked, even on terminal cancers.

In January 1971, José Arigo told several people that he would not be seeing them again. His words were prophetic, for a few days later he was killed in a car crash.

❖

Faith-healing, psychic surgery and related topics provoke passionate debate among the medical community, the majority of whom feel that terminally ill and crippled people are offered false hope by such practices. Faith-healing, in many different forms, has been around for thousands of years, but psychic surgery is essentially a phenomenon of the late twentieth century. Although there are a minority of practitioners in Europe and America, the greatest number of psychic surgeons is to be found in the Third World countries of South America and the Far East.

The Philippines has the largest concentration of psychic surgeons (known locally as *curanderos*) in the world and Manila has become a magnet for Asian tourists seeking to have tumours removed from their bodies and other diseases cured. Research among the surgeons there has found, however, that most of the surgery is in fact fraudulent. A fraudulent psychic surgeon can fake an operation very easily by laying a patient on a table and pressing their hands, in the shape of a fist, hard into the stomach. When the hands are pressed down, it is then possible for the surgeon to release from his fists small quantities of animal blood and entrails, making it appear that an incision has been made and the tumour (or whatever) removed. When the hands are removed again the wound has miraculously healed. There are many variations on this theme: some make a small incision with a knife; others need more complex props. Stricter laws and better access to licensed doctors have meant that psychic surgery has never grown beyond the back-street level in developed countries. Instead, there has been an increase in less invasive and controversial alternative healing methods, such as faith-healing, aromatherapy and herbalism.

In 1980s North America there was an increase in Evangelical Christian preachers who would perform miraculous cures at public gatherings. A series of scandals exposed many of the preachers for financial irregularities or just plain fraud. For example, James Randi exposed an Evangelical preacher after finding that a hidden microphone was being used by him to receive information fed to him by his wife. He claimed to have cured many thousands of people in the course of his career and it has been speculated that the rush of adrenalin caused by going up on stage could have led to a temporary suspension of pain or other symptoms in his patients.

The dangers associated with encouraging people to visit non-qualified medical practitioners means that the topic provokes much hostility among the general public. A 1996 BBC programme called *Open Space* featured a documentary about the life of a psychic healer. This generated over 200 phone calls and letters complaining that the programme was not biased enough against alternative medicines.

However, in the case of Arigo there are many documented testimonies of his surgical feats, some of which are very impressive. His humble nature and lifestyle also did not suggest blatant publicity-seeking or pursuit of financial gain. Arigo's eye surgery and other operations would have been very hard to fake, particularly in front of other medical practitioners. Arigo was estimated to have treated over 500,000 people in his lifetime and it has been argued that it would be hard to fool all of them.

Ignoring the weight of evidence against psychic surgery, if Arigo's powers were genuine, then how did they work? Arigo claimed that his powers came from Dr Fritz and, as proof, he was apparently capable of conversing in German during his surgery. Yet, considering that Dr Fritz was meant to have died in 1918, his knowledge of surgery and medicine went far beyond that of even the modern day, let alone 1918. He also seems to have affected the nervous systems of his patients by numbing the pain, slowing down any bleeding and healing the wounds in record time. The benign reaction of his patients suggests that Arigo was capable of removing all sense of fear or resistance to surgery.

Joan Grant

❖

POSTHUMOUS AUTOBIOGRAPHIES

R EINCARNATION FORMS A part of many religions. The use of hypnosis to regress people into their past lives had led to growing interest in many Christian societies. Joan Grant was one of the first pioneers of reincarnation and her series of books, including a number of 'posthumous autobiographies', led to a greater awareness of the subject among the public.

Joan Grant was born Joan Marshall in London on 12 July 1907 into a wealthy family. She was aware of being psychic from an early age and during World War I had many battlefield visions. They became so horrific that she would torture herself to keep awake in order to avoid experiencing them. In 1916, when aged nine, she described going downstairs one morning to find a soldier friend of her father's at breakfast. She told him of a vision she had had during the night in which she was with a soldier at the front named McAndrew who had been killed. She described his regimental badge and some of the slang that he had used to describe life in his trench. Unbeknown to her, her father's friend had recognized Joan's description of the regimental badge as being Canadian and later made checks on her story. In a letter to Joan's father, which was not revealed to Joan for a number of years, he said that a Canadian regiment had indeed gone over the top a few hours before he had spoken to Joan and that a Private McAndrew had been killed. The trench slang also proved to be correct.

While still a teenager she was introduced to psychic research by another friend of her father's, a professor of engineering called C. G. Lamb. Joan amazed him by displaying mediumistic powers, including in one incident playing a piano tune that was associated only with her long-dead grandmother. Aged 16 she discussed her psychic powers with the author H. G. Wells, who advised her to keep them to herself lest she be ridiculed by others.

As a young woman, Joan's first engagement was broken off because her fiancé could not tolerate her strange dreams and visions. It was through one such dream that she met her next romance, a man called Esmond. Apparently both Joan and Esmond had been dreaming of each other for two years before they finally met at a party. They were soon engaged, but before they could marry Esmond was killed in a shooting accident.

She eventually married Leslie Grant in 1927. Her husband was a firm believer in her powers and the two set about experimenting with them. For years Joan had been having vivid dreams in which she felt she was experiencing large sections of other people's lives. With Leslie's help she developed a trance-like state which enabled her to have the dreams without actually falling asleep. All the details of these 'far-memory' dreams, and her other experiences, were meticulously recorded by Leslie.

Grant also found that she was a psychometrist (see Gerald Croiset, page 10) and in 1936 started to remember the life of an Egyptian princess after holding a scarab that belonged to a friend of hers. Joan and Leslie wrote down every detail that emerged about the princess, called Sekeeta, and later, after a further 115 sessions, published the story as a posthumous autobiography under the title *Winged Pharaoh* in October 1937.

The book described the rise to power of Sekeeta, who was a daughter of a Pharaoh who became co-ruler with her brother after his death. Sekeeta trained to be a priestess, a process which included being able to remember at least ten deaths from previous lives. She had to undergo a number of ordeals in order to be initiated into the priesthood, including being sealed in a tomb for four days and fighting a cobra.

The book was acclaimed as a historical novel, but there was much debate as to whether it represented a true case of reincarnation. The success of this book led to Grant writing a whole series of posthumous autobiographies.

The next of these, published in 1939, was called *Life as Corola* and concerned a girl born in 1510, the bastard daughter of an Italian nobleman. Having been abandoned by her father, she was taken in by a group of travelling performers, with whom she learned to play musical instruments. After being tortured in a convent, she was taken in by and eventually married Carlos di Ludovici. They were happy together, but Carlos died in a hunting accident. Broken-hearted, Corola died soon after in the autumn of 1537.

Shortly before the publication of *Life as Corola*, Joan left Leslie Grant and eloped to Wales with the psychologist Dr Charles Beatty. The two of them continued the far-memory work, this time concentrating on the life of another Egyptian, Ra-ab Hotep, who was born 1,000 years after Sekeeta. Ra-ab Hotep, a member of the Egyptian aristocracy, belonged to a resistance movement fighting against a society obsessed with decadence and godlessness. When the Pharaoh Amenemhet was installed, peace reigned over Egypt for three centuries, during which time Joan was born again twice. Ra-ab's story was published as two further books, *Eyes of Horus* and *Lord of the Horizon*, in 1942 and 1943. Further autobiographies followed, including those of a 4,000-year-old American Indian (*Scarlet Feather*), a

Greek philosopher (*Return to Elysium*) and an Egyptian who was a contemporary of Rameses II (*So Moses was Born*).

As well as these, Joan remembered other past lives, most of which ended in agonizing deaths, including being burnt as a witch, being speared at a joust and instructing a Roman court physician to cut her wrists. All her publications sold well.

In 1958 she met psychiatrist Dr Denys Kelsey, who had followed her books with interest. Within a short time the two had fallen in love and began exploring the reincarnation issue from a psychiatric point of view.

Dr Kelsey was a keen advocate of hypnosis as an aid to psychotherapy and through this the couple discovered that many of people's everyday anxieties could be traced back to incidents that had taken place in previous lives. For example, prior to meeting Kelsey, a psychiatrist friend of Charles Beatty refused the offer of a brace of pheasants, saying that he had a phobia of feathers. Joan immediately looked at him and told him that his fear of feathers resulted from an experience he had had in a previous life: he had been left for dead on a battlefield and had had to watch as vultures gathered round him waiting for him to die. After this the psychiatrist friend apparently began to recall the incident for himself. This technique was used by Joan and Dr Kelsey to solve many people's anxieties.

Joan also came up with some theories concerning the mechanisms behind reincarnation. She believed that the human body consisted of the physical and 'supra-physical', and when the energy exchange between the two dissolved, the physical body died but the supra-physical continued on to other incarnations under the direction of an organizing fountain of wisdom called the 'Integral'. It was also the Integral that decided the sex and other attributes of new incarnations. Experience from each incarnation could be carried forward subconsciously into the new incarnation. Although this incorporated many traditional notions of the presence of a soul or astral body within a physical body, it was not widely accepted.

In 1967 Joan and Dr Kelsey published a book of their experiences together called *Many Lifetimes* and Joan published *Far Memories*, an autobiography of her current life, in 1972.

❖

The use of hypnosis to regress people to their past lives is now a common feature on television shows and in magazine articles. The popularity of reincarnation in the public imagination has led to expressions such as 'I must have done something bad in a previous life to deserve this'. There are, as usual, strong arguments from all sides as to the validity of reincarnation as a genuine phenomenon.

1. DRAWING BY GEORGE SCOTT OF GEF FROM PARTICULARS SUPPLIED BY MR. IRVING AND THE 'MONGOOSE' HIMSELF

2. PHOTOGRAPH OF A GREY MONGOOSE AT THE ZOOLOGICAL GARDENS

Frontispiece for *The Haunting of Cashen's Gap* (1936) by Harry Price and R.S. Lambert, about Gef the Talking Mongoose.
Fortean Picture Library

THE WORLD OF TED SERIOS

"THOUGHTOGRAPHIC" STUDIES
OF AN EXTRAORDINARY MIND

JULE EISENBUD, M.D.

Jacket of *The World of Ted Serios,*
published 1967.
Fortean Picture Library

Investigator Maurice
Grosse with some of the
smaller items from the
Enfield poltergeist case
of 1977–8.
Guy Lyon Playfair/
Fortean Picture Library

The greatest physical medium,
Daniel Dunglas Home, levitating.
Fortean Picture Library

Lieutenant-Colonel
Percy Harrison
Fawcett, 1911.
Fortean Picture Library

'The wickedest man in the world', Aleister Crowley.
Fortean Picture Library

Contemporary portrayal of
Springheel Jack, c. 1877.
Fortean Picture Library

Hand of the 'Minnesota Ice-Man'.
Loren Coleman/Fortean Picture Library

Levitation of St Joseph of Copertino.
Fortean Picture Library

Angels of Mons, drawn by A. Forestier and used in Christmas edition
of *London Illustrated News*, 1915.
Fortean Picture Library

Francis Griffiths with fairies, photographed by Elsie Wright
at Cottingley Glen, West Yorkshire, July 1917.
Fortean Picture Library

Harry Price, psychic researcher, from his book *Search for Truth* (1942).
Fortean Picture Library

One of the strongest arguments against reincarnation is that stories of people's past lives always seem to read like the script for a Hollywood film. Joan Grant's posthumous autobiographies illustrate this quite well. Ordinary people seem to have been kings, witches, heretics or Atlanteans in crucial or glamorous stages of human history. Few people are ever regressed back to lives that are mundane or ordinary. As hypnosis is crucial to the revealing of a past life, it has been suspected that the subconscious is responsible for the creation of the reincarnation experiences. The mind is capable of using information gathered from books, radio, television and conversations to build scenarios that, on the face of it, seem plausible. When the majority of cases are studied, few provide enough information to allow the historical individuals to be traced and the facts verified (see the Pollock Twins, page 104, for a further discussion of this).

Joan Grant claimed that modern personality traits are the result of past-life experiences. Recent research by the psychologist S. Pasricha has also found evidence of this. In 1996 he studied 141 Indian children with phobias. After questioning, and in some cases hypnotizing, the children to gain information about their past lives, Pasricha came to the conclusion that the children's phobias could be directly related to their modes of death in a previous life. He also concluded that the prime time for reincarnation signs to be exhibited in children was between two and five years of age. Other work (again mostly done on the Indian subcontinent, where belief in reincarnation is strong) has found similar links between nervous conditions, personality traits and even physical characteristics in people and aspects of their past lives.

It has been argued that, in the case of personality traits, it could be the modern personality influencing the mind to create a past-life scenario. Joan Grant claimed that her own fear of snakes resulted from twice dying from snakebites in previous lives. It could also be that her fear of snakes would allow her subconscious to create scenarios in which they featured prominently. The same may be true for more general personality traits and it has been noticed that when people with occultist or esoteric backgrounds are hypnotically regressed, they are more likely to have been alchemists, court magicians, Atlanteans or suchlike in their past lives. Pro-reincarnationists argue that their current interest in the occult results from their past-life experiences, but most psychologists would argue that it is the other way round.

On a more philosophical note, it has been pointed out that the current level of the earth's population (about 5.2 billion people) is the highest it has ever been and is still rising. This means that not everyone can have possibly lived before as a person – there simply were not enough people in the past to cater for the amount that there are now. In response to this, some religions believe that it is possible for animals to be reincarnated as humans (and vice versa), yet no one has ever regressed to describe living as an animal, and indeed it is rare for people to describe past-life experiences in other cultures, suggesting that people are more likely to be reincarnated as people who lived in their own country.

The use of hypnosis to recover past-life and other memories is becoming an increasing liability for parapsychologists. In the past decade there has been a staggering increase in people reporting alien abduction experiences, parental or satanic abuse, multiple personalities, encounters with angels, etc. under hypnosis. Almost all of them are unprovable and seem to rely on the person's desire for escapism, sometimes with prompting from the interviewer.

Although the current evidence is weak, reincarnation is potentially a phenomenon whose existence could be proved. A researcher would need to get a detailed and unbiased description of a person's past-life experience before beginning any work on the case. If then, after a historical search, the dates, names and other facts from the past-life experience could be strongly linked to a genuine historical character, then solid evidence would exist for the person having lived before (or at least having gained knowledge supernaturally). This approach has been attempted many times, but often runs into difficulties. The first is that by the time the case comes to the attention of the researcher, many other people have had contact with the subject, all influencing the nature and content of the experience. Another major problem is the neutrality of researchers, many of whom are too eager to stretch facts to fit their case (see the Imad Elawar case, page 106). One very strong method of assessing a case's validity is to compare historical words and phrases given during a past-life interview with those actually around at the time of the claimed experience. We have good records of all the European languages from the Middle Ages onward and it is very difficult to fake conversations in old languages. In the 1980s a couple in southern England claimed to have a computer that was possessed with the spirit of a sixteenth-century man. The language used by the 'spirit' in its communications was vindicated by an expert from Oxford University as being authentic, adding much weight to the case, although it must be added that other academics disagreed with this conclusion.

In addition to Joan Grant's past lives, some of her supporters also claim that she possessed some modest mediumistic ability. Her childhood dreams and use of psychometry could have played a major part in the construction of her scenarios. It does not seem to be a coincidence that the subject of her first book, Sekeeta, came to her after holding an Egyptian scarab – she may well have picked up psychometric images from the scarab and started the process there.

Reincarnation, with its religious overtones, is a controversial area and evidence for it at the moment is not strong, although the potential remains for its vindication beyond doubt.

Emanuel Swedenborg

❖

RELIGIOUS MEDIUM

I N HIS TIME Emanuel Swedenborg was considered to be one of the greatest poly-
maths in Sweden, yet he gave up a promising life as a scientist and geologist to
follow a path dictated to him in a number of extraordinary experiences, which
included visits to the spirit world.

Born in Sweden on 29 January 1688, the second son of the Bishop of Skar,
Emanuel Swedenborg showed early signs of high intelligence and developed a
keen interest in mathematics, science, philosophy and languages. He studied
mathematics and science at university and afterwards spent a number of years
touring Europe, where he met and talked to a number of experts in science and
astronomy, such as Edmund Halley. In 1716, aged 28, he returned to Sweden and
was appointed assessor of the Swedish board of mines. This occupied much of his
life for the next 30 years, although his brilliant intellect was also responsible for
the design and building of docks, canals and other grand projects. He was a
prolific writer and published books on mining, astronomy, mathematics, economics,
physiology and physics. A paper published on the nature of atoms in 1734 seems
to have pre-empted much of the work done in nuclear physics in the early twentieth century. In addition to this, by the 1740s Swedenborg could also speak nine
languages and had mastered a number of musical instruments. He was truly a
gifted man of high intelligence.

It was therefore all the more surprising to people when, in the mid-1740s, he
announced that he had been visited by God and was now able to converse with
the dead and even visit their world. His experiences began in April 1744, when
he had a dream in which he heard the sound of a roaring wind which then picked
him up and flung him face downwards. He started to pray furiously, then felt
another hand grab his and suddenly saw Jesus standing in front of him.
Swedenborg conversed with Jesus for a while before awakening suddenly. Over
the following months he had a series of similar dreams, which ranged from
demonic nightmares, such as placing his hand between a woman's legs only to
have it bitten by a vagina armed with teeth, to visions of visiting heaven and hell.

He lessened his scientific studies in favour of writing works on theology, which were published from the autumn of 1744 onwards.

In the spring of 1745 Swedenborg had a vision that frightened him so much he devoted the rest of his life to explaining his ideas to the world. He had just eaten an excessive lunch when the floor of his room started to crawl with reptile and frogs. A man appeared in front of him and said, 'Eat not so much!'. The man reappeared that night, saying that he was God and that Swedenborg had been chosen to deliver a new set of scriptures to the world.

From then on Swedenborg claimed that he was living simultaneously in the spirit and the physical world. He described the afterlife as being similar to life on earth, with heaven and earth existing all around us but in a different state. He believed that there were three heavens and three hells, each of which was inhabited by both angels and devils, all of whom had at some time been human. He said that new souls entering the afterlife were initially helped about by angels until their own desires drew them to associate with similar beings. He also said that the spirits in his world called him 'the unaccountable one', because they could not understand how a human was able to visit them in their world. He wrote of many conversations with eminent people in the spirit world and even claimed to have converted Martin Luther to his way of thinking, although he could not convert John Calvin! His new version of Christianity was explained in a number of theological books, the most important of which, *True Christian Religion*, was published in 1771.

Swedenborg also talked about sensations that today would be described by parapsychologists as astral-travelling or remote-viewing. He claimed to have travelled to other planets in the solar system and to have met with the inhabitants on both Venus and the Moon. He described the people of the Moon as:

> small, like children of 6 or 7 years old, but [they] have the strength of men like ourselves. Their voice is like thunder and comes from the belly for the Moon is in quite a different atmosphere from the other planets.

What has been said about Swedenborg so far could easily be dismissed as a series of hallucinations or as a case of mild schizophrenia. However, in addition to his travels to the spirit world, Swedenborg had also developed considerable clairvoyant powers, and it is for these that he is best known.

The most famous incident occurred on Saturday 16 July 1759, when he was one of 16 guests at a dinner party being thrown by William Castel in Goteborg. At 6 p.m. Swedenborg left the table, only to return a while later looking somewhat shaken. He announced to the party that he had 'seen' the city of Stockholm (located nearly 250 miles away) ablaze and that his house was threatened with destruction. After a tense two-hour wait, he was able to announce that the fire had been extinguished only three houses away from his own. The next day he explained how the fire had started and been put out. The whole story was confirmed by a messenger who arrived on the following Monday.

The next well-attested example of his clairvoyance took place a year later, when the wife of the recently deceased Dutch ambassador to Sweden, Madame de Marteville, contacted Swedenborg for help. She said that she was being pursued by a goldsmith who was demanding payment for a dinner service she was certain had already been paid for by her husband. Swedenborg went away and visited the spirit world, where he contacted the dead ambassador, who promised to sort the matter out. A few days later the dead ambassador appeared to his wife in a dream, telling her that a receipt for the goods lay behind the drawer of a desk. A search revealed that this was indeed the case.

In October 1761 Swedenborg was summoned before the queen of Sweden, who wanted him to contact her brother, who had died three years previously. She was somewhat sceptical of Swedenborg and did not expect anything to come of it. Swedenborg returned three weeks later, asking for a private audience with the queen. On hearing what he had to say, the queen went ashen and said, 'Only God and my brother could have known this!' The next year, on 17 July 1762, he told a group of people of the strangulation in prison of the Russian Tsar Peter III only minutes after it had occurred. He forced the people present to write down testimonies of his description so that it could later be verified (as indeed it was).

Because of his mediumistic powers, Swedenborg was regarded with some wariness in Sweden during his lifetime and in his final years spent much time living in London, where his beliefs were more tolerated. It was here that he died on 29 March 1772.

In the years following his death, Swedenborg's supporters founded a religion based on his writings. The first church was established in 1778 in London and the religion spread to America in 1792. The Swedenborg Society was founded in 1810 and still continues to publish and promote Swedenborg's theological works. Although he never had a large following, Swedenborg still has his advocates today and his thoughts about the afterlife have been incorporated into Spiritualism and other related religions.

At the request of the Swedish government, Swedenborg's body was moved from London to Uppsala in 1908.

❖

In many respects Swedenborg's life followed a pattern of events that would later be repeated by other spiritualist evangelists such as Benjamin Creme (see page 118), the Fox Sisters (see page 122), Madame Blavatsky (see page 127), Dr Steiner and others. This pattern involves the prophet being contacted by a higher being/power of some kind with the intention of acting as their intermediary for a set of ground-breaking messages that must be proclaimed to the world. The prophet has usually either displayed previous psychic ability or had a strong interest in esoteric matters before being chosen to deliver their galactic message. Swedenborg had been keenly interested in theology, philosophy, collecting his dreams and experimenting with meditation prior to the onset of his visions. His writings also follow a similar pattern to those set by Blavatsky and others in their concentration on describing the nature of other worlds and their relationship to human existence and survival after death. Most interesting is Swedenborg's description of other planets and the alien races on them which have been rendered absurd by interplanetary probes: for example, two human-like civilizations living on Venus, a planet we know to be under extreme temperatures and pressures. There does appear to be a trend within supernaturally dictated scripts for there to be some mention of other civilizations, whether they be on Atlantis or Mars, or are simply telepathic alien life forms, which are superior to our own.

Swedenborg's description of the afterlife and the people he met there seem to be fantastic, making some psychologists think that he was suffering from hallucinations or some form of altered state of mind. While Swedenborg was still alive, the psychologist Henry Maudsley did a mental pathology on his mental behaviour and concluded that he had developed a messianic psychosis in middle life – probably monomania due to epilepsy.

Epileptic or not, there are some impressive testimonies to his clairvoyant powers, particularly his ability to glean information from dead personalities. It is possible that this was an expression of psychometric ability or extrasensory perception, rather than anything to do with his actually visiting the spirit world and talking to the people concerned. Having said that, there are some similarities between Swedenborg's description of three heavens and hells as places which exist in a different state to the physical world and Robert Monroe's (see page 87) description of three astral planes which vibrate at different wavelengths to our own world where the dead go and where, under special circumstances, the astral body can visit too. Even Monroe's description of finding the third astral world (Locale III) by turning his astral body over so that it faced downward sounds likes Swedenborg's description of being thrown face downwards by a wind in his initial 1744 experience.

Wilson van Dusen (in *The Presence of Other Worlds*) suggests that Swedenborg was describing dreams he was having on the edge of sleep (hypnagogic dreams), which explains the afterlife visions but does not explain the waking clairvoyant experiences. B. P. Cashin compares Swedenborg's experiences to those of tribal shamans who act as intermediaries between the world of spirits and the human world. Colin Wilson (in *The Psychic Detectives*) notes the strange way in which Swedenborg's suspect descriptions of the afterlife and alien races can contrast with genuine clairvoyant powers.

It is clear that whatever the truth behind Swedenborgism as a religion, the man himself was not stupid, deluded or a publicity-seeking charlatan. It is a credit to his standing within Swedish society that he was not publicly humiliated for his beliefs and that he was still invited to society dinners and functions, where some of his best-attested examples of clairvoyance come from. His works are still read today and much of his unusual brand of theology paved the way for the spiritualist movement that was to begin less than a century after his death.

The Pollock Twins

❖

REINCARNATION

THIS IS A relatively short but often quoted story. Is it a case of genuine reincarnation or of wishful thinking by a heartbroken parent? As a young man, John Pollock, a devout Catholic, was so convinced of the existence of reincarnation that he was frequently scolded by his priest for praying to God to provide him with proof. He married a girl called Florence and settled down in the town of Hexham, Northumberland. By 1957 the couple had two daughters, Joanna (aged 11) and Jacqueline (aged 6). However, tragedy was soon to strike the family.

On 5 May 1957 Joanna, Jacqueline and a friend, Anthony Layden (aged 9) were walking to church when a speeding car left the road and ploughed into the children. All three were killed instantly. The driver of the car was a depressed widow called Marjorie Wynn, who had taken an overdose of barbiturates and had intended to kill herself by crashing the car. Ironically, she survived the crash.

John Pollock initially took the tragedy as retribution from God for having persisted in his belief in reincarnation, but he soon became convinced that it was actually God's way of proving to him that reincarnation did exist.

At the start of 1958 Florence Pollock became pregnant again and John soon became obsessed with the idea that his dead daughters were going to be given back to him. He was absolutely convinced that his wife would give birth to twin girls, despite their gynaecologist's insistence that he could see only one set of limbs and could hear only one heartbeat. Florence, having recently converted from Baptism to Catholicism, was not at all pleased with her husband's eccentric behaviour. Despite this she gave birth to twin daughters on the morning of 4 October 1958. John noticed that the second twin, called Jennifer, was born with a white line on her forehead, where her dead sister, Jacqueline, had had a scar from falling off her bicycle. She also had a birthmark on her hip in an identical location to where Jacqueline had had a birthmark. Despite being identical twins, there were no similar marks on the elder twin, Gillian. Four months after their birth the family moved 30 miles away from Hexham to the town of Whitley Bay.

John's belief that the twins had been reincarnated was reinforced when, approximately three years after moving, the couple returned to Hexham with the twins on a day trip. To their astonishment the twins acted as if they had lived there before, recognizing their old house and saying things such as; 'Our school is round the corner!' and 'There's the playground where we used to play!' Everything they said apparently related to the previous lives of Jacqueline and Joanna.

Soon after this the parents gave the twins a box of their dead sisters' toys which had remained hidden in the attic since moving from Hexham. On seeing the toys the twins immediately grabbed at the dolls. Jennifer said, 'This is Mary and there is my Suzanne! I have not seen them for years! And there's your wringer!'. She had given the dolls the same names that Joanna and Jacqueline had done. This scene was witnessed by both parents and seriously disturbed Florence. Worse was yet to come.

The twins were outside in the yard one day when a car across the road had its engine started up. The parents heard the girls screaming loudly, which brought them outside quickly. They saw both girls clinging to each other, shouting, 'The car! Its coming at us!' John noticed that the car was at the same angle to the girls as the one that had hit Joanna and Jacqueline. The last incident occurred when Florence found Gillian holding Jennifer's head at an angle and saying, 'The blood's coming from your eyes. That's where you were hit by the car.' After the twins' fifth birthday the strange occurrences stopped and the family grew up as normal, save for the occasional newspaper article.

❖

On the face of it, this story seems to provide good evidence for the existence of reincarnation. Unfortunately, the whole story does rely quite heavily on the testimony of John Pollock.

The most obvious point to make is that even before the birth of Joanna and Jacqueline, he was obsessed with the idea of reincarnation. It is therefore not surprising that his wife's pregnancy, following the tragic death of their daughters, would be leapt on by him as proof of his dead children's rebirth. In the 1950s technology such as ultrasound and fibre-optic cameras were not in medical use, making twin pregnancies much harder to detect than today. John was so keen on the idea of reincarnation that, after the twins' birth, he got in touch with Dr Ian Stevenson, a leading parapsychologist with a keen interest in reincarnation. It was Dr Stevenson's suggestion that the twins be taken back to Hexham to see if they could recognize any landmarks from their previous existence. It is easy to imagine an over-keen father inadvertently prompting his offspring into some of the incidents that occurred. To complicate matters, Florence, who died in 1979, remained uncooperative with any attempts to investigate the case and so we are left only with John's version of events.

Investigation of reincarnation cases like this one has proved controversial. In 1974 Dr Stephenson published *Twenty Cases Suggestive of Reincarnation*. The book has been used by many authors and philosophers as evidence of the existence of reincarnation. In 1992 Leonard Angel thoroughly examined what Dr Stephenson considered to be his most impressive case, that of Imad Elawar. Here, Dr Stephenson was able to interview the young Indian boy concerned before anybody else tried to verify any of the memories of reincarnation. Elawar claimed that he had lived before as a man called Mahmoud Bouhamzy, who died after being run over by a truck. He claimed to have lived in a village called Khriby, had a wife called Jamilah and provided names and details connected with his past life. In total Stephenson recorded 57 facts about Elawar's past-life experience, all of which were linked to a man who had died a few years previously in the village of Khriby.

Examination of the case has revealed a number of inconsistencies. The name of the village given by the boy turned out to have been provided by a resident of Khriby who thought that he recognized Elawar in the street. No Mahmoud Bouhamzy had lived in the village, but one Ibrahim Bouzhamy, who had an uncle named Mahmoud, had. Dr Stephenson linked the name with the boy and assumed that Elawar's past life was that of Ibrahim Bouzhamy and that his mention of Mahmoud was just a sign of confusion. Unfortunately, neither Ibrahim nor Mahmoud Bouzhamy was killed in a truck accident – something that Stephenson described as 'baffling'. Other details were loosely connected to Bouzhamy's life: for example, Elawar's description of an empty and a full well in Khriby village was taken to mean a large and a small wine vat in the village. Other details were verified only after leading questions from Stephenson and the researchers. There is the same worry here that an over-eager father and/or parapsychologist could inadvertently have prompted the twins to remember events connected with the dead girls when being shown their toys or taken around their old town.

In the case's favour is the fact that Florence absolutely refused to allow talk of reincarnation in front of the twins, who knew nothing of their father's beliefs. It was only in 1979, when aged 21, that the twins were inadvertently given an article about themselves and were told the truth about their childhood.

Reincarnation features in many Eastern religions and there are many stories from the Indian subcontinent similar to that of the Pollock twins. Indeed, claims of reincarnation are so common in India and Thailand that some scientific investigation of the subject has occurred, although no conclusions have been reached.

The possibility exists that something unusual did occur to the Pollock twins and their family. It may have been a case of reincarnation or even telepathy between father and daughter; it may also have been a case of autosuggestion or wishful thinking on the part of John Pollock.

Colonel Percy Fawcett

❖

MEDIUMSHIP

COLONEL FAWCETT WAS an eccentric character who had a passion both for esoteric matters and for exploring the jungles of South America. His disappearance while searching for a lost city sparked a wave of contradictory sightings and rumours. To add to the matter, he was claimed to have telepathically told people of his fate within the jungles.

Percy Harrison Fawcett was born in England in 1867. He joined the army at an early age and rose quickly through the ranks. During his time there he developed a keen interest, as did many Victorians, in exploring the remote tropical areas of the world.

After qualifying as a cartographer, he was seconded to carry out land and border surveys in the then remote area of the western Amazon basin. World War I drew him back to Europe and into the army again. After the war he distanced himself from things military and began to organize his own expeditions to the Amazon.

Fawcett had always had more than a passing interest in the paranormal and mysticism. He was known to subscribe to, and to have corresponded with, a number of occultist magazines and to have expressed a belief in poltergeists, ghosts, telepathy, psychometry and Spiritualism. He was also fascinated by the thought of lost cities and civilizations hidden beneath the Amazon's rain-forest canopy. The discovery of Machu Picchu in 1911 seemed to prove to him the viability of these lost kingdoms and he set about trying to find lost cities of his own.

It was after World War I that Fawcett found an obscure report of a 1753 expedition that had fruitlessly searched the central Amazon for a fabled silver mine. The report's author, a man named Raposo, wrote that his expedition had stumbled across a deserted city of gigantic proportions with evidence that it had been inhabited by an unknown civilization with an advanced form of writing and craftsmanship. The idea of this appealed to Fawcett's sense of romance and he at once made plans to travel to the Amazon to hunt for the lost city.

The first expedition he organized was unsuccessful and returned in 1920. It did, however, offer him enough hope to try and organize a bigger and better expedition, which, he felt sure, would end in the discovery of his mystical lost city. It was five years before this second expedition was ready to leave.

In early 1925 Percy Fawcett, his son Jack and the explorer Ralph Rimmel set off. Despite his promise to be better organized, Fawcett and his party seem to have been unfit, poorly supplied and without a plan. They departed from the central Amazonian town of Cuiaba on 20 April 1925. They headed north to Baccairi and from there further north to a camping place they had used in the previous expedition called Dead Horse Camp. Here, on 29 May 1925, he made a rather average entry in his journal about bathing and bothersome insects. It was to be his last confirmed message to the outside world, for neither he nor any of his party was seen again.

The expedition was not due to return until 1927 and so, despite no communication for two years, no undue concern was expressed. However, in 1927 a French explorer, Roger Courteville, returned from South America, claiming to have met a confused and weary old man in north-east Brazil who called himself Colonel Fawcett. This was disregarded at first, but as time marched on people started to suspect that Fawcett was unlikely to return. Speculation began about his party's fate and Courteville's sighting proved to be the first of many, often contradictory, encounters reported about Colonel Fawcett.

An American search party, led by George Dyott, set off to look for the Fawcett expedition in 1928. He soon discovered that much of the information written in Fawcett's journals was designed to throw any pursuers off his scent. None the less, Dyott found Dead Horse Camp and some local Indians who had a number of possessions that had belonged to the party. The Indians claimed that Fawcett had given them the objects before setting off into the jungle. They were convinced that Colonel Fawcett and his friends had fallen prey to vicious Indians, a conclusion that Dyott eventually agreed with.

However, Fawcett's wife, Nina, who had a keen interest in occultism, was convinced that her husband was still alive. In May 1930 she received a letter from a Californian medium who claimed to be in contact with a telepathic tribe of New Mexico Indians. The Indians said that they knew that Colonel Fawcett was alive and being held captive by a friendly tribe in the Amazon. Soon afterwards Mrs Fawcett began receiving direct telepathic messages from her son and husband, who apparently announced that they were about to emerge from the jungle and come back to civilization.

Shortly after this, in 1931, there was a whole barrage of sightings and rumours concerning the colonel. He and his son were seen in the Ria das Mortes by Miguel Trucchi, who claimed that they were hiding for personal reasons. At around the same time they were also spotted in the Matto Grosso region of Amazonia by Tom Roch. Most intriguingly, on 16 October 1931 the explorer

Stefan Rattin was temporarily held captive by a central Amazon Indian tribe. He claimed the Indians had also captured a tall, blue-eyed Englishman who fitted Fawcett's age and claimed to be a colonel, although he would not divulge his name. The man asked Rattin to contact a Major Paget (a friend of Fawcett). Although this sounded hopeful, a large number of inconsistencies in the story, including the man's description, his refusal to give a name and his inability to converse in Portuguese (Fawcett was fluent) led people to the conclusion that the story was false or that some other unfortunate was being held by the tribe.

In May 1932 Mrs Fawcett announced that she had lost telepathic contact with her husband and began supposing that he was dead. However, soon after this the medium Estelle Roberts received a message from Colonel Fawcett at a seance. He announced he was still alive but growing physically weak. Later in the year he made contact with Roberts again and confirmed that he had indeed met the explorer Rattin in October 1931.

In July 1933 another report suggested that the members of Fawcett's expedition were now the chiefs of an Indian tribe called the Aruvudu. One of the colonel's remaining sons, Brian, found this believable, but by now stories about his father were emerging from every part of Brazil. In addition to these, children claiming to be the offspring of members of the party also started to appear in various locations.

On the psychic front, a New Zealand spiritualist who claimed to have been in contact with Fawcett for two years said that he was now dead. Through the medium he claimed to have found his magical lost city but said that he and his companions had died of hunger trying to return to civilization.

In 1937 a missionary, Martha Moenich, sent photographs of a white Indian boy to Mrs Fawcett claiming that he was the son of Jack Fawcett. A covering letter said that the Fawcett expedition had been forced, through illness, to spend a year living with the Kuikuro tribe and during this time Jack had fathered the Indian boy, who had subsequently been named Dulipe. After recovering, the expedition had then apparently pressed on with guides from the Kalapalo tribe. After running out of food and placing themselves in great danger, the Kalapalo guides killed the members of the expedition in order to both free themselves and save the explorers from dying of starvation.

In 1943 the explorer Edmar Morel set off into the Amazon to find Fawcett. He was unsuccessful and seemed to be convinced that Fawcett had indeed been killed by the Kalapalo tribe. He managed to extract a confession from the chief of the tribe, who admitted spearing the party to death. He also brought out of the jungle the supposed son of Jack Fawcett, Dulipe. Morel contacted Brian Fawcett with a view to his adopting his alleged nephew. Brian was indignant, claiming that the boy was almost certainly an albino and that he had no connection with the Fawcett family. A few years later, in 1952, he was proved to be correct when a Brazilian newspaper declared that the boy was indeed an albino and not related to any member of the Fawcett expedition.

By the early 1950s it was widely accepted that the members of the 1927 expedition must by now be dead. In 1951 another explorer, Orlando Vilas-Boas, also extracted a confession of murder from the Kalapalo chief. Vilas-Boas was shown the remains of the colonel (but not the others, whose bodies had been thrown into a lake). He managed to get the remains examined by forensic experts from London, who, on comparing them with the colonel's medical records, declared them not to be Fawcett's.

Also in 1951 a close friend of Percy Fawcett, Ralph Paget, contacted a well-known medium, Mrs Nell Montague, to see if she could solve the mystery of the Fawcett expedition's fate. On being handed a scrap of paper from a letter written by the colonel, the medium immediately had a vision of him, his son and Rimmel being savagely attacked by native Indians. She saw their lifeless bodies then being carried away in triumph. This fully convinced Paget that his dear friend was indeed now dead.

The final chapter in the Fawcett saga must go to the medium Geraldine Cummins, who published *The Fate of Colonel Fawcett* in 1955. The book was based on a large number of automatic writings apparently received from Colonel Fawcett through Mrs Cummins. It follows much in the pattern of dictated books from the previous century (see Madame Blavatsky, page 127), concerning itself with the evolution of mankind, the lost civilizations of earlier periods, including Atlantis and those of the lost city that Fawcett himself was searching for. Allegations were again made that Dulipe was Jack's son (even though he clearly was not) and it was said that the Vilas-Boas bones had been deliberately buried to confuse people and that the party had been held captive elsewhere. The remaining members of the Fawcett family were not impressed with this book and even Mrs Cummins herself acknowledged that the writings could easily have come from her unconscious.

The 1955 book was the last major work to be published on the subject of the disappearance of Colonel Fawcett. His son Brian had previously collected together some of his father's notes and writings and published them in a book entitled *Exploration Fawcett* in 1953. To date there has been little further speculation about the fate of the expedition and no remains have ever been recovered. At the time of writing, a new expedition to look for him is being planned by his descendants.

❖

Colonel Fawcett's story seems to have followed a similar pattern to those of other larger-than-life characters who have gone missing. For years after the disappearance of the suspected murderer Lord Lucan, he was reportedly sighted in half the countries of the world. Elvis Presley, Jimi Hendrix and Jim Morrison are still sighted from time to time and have become standing jokes in films and magazines. They too have reportedly contacted people from beyond the grave. For example, in 1995 Elvis was said to be haunting a south London council house, despite the fact that he never visited England while alive!

It would seem that the 1927 report of a distressed man claiming to be Fawcett probably sparked the notion that he was still alive somewhere in the jungle. Once caught in the public imagination, the sightings and rumours spread like wildfire. Nina Fawcett's interest in Spiritualism led to her taking seriously some of the reported contacts with her husband, even though most of the information provided by him, including her own telepathic communications, proved to be wrong. The majority of the psychic communications seem to have been based on rumours or alleged sightings that had already taken place. Very little credible original material was produced psychically. Most of the communications also contradict each other quite definitely.

It seems strange that all the theories concerning Colonel Fawcett's party are romantic or swashbuckling notions of the expedition being held captive by, or dying at the hands of, Indians or of starving to death after finding a vast lost civilization. These were popular themes in many films of the day, including the hugely successful *Tarzan* series. These days, the fate of missing people is sometimes attributed to more modern reasons, such as alien abduction, government conspiracy or a desire for personal privacy.

Any number of comparatively mundane things could have led to the expedition's demise, including accident, illness and exhaustion. It is unlikely that the true fate of the expedition will ever be known or whether Fawcett's mystical city is still lying out there, waiting to be discovered.

The expansion of civilization into even the most remote areas of the world has now all but robbed people of the romantic notion of hidden cities. The oceans, however, are still largely unexplored. Perhaps it will be there that a new wave of treasure-seekers turn in their search for fame and fortune.

CULT FIGURES

INTRODUCTION

PERHAPS BECAUSE OF its similarity to religion in its requirement of faith in often seemingly impossible phenomena, the paranormal has always had its cult figures.

In this book a cult figure is defined as somebody who, intentionally or inadvertently, has become the icon or figurehead of a movement that requires belief in some supernatural phenomena. This criterion is quite broad and would also include within it many religious figures, including Christ.

The origins of supernatural cults in the Western world are, as with many things, linked to the marked decline in the power of the Church in the eighteenth and nineteenth centuries. In the days when the powers of the Church and the state were inseparable, to suggest that there was any popular alternative to Christianity was blasphemous and, at the very least, resulted in social ostracism. Sometimes, as with witch trials, the consequences were far more extreme. Although the growth of democracy, literacy and Darwinism released people from the stranglehold of the organized Church, many of the early paranormal cults still based their beliefs on Christianity, enabling them to appeal to a wide audience and minimize offence. Examples of this are provided by Swedenborg's followers (see page 99) and, most importantly of all, the advent of Spiritualism.

Spiritualism was also the first organized religion to, in a minor way, threaten Christianity on its own ground and as such found itself trapped between the scientific community (which was keen to stay free of organized religion) and the Church (which was equally keen to keep its followers). It was therefore doomed never to succeed in a major way and has declined since the turn of the century. Spiritualism itself created many offshoot cults that were based on the variety of psychic phenomena it brought to the public attention, such as Madame Blavatsky's Theosophical Society (see page 127).

It is the post-World War II society that has seen the largest growth in the popularity and number of cults, both religious and paranormal. Entire books have been written about the philosophy and psychology behind the rise in popularity and diversity of cults in the late twentieth century. Blame is generally placed firmly on the breakdown of the family, the Flower Power generation and a decline in religious and moral values. Whatever the cause, from the late 1960s onwards a series of fanatical and dangerous cults, all centred around one individual, made themselves known to society at large. This included Charles Manson, responsible for murders in California; the Reverend Jimmy Jones, whose 700 followers committed ritual suicide in 1978; David Koresh, many of whose Branch Davidian followers died in an FBI siege in 1994; and the Heaven's Gate cult, whose 39 members committed suicide in order to join aliens hiding behind the comet Hale-Bopp in March 1997. It is therefore not surprising that in modern society cults, particularly personality-oriented ones, are extremely unpopular. Fortunately, most paranormal cults can be distinguished from the more extreme religious ones and tend to be curious rather than dangerous in nature.

Some cults, such as those of Benjamin Creme and the Swedenborg Society, give regular talks or publish literature. Attending these talks can be fascinating and revealing, although there is little point in arguing any finer points during discussions as the majority of speakers rely on preaching to the converted. I have had to bite my tongue quite a few times during talks: for example, during one given by the Aetherius Society the speaker claimed to have a friend who had to duck when a UFO buzzed him on Silbury Hill. On questioning, the Aetherius speaker believed in the low-flying UFO story because he had known the friend it had happened to for a long time and thought that he was scrupulously honest. It never crossed his mind for a moment that the story might, at best, be an exaggeration of the truth.

It seems to be the case that whatever opinion or point of view exists, there will always be somebody willing to believe in it or follow it. The majority of cults rely heavily on people's faith in their beliefs, however improbable they may be.

Aleister Crowley

❖

SATANISM

THE SO-CALLED 'wickedest man alive' was born Edward Alexander Crowley on 12 October 1875. He was the only son of a highly religious brewer and his wife, who lived in the English town of Leamington Spa. Both parents were members of a strict and puritanical Christian sect known as the Plymouth Brethren and tried to bring up their son according to its precepts.

Despite later protests, Aleister Crowley had a very spoilt childhood and was reported to be a normal child until, aged 11, his father died, leaving him to be brought up by his fanatically religious mother. After this, he became progressively more wild until, at the onset of puberty, he was sent away to a Plymouth Brethren College in Cambridge. Here his rebelliousness increased dramatically. He acquired a hatred of the Brethren and hence of Christianity and his strict mother, who on more than one occasion accused him of being the beast described in the Book of Revelation.

After a brief spell in public school, he went to study at Trinity College, Cambridge, during which time he inherited a £30,000 fortune. He developed an interest in poetry, rock-climbing and, more significantly, the occult. This was initially sustained by reading books on ceremonial magic and other occultist subjects, until eventually, through an alchemist named George Cecil Jones, he joined the magical society the Order of the Golden Dawn in 1898.

It did not take him long to develop an arrogant contempt for the Order, but he did admire one of its higher members, Allan Bennette, and ended up sharing a flat with him in central London. Here the two of them erected a White Temple and a Black Temple and carried out many occult rituals and experiments, including some minor animal sacrifices.

One evening, according to Crowley, he and Bennette returned to the flat to find that the door to the White Temple was unlocked and that all the furniture was overturned and the magic talismans scattered everywhere. Although this may have been only a burglary, both men are reported to have clairvoyantly seen an army of semi-materialized demons marching around the room. Similarly, a mansion which Crowley had bought near Loch Ness, called Boleskin House, had also apparently become filled with an abnormal darkness, even in the daytime, and shadowy figures were constantly seen moving around the corridors. It is certainly true that the lodgekeeper of Boleskin House went mad and tried to kill his family.

After some serious infighting, Crowley left the Order of the Golden Dawn in 1900 and spent the next few years wandering the world in pursuit of his poetry, mountaineering and occult practices. In 1902, while on his travels, he married a strange and mentally unstable girl named Rose Kelly who, despite her initial lack of interest in the occult, he renamed Ouarda the Seer. The two continued to travel, eventually settling in Cairo, where Crowley adopted the name Prince Chioa Khan. In 1904 Crowley attempted to invoke the spirits of the air into Rose, producing a result that was to change his life permanently. During the cere-mony, both Rose and Crowley received the same mental message, which stated that Crowley was to be the prophet of a new era in the history of mankind. On Rose's request, he performed a ritual that placed him in contact with both his own Guardian Angel and the demon Horus. He wrote down everything that was dictated to him by the demon on the assurance that the product would provide the solution to all worldwide religious problems. The result was 'The Book of the Law', a prose-style poem that repeatedly asserted the libertarian phrase 'Do what thou wilt'. The book seems to suggest that all the major religions will be replaced by a very liberal faith whose aim was personal self-fulfilment.

After a time of doubt and apathy, Crowley finally accepted the revelations of 'The Book of the Law' and devoted his life to its promotion, claiming himself to be 'the Great Beast of the Apocalypse' and a new messiah. By 1910 he had divorced Rose (whose sanity was now in doubt) and was experimenting with the drugs opium and mescaline in order to induce higher religious states.

Feeling that the time was right for public promotion, he and his small band of followers rented London's Caxton Hall, where, on seven consecutive Wednesdays, he gave public performances of occult ceremonies. For this, and for the occult publications he had produced, Crowley and his followers received some serious attacks in the press. He was accused by the occultist MacGregor Mathers (who was an initial inspiration for Crowley) of giving away secrets from the Order of the Golden Dawn and accused by Theodor Reuss of revealing aspects of sexual magic performed by another group, the Ordo Templis Orientis. Despite this, Reuss authorized Crowley to set up his own branch of the Templis. This provoked Crowley into a serious interest in sexual magic, which in turn seemed to encourage the sadist within him.

To escape from World War I, and a certain amount of hostility he was receiving for having written pro-German literature, Crowley went to America to spread the word about The Book of the Law'. His six years there were described by him as 'a period of poverty and humiliation'. He returned to England in late 1919 with two mistresses and, after receiving another legacy of £3,000, moved into a farmhouse on the Sicilian coast.

The Sicilians seemed tolerant of Crowley and left him, his mistresses, disciples and visitors to perform their sexual magic and rituals in peace. He was by now hopelessly addicted to opiates and his life was sliding downhill rapidly. Things became worse after the visit to Sicily of a brilliant Oxford graduate, Raoul Loveday, and his wife, Betty May. During the course of a ritual, Loveday was persuaded to drink blood from a sacrificed cat, but he became very ill and within a few days was dead. Betty May was distraught and returned to England, where she started a press campaign against Crowley. The English press, then as now, loved nothing more than a society scandal and the ensuing outrage was enough to persuade Mussolini to order Crowley and his followers out of Italy.

Crowley, his mistresses, offspring and a new disciple, Norman Mudd, moved their operation from Sicily to Tunis. Here Crowley lived in a drug-induced haze but still occasionally wrote poetry and indulged in both heterosexual and homosexual relationships. The debauchery of his lifestyle caused him to desert his Tunisian friends for Paris. Unfortunately, his reputation had gone before him and he was ordered out of France in 1929. He returned to England and married a previous mistress, Teresa de Miramar, but England did not react favourably to the self-styled 'beast'. His autobiography was refused for publication and lectures and exhibitions of his paintings were banned. He moved to Lisbon and then to Berlin, but physically and financially Crowley was now far past his peak and the rest of his life was spent travelling in Britain and Europe, imposing himself upon friends, disciples or anyone who could tolerate him. His addiction to heroin and alcohol was chronic, although he did still seem to be able to find mistresses wherever he went. He died, aged 72, on 5 December 1947. There was considerable fuss regarding the reading of one of his poems at his funeral, but other than that his death was rather uneventful, his prophecies remaining unfulfilled.

Ironically, a revival of interest in Crowley's writings and magic began about ten years after his death and is still around today. Many people still obsessively study 'The Book of the Law' and treat it as many Evangelical Christians treat the New Testament. Many books have been written about his life and works, and a play, *The Number of the Beast*, was performed in the West End of London in 1982. Crowley has also entered pop culture for, if you look carefully at the cover of the Beatles' *Sergeant Pepper's Lonely Hearts Club Band* album, you should be able to see Crowley's face in the back row, second from the left.

❖

The traditional classification of Crowley as a fraud or a charlatan is perhaps a bit harsh. Although his claims of mastery over the dark occult powers are highly suspect, there is no doubt that he did have a power over people and was a highly intelligent individual. His disciplines, obsessions with sex and religion bear many similarities to some of today's more modern cults, such as David Koresh's Branch Davidian sect, the subject of the tragic 1994 Waco siege, where a bungled FBI rescue attempt led to the burning to death of a number of his followers. A look at the people who were attracted to Crowley during his lifetime shows that they were generally weak-willed, unstable or lonely people. These are characteristics of the type of people preyed upon by modern cults. Similarly, his anarchic image and ability to upset the general public also attracted people trying to rebel against society at large. The fact that Crowley's name is now to be seen on the T-shirts and school bags of fans of the more image-conscious heavy-metal bands shows that his status as a rebel has lasted. Crowley seems to have had a passion for adopting and giving titles and at different times went under the name of the Laird of Boleskin and Prince Chioa Khan, as well as the Great Beast. He gave all his various mistresses and students demonic or pagan-sounding titles, encouraging them to believe they had power and status within his organization.

Crowley wanted both to shock people and to be accepted as a genius. His obsession with the occult seems to have been a direct rebellion against his own strictly Christian childhood and it may well have been his mother's insistence that he was the 'beast' that caused him to adopt this role. However, in retrospect much of what Crowley did is shocking only for the times in which he lived. Although he claimed to be the Antichrist, he never (as far as is known) actually committed any serious crimes other than sexual perversions (some of which were then illegal), animal sacrifice, mild sadism, etc. He also, in his later years, did not seem to live under the protection of any divine force and suffered from ill heath, drug addiction and a fair share of bad luck.

In his favour, interviews with Crowley show him to have genuinely believed in much of what he preached and many people believe that he did possess psychic powers. His description of the ransacking of the White Temple in London has some similarities with poltergeist activity and there is speculation that a telepathic link between himself and his first wife, Rose, might have existed.

However, much of Crowley's life seems to have been devoted to shocking what he saw as the conservatism and hypocrisy within English aristocratic society. The genuine outrage that he caused was to backfire on him in later life when he was expelled from various parts of Europe. A similar example today might be the Marquis of Blandford, who, despite being heir to a fortune, has been arrested and imprisoned for drug abuse, bad debt and theft. Had Crowley been born 70 years later, he might well have used more orthodox means to express his rebellion, such as hard drugs and rock 'n' roll.

Benjamin Creme

❖

THE SECOND COMING

ONTACT WITH JESUS is a common claim by many modern cults, religions and
individuals. However, it is not often that the claim is made that Jesus is
alive and well and living in the East End of London.

Benjamin Creme was born in 1922 in Scotland. His interest in the esoteric
began when he was 14 and after reading the book *With Mystics and Magicians in Tibet*
by Alexander David-Neal. Creme claims to have discovered that he himself had
some of the powers outlined in the book, including limited healing abilities and
autosuggestion. Over the years his interest in Spiritualism and esoteric religions
increased and he began to have mystical experiences that placed him in touch
with the etheric plane, resulting in a host of spiritualist phenomena.

By 1957 he had become vice-chairman of the Aetherius Society, a British
semi-cult that claimed mental contact with purposeful extraterrestrial beings.
The Aetherius Society routinely used 'channelling' as a means of communicating
and receiving instructions and, most interestingly, claimed to have contacted
Jesus during public meetings in London in the 1950s. Despite still being a
believer in the Aetherians, an unspecified reason caused him to leave the society
in 1958.

Creme was placed on his current path early in 1959, when, as he was emerging from the bath, he received a telepathic message instructing him to go to a
specified location where he would meet a group of people with an important
message for him. Creme duly went and was indeed met by a collection of people
who told him to prepare himself for a great event. The telepathic messages
continued until, in late 1959, a voice told him that he had been chosen to prepare
the world for Christ's second coming. The voice, which was to become Creme's
full-time 'control', claimed to be a senior member of the Spiritual Hierarchy of
Masters, a group of entities who had been shaping the progress and evolution of
human existence for thousands of years.

It was in 1972 that the voice began to prepare Creme so he would be able to
carry out the masters' work on earth. He says that he underwent a lengthy process
of training, the objective of which was to make him mentally ready for the rigours
and abuse that he would receive once his mission became public. He also formed

a mental link between himself and his voice, which, from his description, seemed akin to some form of minor possession, with Creme's master being able to feel and experience everything that Creme could.

Benjamin Creme began lecturing on his experiences and beliefs in 1974. He proclaimed that the earth was nearing a spiritual watershed and that the Day of Deliverance, when Christ would return, was close at hand. His claims are that Christ is just another incarnation of a spiritual master who has also appeared previously as Christ, Buddha, Krishna and others. According to Creme, the real name of this spiritual master is Maitreya and he has spent the last few hundred years living in a high mountain retreat in the Himalayas. At the many meetings Creme gave, Maitreya's messages to the world, as channelled through Creme, were delivered to the audience. These messages range from a pessimistic analysis of modern world problems to a message of hope and goodwill that would be apparent after his announcement to the world.

In 1977 Creme announced that on 8 July that year Maitreya had descended from his 20,000-foot Himalayan retreat and, after a few days in Pakistan, had come to London, where he moved into the East End Asian community there. Creme kept in touch with Maitreya's progress. This seems to have involved rising to become a spokesperson and educator for the poor in the area.

In January 1982 Creme threw himself into the public arena by founding Share International, an organization for the promotion of his beliefs and teachings. Shortly afterwards, he spent £100,000 on advertisements in 17 newspapers worldwide, announcing the arrival of Maitreya. He claimed that Maitreya was waiting for the world to invite him to come forward and challenged a very sceptical media to issue this invitation. Perhaps not surprisingly, it was never issued by the press and Maitreya remained in hiding.

In early 1984 a collection of journalists accepted Creme's long-standing offer and expressed a desire to meet with Maitreya. Months of debate followed until Creme announced that Maitreya was prepared to meet the journalists in a Brick Lane curry house in the East End. A sizeable number of journalists turned up, but Maitreya did not appear, leading to a series of sceptical and comical articles in the national and local press. Creme predictably blamed negative and sceptical energies for Maitreya's refusal to appear, but the press did not buy this and he was treated as a crank. However, one unusual incident that Creme still refers to did occur on that day.

About 18 months before the Brick Lane no-show, a sceptical journalist attended one of Creme's London meetings and had a vision in which she clearly saw Maitreya. While she was among the other journalists in Brick Lane, she claims that she saw the man from her vision standing in the restaurant and he recognized her before fading away. The journalist concerned is now utterly convinced of Creme's claims and of the existence of the Maitreya.

After Maitreya refused to appear in Brick Lane, Creme was not taken seriously by the media and was forced to continue his publicity by international lectures, although he did selectively target certain media.

In 1986 he accused the BBC of being part of a conspiracy to silence the existence of Maitreya. He accused them of having being contacted by Maitreya and afterwards refusing to announce his messages to the world. His protests were dismissed and just as it looked as if Creme was destined never to get a favourable press, Maitreya made an unannounced appearance before a crowd of 6,000 in Kenya.

Maitreya apparently materialized from nowhere in front of a prayer meeting in the Kenyan village of Kawangware on 11 June 1988. A first-hand report was provided in the *Kenya Times* by journalist Job Mutungi, who also managed to photograph Maitreya.

According to Mutungi, the healer Mary Akatsa interrupted the meeting to announce that God had spoken to her and an important guest would be making an appearance. Whispers of 'Jesus' went through the crowd. Five minutes later a tall Asian man 'appeared from nowhere' and began to move among the now hysterical crowd. After delivering a speech, the man departed by (rather oddly) accepting a lift from a local man with a car. This man said that after letting the Asian man out at a bus stop, he disappeared. Creme claims that this and a number of similar appearances worldwide, including one in Edinburgh in 1992, were the work of Maitreya.

From the late 1980s onward, a series of prophecies made by Maitreya were released through Creme. In September 1988 he predicted that Nelson Mandela would be released from prison; this occurred 18 months later. He also predicted that Margaret Thatcher would retire as prime minister, that Beirut hostage Terry Waite would be freed and that a Democrat would be elected American president in 1992. These are fairly generalized prophecies that would attract low odds from a bookmaker. Other predictions, such as Prince Charles being king of England by 1990, were not so accurate. In recent times Creme has announced that Maitreya has moved from the East End to south-west London in order to escape media harassment.

From 1982 to the present day, Creme's (and therefore Maitreya's) following has steadily increased so that his monthly magazine has a circulation of 150,000 and he now spends half the year lecturing abroad. He still makes occasional appearances on chat shows and in magazines, and has written two books on the subject of Maitreya and the Day of Deliverance. He does, however, still largely remain the object of much ridicule.

Having personally heard Creme speak, it is hard to doubt the sincerity of his belief in Maitreya and the forthcoming Day of Deliverance. It does, however, worry me that much of what he claims falls into a rather predictable pattern shown by other messianic cults. Many modern cults have a prophet or representative on earth who has been contacted by a higher being (aliens, Christ, etc.) in order to make the human race ready for their arrival. The prophets normally rely heavily on people's faith in them and rarely provide proof of the substance of their claims. Despite this the prophets may claim to have seen such proof themselves: for example, they have been taken to another planet or are in contact with higher beings. Sometimes a cult leader will announce that proof is on the way: for example, the end of the world will occur on a certain day or the aliens will appear in a certain place. The regular failure of these stunts is put down to negative energy emanating from non-believers. Although his claims are not as extreme as some, they do broadly follow many other cults, including Creme's old associates, the Aetherius Society.

His claims that Maitreya has previously appeared as Christ, Buddha and Krishna are also a bit suspect. The teachings of these people do not overlap much with each other and do not show any awareness of periods of time beyond that in which they were living, suggesting that they are the products of different individuals.

It may have been that Creme got many of his ideas from his time with the Aetherius Society, which, after all, claims to have channelled Jesus – something that Creme publicly defended at the time. The voices in his head do not seem to be abnormal when compared to other mediums, and the claims he makes are not as outlandish as those of other people who have channelled religious figures, such as Sophia Richmond, David Ike and George Adamski. Creme is sincere in what he does, derives no money personally from Share International and has received much sarcasm and abuse from the press, yet he still continues with his work. Despite this, his claims are at the moment unsubstantiated and Maitreya still remains hidden in London's sprawling suburbs.

The Fox Sisters

❖

SPIRITUALISM

IN 1848 THE Fox family consisted of two parents, James and Margaret, and six children, only two of whom, Margaretta (14) and Catherine (12), remained at home. The family lived in a simple timber house in the village of Hydesville, New York State. It was here, during the last two weeks of March that year, that the family became disturbed by a nightly knocking on the walls and by mysterious vibrations throughout the house. The previous tenant, Michael Weekman, had complained about similar noises and told the Foxes that he thought a restless spirit was responsible.

On Friday 31 March the entire family retired to bed early to try and make up for the sleep they had lost because of the noises. As the two girls had been frightened by the disturbances, they moved into their parents' room for the night. When the knocking sounds began again Catherine plucked up her courage and said aloud, 'Mr Splitfoot, do as I do!' and started rhythmically snapping her fingers. To the family's amazement, the knocking imitated the pattern of her snapping. Margaretta joined in by clapping her hands and again the noises copied her exactly. Mrs Fox, thinking that someone was playing tricks, asked if the entity could knock the ages of the two girls. It did this correctly. She then asked it to knock the ages for all her children. This too was correct and ended with three faint knocks for the seventh child, who had died aged three.

Mrs Fox then asked a series of questions using two knocks for yes, one for no. With this and other codes, she found that the knocking entity claimed to be an injured spirit who had been murdered in the house when aged 31. Over a dozen neighbours were called in, one of whom, William Duesler, asked the spirit more questions and determined that the murdered man had been a pedlar named Charles B. Rosma, who had been killed five years previously by the then tenant, Mr Bell. It claimed that the body had been buried in the cellar and the murderer would never be brought to justice. A dig in the cellar the next day revealed nothing.

News of the noises travelled fast and when they commenced again on the Saturday evening over 300 people turned up to witness them. On Tuesday 4 April Mrs Fox wrote an account of the previous week's events.

Interest in the phenomenon grew so rapidly that a committee was set up to monitor events and it was soon apparent that the noises occurred only when Margaretta and, in particular, Catherine were present. Suspicious, the committee stripped the children, searched them, stood them on cushions, tied them up and observed them closely. The noises still occurred and no allegations of fraud were made.

In an attempt to escape public attention, the two sisters and Mrs Fox moved to Rochester to stay with Mrs Fox's 34-year-old daughter Leah. To everyone's amazement, the noises followed the daughters to Rochester and in addition objects were thrown and people would be pinched, jabbed and punched by invisible forces. The phenomenon now seemed to be in two places at once, for the noises continued in the Hydesville house. It also followed Margaretta when she moved to Auburn to stay with her brother David. Here she managed to communicate with spirits other than that of the murdered pedlar. In Rochester Leah discovered that she too could induce the noises and communicate with the spirits.

The whole family moved to Rochester, where the volume of the banging would keep the neighbourhood awake for hours on end. After a particularly active question and answer session, the spirits suddenly told the Fox family, 'You must proclaim the truth to the world. This is the dawning of a new era...God will protect you and good spirits will watch over you.'

Under instruction from the spirits, the world's first-ever seances were held at the Fox family home. These were small affairs but phenomena occurred there which are now synonymous with mediumship (see Daniel Dunglas Home, page 81), such as musical instruments playing themselves, moving furniture, the manifestation of limbs and rapping noises. Under instructions from their invisible guides, the Fox sisters rented a public hall in Rochester and, on 14 November 1849 the world's first spiritualist meeting was held.

Spiritualism was an instant success and before long the girls were national celebrities, embarking on a long run of public meetings. Their seances would be mobbed by curious members of the public and the controversy created was such that the girls were frequently attacked, both verbally and physically, at their meetings. An official committee was set up by the Rochester authorities to test the sisters. It cleared them of forgery. This was not the result the authorities were looking for and a second more sceptical committee was appointed. It too could find no evidence of deception.

A normal existence became impossible and soon the sisters moved from Rochester to Troy, in Albany. The public storm they had caused followed them and they moved again, this time to New York itself, where they arrived in June 1850. By this time, hundreds of other people had discovered that they too were capable of producing the same type of phenomena as the Fox sisters, causing the rapid spread of parlour-room seances.

The first blow to the Fox sisters' reputation came in 1851. Three professors from the Buffalo School of Medicine attended some of their seances and claimed to have found evidence of trickery. They said that if the sisters' knees were held, the noises would stop. They therefore concluded that the noises were produced by 'popping' (dislocating) the knee joints. When they could not explain exactly how this was done, they favoured the popping of the toe joints instead. This was confirmed by a statement made on 17 April 1851 by a distant relative of the sisters, Mrs Culver, who claimed that Catherine Fox had revealed to Mrs Culver that the noises were indeed made by cracking the toes; indeed, she said that Catherine had taught her how to do this herself. Despite these attempts at explanations, panel after panel of journalists and scientists came out on the girls' side. This included a lengthy investigation of Catherine Fox during a later stay in England by the eminent scientist Sir William Crookes. Crookes tried every method possible to stop the noises or to catch Catherine cheating, including suspending her in the air, holding her hands and feet, enclosing her in a suspended wire cage, etc. His conclusions were that the noises were 'true objective occurrences and not produced by trickery or mechanical means'.

All the attention and controversy started to take its toll and by 1855 Margaretta and Catherine were drinking excessively and were thoroughly disillusioned with the whole business of Spiritualism. Margaretta attempted to leave the act but was forced to stay by her parents. The seances were finally stopped when Margaretta's fiancé, Elisha Kane, died shortly before their marriage. She became extremely depressed and the family separated her from Catherine in an attempt to control her alcoholism, although this was only partially successful. Leah left the family in 1857 to marry a wealthy businessman and Margaretta converted to Catholicism, thus formally ending her involvement with the family's public performances. Catherine continued to perform and was credited with many spectacular feats, including backwards automatic writing and manifestations of the spirits of the dead. While in England she married Henry Jencken and they had two sons, the first of whom was alleged to have shown mediumistic powers by the age of five. After her husband's death in 1885, Catherine returned to New York.

Many of the doubts cast on the sisters seemed to be confirmed when, in New York on 21 October 1888, Catherine and Margaretta publicly confessed to having faked all their seances. Margaretta explained that all the noises had indeed been the result of toe-cracking and blamed Leah for leading her and Catherine on. Catherine kept quiet during her sister's confession and later said she did not agree with her. Leah said nothing.

There was much disbelief of the 'confession' among spiritualists but this was just what the Church and the scientific establishment had been waiting for. News of the event was reportedly greeted with cheers in some learned societies.

In 1891 Margaretta withdrew her confession, saying that extreme pressure from the Catholic Church, to which she had converted years previously, had made her make her statement in the first place. Confusion over the issue still continues to this day.

Living life in the public gaze had proved too much for the sisters and on 1 November 1891 Leah died. Catherine followed soon after, drinking herself to death on 2 July 1892. Margaretta died poor and destitute on 8 March 1893. It was a tragic ending to a chain of events that had begun as a neighbourhood curiosity in Hydesville in 1848.

The story has one final twist. On 21 November 1904, many years after the Fox sisters' deaths, a cellar wall collapsed in their old Hydesville house where the knocking had first begun. The collapsed wall uncovered a second false wall which, when excavated by workmen, revealed the skeleton of a man and a pedlar's tin box, confirming the story first rapped out in 1848. The house itself burnt down in 1955, but has since been replaced by a replica for tourists.

Perhaps the greatest legacy left by the Fox sisters is their creation of the religion of Spiritualism. It was their public seances that led to many thousands of people visiting mediums within months of their 1849 Rochester performance. Spiritualism was founded as a means of explaining many of the phenomena occurring at seances. Its followers believe that the soul is immortal and that it is possible to contact the souls of the dead using mediums. Although it is not anti-Christian, it has always been given a rough ride by the Christian Church, especially in its heyday, when it was stealing large numbers of people from the Christian congregations. In 1855 it was estimated that Spiritualism had 2 million followers in America alone. Apart from the Church, Spiritualism suffered badly at the hands of the late nineteenth- and early twentieth-century psychical research organizations, which largely seemed to focus their 'research' on the debunking of mediums. Although Spiritualism is still around today, like many religions in the West, it has suffered something of a decline in the latter half of the twentieth century. It does, however, still owe its existence to the two barely teenage Fox sisters and, depending on your point of view, their attempts to try and either enlighten or dupe the world.

❖

As already mentioned, the truth behind the Fox sisters' seances is still a matter of debate, with much of the controversy hinging on the confession to fraud and then its later withdrawal.

In their favour is the way in which the haunting of their house and their subsequent acquisition of mediumistic powers seem to follow the pattern of other mediums. The manifestations at their seances were, in many respects, far more tame than those of other later mediums, such as Daniel Dunglas Home. They also satisfied scientific and every other type of panel that set out to unmask them, although it has been argued that the examiners, being new to Spiritualism, were unaware of what tricks to look for. The confession by Margaretta that the initial rapping sounds were produced by bone-cracking seems only to mimic what had been earlier proposed by the Buffalo professors. The role of the Catholic Church in the confession has never been fully sorted out. The confession was also never formally agreed to by either Catherine or Leah and never fully explained many of the phenomena which had been witnessed at their seances by thousands of people.

Against the girls is the fact that the public seances were not free and that their parents treated them as a source of money, even forcing the girls to carry on long after they had grown weary of the performances. Then there is the simple fact that despite having passed many panels, the people on those panels did not really know what they were looking for. Later in the century the tricks that mediums used became more widely known and the debunking of mediums became a common occurrence. Also, the confession does cast doubt on their reliability and thus strongly diminishes the value of any evidence that they might have contributed to psychical research.

Madame Blavatsky

❖

THEOSOPHY

MADAME BLAVATSKY WAS born Helena Petrouna Halin on 31 July 1831 in Ekaterinoslav, Russia. Her mother was a well-known novelist and her father a colonel in the Russian army.

Her spiritual career began by accident when, as a young girl, she was day-dreaming while holding a pen in her hand. Without consciously willing it, her hand began to write coherent messages. The spiritual author of these messages claimed to be one Telka Lebendorff who said that she was the aunt of one of the soldiers in her father's regiment. Disbelieving, Helena's father used his access to government files to check the claims of 'Lebendorff' and was amazed to find that they were true. Both he and Helena were even more surprised to discover that Telka Lebendorff was in fact alive and well and unaware that she had apparently been writing messages through Helena.

The young Helena would appear to have been quite an awkward and stubborn child, for when aged 16 she became engaged to a 40-year-old man called Nicephore Blavatsky in order to upset her family and governess. Her spitefulness backfired when, aged 18, she was forced by her family to marry him. Before the marriage could be consummated she ran away from home and, from 1848 to 1873, wandered around Europe, India, Tibet and the Near East. She had many part-time jobs around the world before a chance meeting with the physical medium Daniel Dunglas Home (see page 81) brought back her interest in Spiritualism. Between 1848 and 1858, her so-called 'veiled period', she claimed to have learned much esoteric mysticism from Mahatmas (spiritual masters) in Tibet. In 1873, after a period working as a spiritualist medium in Russia, she took this knowledge with her to America, where she went in search of the wave of Spiritualism that had swept through the country.

After a short period of abject poverty, she met a lawyer called Colonel Henry Steel Olcott who was also the spiritualist correspondent for a local newspaper. Helena demonstrated her mediumistic powers to Olcott by producing many common seance effects, including raps, moving furniture and musical instruments playing themselves. He was immediately impressed and shortly afterwards he and Helena (or Madame Blavatsky, as she now preferred to be called) founded the Theosophical

Society, whose aim was to promote the knowledge and wisdom of the ancients.

Olcott left his family and moved into a house with Madame Blavatsky. Here she used her automatic-writing skills to produce a large manuscript, parts of which were reportedly written while she was either in a trance or asleep. The writing looked to have been done by several different hands and the result was a two-volume book entitled *Isis Unveiled*, which was published in 1877. The initial print run was only 1,000 and copies were very expensive – the publishers were openly doubtful about the likelihood of either critical acclaim or financial success. However, despite some appalling reviews, all the books were sold within two weeks of issue and the first of many reprints was made.

Isis Unveiled, written as a philosophical work, recounts the spiritual history of mankind and tries to explain the existence of certain types of psychic phenomenon. It hinges around the theory that our universe is permeated by a psychic ether that is capable of many things, including storing information from both the past and the present. This ether was dubbed 'Akasa' and Madame Blavatsky claimed that waves of energy travelling through the ether could be detected by people who were sufficiently sensitive. This was used to explain a range of phenomena including telepathy, clairvoyance, psychometry and, as the future is also recorded in the ether, precognition. Interestingly, Madame Blavatsky also stated that the majority of spirits contacted through seances and Ouija boards, etc. are dishonourable beings obsessed with mischief-making.

The book and the Theosophical Society were popular, but at the same time caused complete uproar among religious leaders and scientists. The pressure became too great for Madame Blavatsky and Olcott and they moved themselves and their society's headquarters to Bombay in 1878. Here the Theosophical Society flourished and before long branches were set up across the Indian subcontinent. Madame Blavatsky claimed that she was in supernatural contact with a group of Tibetan Mahatmas, who were said to be able to project their images to the Theosophists and were also responsible for a number of letters that had supposedly materialized during seances.

In 1884, the Society for Psychical Research (SPR) sent one of its keenest new members, a 29-year-old man called Richard Hodgson, out to India to investigate the claims of Madame Blavatsky and her Theosophists. Shortly before Hodgson left, Madame Blavatsky's former housekeeper, Emma Coulomb, published some letters written to her by Madame Blavatsky stating that her seances were fraudulent. Hodgson arrived with this news and during his three-month investigation found widespread evidence of fraudulent actions, including some sliding panels in the seance room behind which people and objects could be hidden during performances. In addition, Emma Coulomb and her husband demonstrated how they had faked seance phenomena, including apports and the famous materializing letters from the Tibetan masters. Despite vigorous protests of bias from the Theosophists, Hodgson published a highly critical report of Madame Blavatsky and her society in 1885. The Theosophical Society formally broke relations with the SPR and Madame Blavatsky was forced to leave India to retire in London, where she was discovered to have Bright's Disease. She undertook to write a mammoth work entitled *The Secret Doctrine*, but died aged 60 in 1891, shortly before the manuscript was published.

Together with *Isis Unveiled*, *The Secret Doctrine* draws upon the Akasaic Records (the history of the world as recorded in the Akasa ether) to give a history of intelligent life on earth. According to Madame Blavatsky, there have been five great intelligences on earth. The first generation comprised purely spiritual beings, but each successive generation of beings became less spiritual, further removed from the Akasa and more solid. Our own fifth-generation civilization is so far removed from our spiritual side that we find it difficult to be in contact with the Akasa ether at all. Some of the aspects of Madame Blavatsky's history are rather implausible. She places the fourth generation of beings (our forebears) on Atlantis and rewrote much of the known geological timescale to suit her version of history. It was these works that started the great debates over the existence of Atlantis and other lost continents, such as Lemuria, that continue today.

Theosophy continued after Madame Blavatsky's death and underwent a resurgence when, in 1900, Dr Rudolf Steiner joined the society. He was enthusiastic, charismatic and intelligent and within a short time was seen as a natural leader for the society. He was duly appointed as such and was soon adding volumes to the philosophical works of Madame Blavatsky through his lectures and writings. He claimed to be able to read the Akasaic records himself and spoke knowledgeably about important periods of history that he claimed to have seen personally. His fame and ego grew enormously. Many of his followers were convinced that he was a new messiah and, in 1912, he broke away from the Theosophical Society to form his own Anthroposophical Society, taking many of the Theosophical Society's membership with him. His position in the Theosophical Society was taken by a new religious messiah called Jiddu Krishnamurti, a young Hindu boy who led the society at the behest of its then leaders.

World War I shattered Dr Steiner's dreams of founding a new religion. Despite ongoing popularity, both the Anthroposophical and Theosophical Societies suffered a decline in a turbulent post-war world. After the war Dr Steiner founded a series of educational establishments known as the Waldorf Schools in Germany. They were built around his life and writings and had a unique structure for their time, being wholly controlled by the teachers, with a heavily arts-influenced curriculum. The ideas and theories of the Theosophical and Anthroposophical Societies were also taught directly and indirectly to the pupils. Exhausted by his life's efforts, Dr Steiner died in March 1925.

In the meantime, the Theosophists declined further after Krishnamurti renounced Theosophism in 1929. It is still around today, but as a very minor religion. In 1986, the SPR tried to patch up their differences with the Theosophists by suggesting a re-examination of the Coulomb letters which had exposed Madame Blavatsky in India in the 1880s.

❖

Madame Blavatsky and the Theosophical Society have spent many years surrounded by confusion and accusations of fraud. Even though there is now considerable doubt surrounding Madame Blavatsky's claims to mediumship, she is undoubtedly an important figure in the world of the paranormal.

Madame Blavatsky was one of the first people to suggest a mechanism that was capable of explaining a wide range of psychic phenomena. She was also therefore one of the first people to make connections between certain types of phenomenon. The concept of the Akasa psychic ether and its ability to store both past and future information concurrently does go a long way to explaining many aspects of clairvoyance and extrasensory perception. If the subconscious was able to access the Akasaic Record of an individual or object, then the phenomena of psychometry, telepathy, remote-viewing, precognition and clairvoyance are all explicable. However, as with other claims of hidden astral planes and worlds (including heaven and hell), there is no quantifiable proof for the reality of the Akasa, although the theory is as workable as some that have been used to explain psychic powers.

What is perhaps less plausible is the history of mankind outlined in *Isis Unveiled* and *The Secret Doctrine*. In common with other psychically dictated scripts, Madame Blavatsky's writings focus on the existence of ancient, more spiritually advanced beings who ruled the earth before ourselves. In common with some other transcripts and many past-life regressions, there was a fixation on Atlantis and the civilization that lived on the legendary continent. Madame Blavatsky was, by suggesting this, one of the first people to comment on a trend that has grown progressively stronger throughout the twentieth century.

There is a belief that our ancient ancestors (whether spiritual or physical) maintained a symbiotic relationship with the earth by utilizing hidden forces and natural energies that we have since lost touch with. Today there is a strong belief among many occultists that ancient monuments such as stone circles, hillforts and tumuli were built to channel hidden earth energy into specific locations or into ley lines. Many dowsers and psychics claim to be able to detect these energies and in more recent times these features have been linked to more recent phenomena such as UFOs and crop circles. In a similar fashion, Madame Blavatsky's ancient beings had fuller access to natural earth energies than ourselves and as such were able to use the benefits of a closer spiritual bond to nature, including psychic powers such as precognition and telepathy.

There is no fossil evidence for the existence of any ancestors other than the lineage that can be traced to *Australopithecus afarensis*, 4.4 million years ago, and ends with ourselves. Having said this, Madame Blavatsky's ancestors were supposedly more spiritual than physical in nature and one would therefore not expect to find the fossil remains of non-physical beings. Some of the generations of these spiritual beings also apparently lived on the legendary island of Atlantis, the site of which has never been formally identified.

Arguments for and against the existence of Atlantis could fill several volumes. Suffice to say that although the continent apparently disappeared only 11,500 years ago, there is no evidence of its existence on sea-floor geographic maps. Some people have suggested that the Atlantis legend represents the drowning of many lowland areas with the rise in sea level that accompanied the end of the last Ice Age, which occurred approximately 10,000 years ago. Others think that it may represent the mammoth explosion of a volcano on the Greek island of Thera 3,500 years ago or even the marine flooding of the Black Sea 7,500 years ago. Whatever the truth, the legend of Atlantis does feature strongly in many people's past-life regressions and in numerous channelled entities.

As for the structure of the Theosophical Society itself, it seems to have been a minor religion based around the strong personality of Madame Blavatsky. After her death the society was fortunate enough to encounter the pseudo-intellectual and authoritative Dr Steiner. Sadly, he had greater ambitions than the Theosophical Society and left to form a messianic religion around himself. The Theosophists tried replacing Dr Steiner's strong personality with that of the cult figure of Krishnamurti. Although this prolonged the society's life for a while, without the progressive thinking of Blavatsky and Steiner interest soon waned.

This pattern can be seen in many cults, spiritualist societies and political doctrines, where the death or removal of the founding figurehead causes unrest, a decline in interest and a lack of faith among the followers. Even the spiritualist movement witnesses this same decline in public interest following a series of attacks on their founders, the Fox Sisters (see page 124).

Theosophists are still around today, although it really is a minority religion. None the less, Madame Blavatsky's works still make interesting reading and do at least propose a mechanism for some of the religion's stated beliefs.

MYSTERIOUS
PEOPLE

INTRODUCTION

THE PEOPLE INCLUDED in this chapter are diverse in character and nature but all have an unsolved mystery associated with them. In this book a mystery is defined as being an aspect of a personality, event or associated quality for which there is a probable answer if only the full facts of the case were known.

Many of the people described here have, to varying degrees, got the answers to the mysteries themselves, if only they were prepared to reveal them. For example, Frank Hansen (see page 141) knows whether his 'missing-link' iceman is the real thing or just a made-up exhibit for a side-show; it is up to him to tell us either way or take the truth to his grave. Some people who have created false enigmas around themselves have chosen to come clean about it, as was the case with the Cottingley Fairies (see page 173), and can therefore be dismissed as hoaxers. Other cases can be resolved only if further evidence comes to light, but at least the potential to solve them is there. This is unlike many areas of the paranormal, such as life after death, that will never be resolved to most people's satisfaction.

Mysteries tend to be at the less extreme and therefore more user-friendly end of the paranormal spectrum. Many people do not like to get bogged down in the complex arguments, psychology and fanaticism associated with broad topics such as UFOs, poltergeists, ghosts, etc. The simple, compact and interesting nature of a mystery, and the fact that most of its main points can be summarized into a short article, mean that they have wide appeal among the public at large. Some mysteries, although not many from this book, are ongoing affairs which surface in the media from time to time. Barely a year goes by without a new sighting of the Loch

132

Ness Monster or a theory being put forward about the Bermuda Triangle, the Roswell UFO crash or the Yeti.

Of the mysteries associated with individuals, some are created by the people themselves, while others are associated with them later on (usually posthumously). Whatever the means of association with an individual, each mystery is entertaining in its own right and very often the solutions to some of the enigmas are as fascinating as the original mysteries themselves.

Arnold Paole

❖

VAMPIRISM

MANY PEOPLE ARE selective in the areas of the paranormal in which they believe. Some may have faith in horoscopes even though they do not believe in UFOs. Others believe in ghosts but not in an afterlife. There are, however, some aspects in which virtually no one has any faith at all, and vampires are a good example. Despite hours of Hollywood and Hammer film footage devoted to Dracula and his kin, there are very few accounts of true vampirism, or in fact of people returning bodily from the grave at all. There is, however, a well-documented case from eighteenth-century Serbia which centres around the soldier Arnold Paole.

The available literature tells us little about his early life. He is thought to have lived just before or at the turn of the eighteenth century in the Serbian village of Meduegna.

As a young man he joined the Serbian army and before long was fighting the Turks in the north-eastern Serbian region of Cassova (some accounts have him stationed in Greece). The region itself is mountainous and close to the now infamous Romanian territory of Transylvania where, in the eighteenth century, belief in vampirism was very strong indeed.

According to Arnold himself, while he was stationed in Cassova he was attacked by a vampire and partially drained of blood. After taking local advice, he was warned that the vampire would keep returning to feed on him until he was dead, at which point he would join the ranks of the undead. Arnold, being strong-willed, somehow (exactly how is not clear) managed to find his attacker's grave and proceeded to destroy the vampire. In an attempt to prevent the onset of vampirism in himself, he ate dirt from the grave and smeared the vampire's blood on to himself.

Understandably frightened, Paole quit the army and returned to Meduegna. He is thought to have arrived there in the spring of 1727 and then to have led a semi-reclusive existence as the farmer of a small farm. Before long he married a neighbouring farmer's daughter called Nina and it was to her that Paole confided the story of his attack in Cassova. He also told her of his fear that he was now cursed and would die ahead of his time. His prediction turned out to be true, for after being married only a short time, Arnold Paole was killed in an accident involving a haycart.

Within days of his burial, Paole was reportedly seen wandering the village at night. Soon afterwards some villagers claimed that his ghost had attacked them during their sleep. The people who claimed to have been attacked began to fall ill, becoming tired and listless. Within four weeks of his burial, four of the villagers had died, all of them apparently victims of Arnold's ghostly attacks. Panic ensued as the villagers became convinced that they had a vampire in their midst.

Luckily for the historians, the villagers approached the district authorities for permission to exhume the body of Paole to check for signs of vampirism. The authorities agreed and six to seven weeks after his death a group of administrators, doctors, soldiers and officers gathered to open the grave. When the coffin emerged, the worst fears of the villagers were realized.

According to a translation of a report by Abbot Augustere Dom Camlet, published in 1749, Paole's body had shifted position within the coffin and had blood smeared around its mouth. It also appeared to show some signs of life, including supple limbs, liquid blood and growing hair and nails. Convinced that they had found a vampire, a stake was driven through Paole's heart – the 'corpse' allegedly screamed as this was carried out. Other precautions were taken, including beheading and cremating not only Paole's body but those of his four victims. No more attacks or strange deaths were reported after the exhumation and peace descended on the village once more.

However, in September 1731 people again began to fall ill, showing symptoms of anaemia and extreme tiredness. The son of a man called Millo died of the disease and, as with Paole, his ghost was reported to be attacking people, giving them the same vampiritic symptoms as before. By midwinter an epidemic was under way, with some 12 villagers dying under suspicious circumstances. In an attempt to link the deaths to the previous vampiristic episode, the villagers decided that Paole must also have attacked local cattle and that infected meat had caused this second episode. Another appeal for help was made to the authorities.

This time the appeal seems to have touched a raw nerve high up in the Serbian government and an official inquiry was ordered by the Emperor Charles VI.

Heading the inquiry was the governor of Serbia, Duke Charles Alexander of Württemberg, who assembled together over 1,000 officers, administrators, doctors, respected figures and people of good character – all of whom were placed under oath to tell the truth about what they witnessed.

Before any physical action was taken, extensive statements were taken from the villagers and inquiries were made into the claims of the Arnold Paole affair a few years previously. After this it was decided that the body of the supposed initiator of this episode, the son of Millo, should be publicly exhumed.

Despite nearly three months underground, the body was fresh, supple and full of warm blood. It was deemed vampiritic and dealt with in the same manner as the five 'vampires' in the previous exhumations. A frenzy of grave-digging ensued during which over 40 corpses were exhumed. Of these, 17 were deemed vampiritic – descriptions of their conditions referred to warm blood and healthy complexions. One 60-year-old woman was described as being found in a better condition than when she had died! All 17 were dealt with by beheading, staking and cremation. The reported attacks and mysterious deaths stopped once more.

The official report of the inquiry was signed by the surgeon-in-chief, three military surgeons and a handful of high-ranking officers and doctors. It was submitted on 7 January 1732 and concludes the last known outbreak of vampirism reported in the village.

❖

The whole affair could be written off as superstitious legend that had become exaggerated over the years were it not for the findings of the Emperor's report. The calibre and number of people who witnessed the report can leave little doubt that there must indeed have been some very lifelike corpses dug up months after they had been buried. Even so, as was mentioned in the introduction, it is difficult to believe or prove that vampirism was responsible for the deaths and subsequent incorruptibility of the bodies. Various authors have commented on the case and have come up with broadly similar conclusions.

The most popular theory is that the unfortunate villagers fell prey to an illness that placed them in a cataleptic state, during which the body appears dead when it is in fact comatose, and they were buried alive. While moving a seventeenth-century graveyard in Paris it was estimated that one in three coffins showed signs that their occupants had been buried alive. Even today such mistakes are not impossible to make. For example, on New Year's Day 1996, a British woman, Daphne Banks, collapsed and was pronounced dead at her home. Her body was placed in a bag and moved to the local mortuary. The next day one of the undertakers saw slight movement in her eyes and called in a medical team. After two days in intensive care she recovered completely and is now living a normal life.

If a mistake like this can be made by modern medicine, it is easy to imagine the highly superstitious villagers of Meduegna (something commented on in the official report) burying bodies as quickly as possible in order to avoid spreading disease (or even vampirism) without checking them thoroughly first. It is, however, hard to imagine how even a comatose body could survive for up to three months underground without food or water or that so many mistakes could have been made in such a short space of time.

It was suggested by Abbot Calmet that the soil in the village might be sterile or act as a preservative to stop the bodies decomposing. However, it has been pointed out that some of the 40 corpses dug up after the second epidemic showed signs of decomposition, even though they had been in the ground less time than the vampire corpses. This selective decomposition makes the preservative qualities attributed to the soil unlikely.

It seems probable that the superstitious villagers could indeed have been struck down by a contagious disease of some sort and quickly blamed it on vampirism. In the hysteria that followed, they may well have prematurely buried some of the bodies. It should also be borne in mind that the only person Arnold Paole reportedly told about his attack was his wife and so we have only her word for this explanation. We do know that the poisoned-cattle theory was thought of by the villagers only as an explanation to their second epidemic – there was no mention of any cattle being attacked during the first.

A possible example of a further hysterical vampiritic episode comes from a small village in nineteenth-century New England. The village was severely affected by tuberculosis and a rumour started that the deceased victims were returning from the grave, causing the living themselves to waste away. As in Meduegna, panic spread quickly among the villagers and in the end many of the tuberculosis victims were exhumed and destroyed.

There are, in general, a whole number of arguments against the existence of vampires in the Hollywood sense of the word. The first and most obvious is that it must be impossible for these creatures to dig themselves out of their graves. Some vampire lore has them travelling in and out of their graves in a gaseous form. Hollywood solves the problem by always placing them in a crypt or cellar.

If they do exist, then vampires should also be much more in evidence than they are. If a person bitten by a vampire also becomes a vampire, then their species would have spread exponentially throughout the world. Despite this, there are few credible modern tales of actual attacks on people. It is interesting that some authors have noted similarities between vampirism and entities that, in some Eastern cultures, are responsible for draining the psychic energy out of people.

In the modern world, vampires are being used as political weapons in Madagascar. During the last century rumours grew about supernatural beings that wandered round Madagascar stealing people's hearts. Political parties on the island have used the stories to create a climate of fear and to discredit their opponents. There have been no formal sightings or indeed victims of these vampires.

It is worth noting that the Vampire Research Society of New York claims to have found 810 examples of modern vampires. The majority of them do not hail from Transylvania but California – possibly not a good idea for creatures that are supposed to loathe sunshine.

Spring-heeled Jack

❖

VICTORIAN TERROR

SPRING-HEELED JACK was one of those mysterious characters whose antics, like those of Jack the Ripper, blossomed in the slum conditions and dark, narrow alleyways of Victorian London. Although the legends surrounding him are now mostly forgotten, at the height of his fame he had a series of penny-dreadful comics named after him and mothers would threaten uncooperative children with a visit from Spring-heeled Jack.

It is believed that the first reports of a strange man capable of performing amazing leaps and bounds originated around 1817, but it was not until 1837 that the first newspaper reports of his antics appeared. There had been rumours of a series of attacks on women by a man dressed as an animal (usually a bear) for some time before the Lord Mayor of London, Sir John Cowan, held a public meeting on 8 January 1838. Here he revealed that he had been sent an anonymous letter from 'a resident of Peckham' claiming that a high-ranking person had taken a wager, the objective of which was to put on disguises in order to try to scare 30 people to death. After this, letters describing encounters with monkeys, white bears and mysterious lamplighters, all of whom could escape by bounding away over walls and fences, flooded into newspapers, town halls and police stations. The leaping ability was put down to springs located within the bounder's shoes and the name Spring-heeled Jack was born.

The first confirmed attack took place on Wednesday 20 February 1838. Spring-heeled Jack had dressed as a policeman and violently rang the bell at the front gate of a well-to-do house in Bearbinder Lane, east London. When 18-year-old Jane Alsop came to see what the fuss was, the policeman said to her, 'Bring me a light, for we have caught Spring-heeled Jack!'.

Jane fetched a candle but, on handing it to the policeman, he shed his cloak to reveal a tight-fitting white oilskin suit. Again, the mysterious figure sprayed flame into the face of his victim and clawed at Jane's clothes before her screaming drew the attention of her sisters and the door was slammed in his face. He unsuccessfully tried this approach again within a week, but fled after he had aroused the suspicions of his intended victim. A witness described seeing an ornate crest on his chest bearing the letter 'W'.

On 28 February, in Limehouse, east London, Jack struck again. Two teenage sisters, Lucy and Margaret Scales, were passing an alleyway when a strangely clad figure leapt out at them. He breathed fire into the face of Lucy and then disappeared with a series of terrific leaps, leaving the girl terror-struck on the ground.

It was after this that his fame reached its height and he featured, sometimes as a hero, in several penny-dreadful comics. There followed a whole series of unconfirmed attacks attributed to Jack, although some of them, such as the one in March 1838, were carried out by imitators. All this attention seemed too much for the real Spring-heeled Jack, whose presence was not reported again for several years.

In 1845 reports again circulated about a figure leaping over walls and hedges in Ealing and Hanwell, west London. This turned out to be a humorous butcher from Brentford. However, another attack, this time with serious consequences, occurred in November 1845, in one of the most wretched areas of Dickensian London, Bermondsey. It was here that Spring-heeled Jack accosted a 13-year-old prostitute, Maria Davis, on a bridge and breathed fire into her face. He then hurled the girl into a muddy ditch where she drowned screaming. Jack was now a murderer, adding even more notoriety to his legend. Unsurprisingly, he again vanished from the public eye.

His next accredited appearance was in Peckham, south London, in November 1872, when a six-foot-tall 'ghost' capable of jumping walls and fences was seen in a number of localities. Five years later, in Aldershot, Jack reportedly bounded across a common and assaulted a sentry on duty there. The sentry fired a gun at him but, luckily for Jack, it was loaded with blanks. This was the last confirmed sighting of Spring-heeled Jack.

Further incidents were put down to Jack, including an attack on some women in Cheshire in 1887 and a story in the *News of the World* on 25 September 1904 described a man bounding over houses in Liverpool's William Henry Street. This last story has been researched and proved to be false. Sadly, the name of Spring-heeled Jack seemed to have been forgotten in the early part of the twentieth century. Possibly his partial namesake Jack the Ripper took away some of his infamy.

❖

The mystery of Spring-heeled Jack was never fully solved, although there is a strong candidate for the early attacks. It would seem that the attacks in the late 1830s differ in character from the later ones. The early attacks all took place in well-off areas of central London and involved the breathing of fire into the face of the victim – an easy enough circus trick to perform using a naked light and a mouthful of paraffin. Is this why Jack requested a candle from Jane Alsop? The purpose of these attacks seems to be more concerned with scaring the living daylights out of the victim than causing bodily harm. As soon as the public attention was on Jack, his antics stopped.

The later attacks are possibly all copy-cat ones and several impostors were arrested by the police, although none was thought to be the original Spring-heeled Jack. Although the murder of the prostitute as described did involve breathing fire, there is little proof for the existence of this crime and it is now suspected to be a case of mistaken identity. The attacks in Aldershot and Cheshire are almost certainly not by the same man who carried out the earlier attacks, as the original Spring-heeled Jack would have been in his mid-fifties at least by then and therefore unlikely to be jumping long distances.

With regard to the initial attacks, contemporary sources put forward a candidate for the true identity of Spring-heeled Jack: Henry de la Poer Beresford, the Marquis of Waterford, who was a notorious and rather unpleasant practical joker. His previous actions include throwing eggs at people, painting the town red (literally!) and evicting 30 people from houses on his estate. He is believed to have committed an attack on a girl in 1837 and his general movements are consistent with the appearances of Spring-heeled Jack. He was married in 1842, after which time his bullying ceased, as did the first bout of Spring-heeled Jack's attacks.

Another candidate was a man named Steven Millbank, who had been arrested shortly after the Jane Alsop attack in Bearbinder Lane wearing a white overcoat that could have been mistaken for oilskins. Despite being the police's prime suspect for the crime, he was released without charge a few days after the attack.

The only memories of Spring-heeled Jack now remain in the penny-dreadful comics and a film, *The Curse of the Wraydons*, which was made in 1946.

Frank Hansen
and the
Minnesota Iceman

❖

CRYPTOZOOLOGY

FRANK HANSEN SEEMS to have inadvertently stumbled his way into the crypto-zoology bible of mysteries. Throughout the 1960s he made his living by touring fairs with exhibits of various kinds. In the mid-1960s he was exhibiting an antique tractor at the Arizona State Fair when he was approached by a man (whom he has said was a Californian millionaire) who claimed to have a frozen exhibit that could be displayed to best effect with the help of Hansen's show-manship. The gentleman refused to be drawn on the details of this exhibit, but he did say that it had been overseas and had been shipped into America illegally. Hansen was dubious, but agreed to look up the man when he arrived in Los Angeles a few days later.

A chauffeur took Hansen to a secret underground freezer, where he was shown a large block of ice which clearly had something inside. On closer inspection, Hansen saw that the ice block contained a large hairy ape that bore a resem-blance to descriptions of the legendary bigfoot or sasquatch. The Californian millionaire explained that the ape needed exhibiting to the public so that they could form their own opinions about the truth behind its existence. He went on to say that, in order not to upset the biblical view of creation, he wanted it to be displayed only as a side-show and not as the subject of any scientific inquiry. Following the signing of a number of contracts, the creature was loaned to Hansen for two years.

After designing a special trailer and a glass 'coffin' to hold the creature, Hansen went on the road. Scared of damaging the original specimen, he commis-sioned a Hollywood sculptor to make a replica, with the intention of switching it with the original at a later date.

The first place to receive a showing of the Minnesota Iceman was Chico, California. It instantly attracted enormous attention and started to draw large crowds wherever it went. The scientific community got wind of the Iceman and questions were soon being asked in government. One evening while Hansen was trying to return from Canada to the United States, customs officials detained him at the border with an order from the Department of Health in Chicago. Apparently somebody at the Smithsonian Institution had used contacts in the government to try and get the Iceman impounded as an illegally transported corpse. Luckily Hansen was able to phone up a friendly senator who pulled enough strings to get him and his exhibit released the next morning.

In December 1968 the story really started to hot up. Hansen received a phone call from two biologists, Dr Bernard Heuvelmans and Ivan Sanderson, requesting a viewing of the exhibit. Hansen refused them a private showing, but none the less both men turned up a few days later at Hansen's farm in the middle of a winter blizzard. After initially refusing to let them see the Iceman, Hansen eventually relented on condition that they told no one else about the visit or wrote about it later. After viewing the ice-bound ape, the two scientists asked if they could photograph it and Hansen reluctantly agreed. While Hansen was out of the trailer for a few seconds, Heuvelmans apparently accidentally shattered the protective glass covering the Iceman, releasing a strange smell into the air. Sanderson rather hysterically declared that the smell was the putrefaction of the frozen corpse and that it had to be placed in scientifically controlled conditions immediately. Heuvelmans then said to Hansen, 'We've discovered the abominable snowman does exist and you've got a baby right here!' When he went on to say that it must be handed over for scientific investigation immediately, Hansen reminded them of their oath of silence. Heuvelmans replied, 'I am a scientist first and a gentleman second!'

Shortly afterwards Sanderson appeared on the high-rating Johnny Carson television show, where he kept his word and only hinted that he had come across the scientific discovery of the century. In the meantime, Heuvelmans had published a paper on the Iceman in which he officially named the creature *Homo pongides*. A friendly sheriff warned Hansen that the FBI were making inquiries and that a pathologist would be arriving the next day to examine the corpse and possibly perform an autopsy.

To try and escape this, Hansen used a neighbour's tractor to dig his way out of the snow and headed south with the original Iceman. The disappearance made headline news. Meanwhile, Hansen contacted the owner, who arranged for the original to be swapped with the replica he had ordered at a secret location. Hansen returned home and called a news conference, during which he declared that the whole story had been a fake from start to finish. He provided the press with details they could check, such as the sculptor's name. This seemed to satisfy the public and also seriously embarrassed Dr Heuvelmans. However, some of the people who had seen the initial Iceman were not convinced and Hansen again found himself pursued by the Smithsonian Institution, although, having claimed to have swapped the original for a replica, he now had nothing to fear.

Interest in the Minnesota Iceman led to a highly successful tour of American shopping malls. Even though Hansen declared the ape to be faked, the curious and often sceptical public seemed to want to look at it anyway. Within a short while other obviously faked exhibits started to appear and, tired of all the attention, Hansen allowed his replica to thaw out and sent it to California, where it remains. He is still a travelling showman, except that now he owns the world's oldest John Deere tractor. When asked about the whereabouts of the original Minnesota Iceman, he claims it is in cold storage in California.

❖

It is difficult to know what to make of this story, as the issue comes down simply to whether Frank Hansen is telling the truth or not.

On the negative side, Hansen is clearly a great showman with the gift of the gab and was probably quite capable of getting a replica made for initial display purposes. He could well have relished the initial attention for the visitors, fame and money it would have brought him. Perhaps when the FBI started to show an interest, he got cold feet and, deciding enough was enough, declared the whole thing an elaborate hoax.

On the positive side, the 'original' Iceman does seem to have had a very favourable press from the people who saw it close up. It was clearly impressive enough for the Smithsonian to want to pursue it, to convince two biologists and to warrant interest from the American government. The putrefying smell reported from the container would also indicate something organic within the ice. Then there is the disappearance of Hansen and the original for a few days. If he had already decided to come clean about a hoax, then why go on the run first? It is all very mysterious.

Hansen claimed that the Iceman had been found floating in a block of ice off the Siberian coast and that it had been rescued, the ice carved and then shipped to California. This again is not inconceivable. The Siberian tundra has yielded a number of deep-frozen mammoths over the centuries, some of which have been so well preserved they are edible!! Then there is the case of the well-preserved Iron Age man found under a receding glacier in 1993 in the Italian Alps. So is it perhaps feasible that a creature like this could have been preserved in such a way? However, in order to be preserved within the ice, the specimen could be no more than 10,000 years old (the age of the end of the last Ice Age) and would have to have been wandering around the Arctic at the time. Humans are currently the only primates that range any great distance north of temperate climates and, even though the Iceman had a fair covering of hair, there is no fossil evidence for primates having been this far north in the past. This does not mean that they did not do so but a lack of fossil evidence, frozen or otherwise, suggests that it is unlikely. Even if we suppose that the Iceman is a true fossil, it is certainly not a missing link or even a close relative of ourselves. Our evolutionary lineage for the last 3–4 million years is quite well known from the fossil record and there is no room in it for an Ice Age ape. Heuvelmans's placing of the Iceman in our genus of *Homo* is completely wrong (based on the morphological features shown in his photographs and sketches) and shows worrying naïvety in biological taxonomy. Biologically the Iceman would have to belong to a separate evolutionary lineage within the primate group of mammals, one for which there has been no evidence whatsoever in the fossil record. It is also worrying that the Iceman displays such a remarkable similarity to descriptions of bigfoot, although if it were a genuine example of the beast, then this is indeed what one would expect.

Andrew Crosse

❖

CREATED LIFE

ANDREW CROSSE WAS said to have been the inspiration behind Mary Shelly's *Frankenstein*, yet he was a mild-mannered scientist whose love of electricity may have led him to create new life.

Born on 17 June 1784, Andrew Crosse was a member of a wealthy English family. He attended school in Bristol and while there developed a passionate interest in science and in particular the then new science of electricity.

In 1805 Crosse inherited the family fortune and lands and started to lead the life of a playboy as the Squire of Broomfield in Somerset. All this changed after a meeting with the obsessive electrical experimenter George John Singer. This meeting inspired Crosse to set up his own electrical laboratory in the family house in 1807. He experimented widely with electricity and in 1836 conducted an experiment that produced quite unexpected results.

The experiment, a simple one, consisted of continually dripping an unspecified liquid on to a piece of iron ore from Vesuvius through which he continually passed an electrical current. Two weeks into the experiment Crosse noted that white crystals were beginning to grow from the middle of the electrified stone. On day 18 the 'crystals' had grown seven–eight filaments and, by day 26, they had formed into perfect but minute insects, complete with eight legs and many long hairs. By day 30 they had detached themselves from the rock and were wandering around of their own free will. He gave the insects the name *Acari*. It appeared to Crosse that these insects had grown in the most inhospitable conditions and he wondered whether he hadn't inadvertently stumbled on a means of creating life.

Crosse did not believe what he was seeing and repeated the experiments using highly controlled conditions to prevent contamination. Eventually, after several months, the insects grew again in the same manner as before. Being a cautious man, he wrote up his experiment and sent it to the Electrical Society of London, which in turn sent a Mr Weeks to investigate the claim. Weeks methodically repeated the experiment, ensuring no contamination at any stage. The insects still grew and the results were published in two noted electrical journals, causing outrage.

Crosse, who had made no supernatural claims for his insects, was accused of setting himself up as God and of being a bad scientist. Perhaps because he had been so methodical and objective in his research, many scientists of the day came to his aid, including Michael Faraday. However, the religious persecution continued, forcing him into isolation. He discontinued his experiments until grief over the deaths of his wife and brother caused him to resume work in his laboratory in 1846. He never repeated the 'insect' experiments. He married again in 1850 and was killed by a stroke on 6 July 1855.

Crosse made no major scientific discoveries in his life and is noted for feeling duty-bound to manage his estates. He was therefore isolated as a scientist. However, at a time when electrical study was in a period of transition from a dilettante hobby to the life work of professionals, he still managed to gain the interest and attention of some of the most eminent scientists of the day.

❖

In the early nineteenth century there was almost no understanding of the complex biochemical and genetic processes that take place within organisms in order to permit them to function. Even now there is little agreement or understanding about what actually defines life and self-awareness within animals.

When it was discovered that passing electricity through a dead animal could cause its muscles to spasm and make it move again, some scientists thought that electricity was the force responsible for life itself. It was this widespread belief that led to the concepts behind Mary Shelly's novel *Frankenstein*. Unlike some other scientists, Crosse does not seem to have been trying to create life using electricity, but merely exploring its potential using simple experiments with everyday materials. When his *Acari* appeared, he was bemused but did not claim to have created life himself. It was others who jumped to this conclusion after the publication of his experiments. None the less, in those pre-Darwinian days, it was blasphemy to suggest that life could be produced by any other means than God and so Crosse found himself in trouble with the Church.

With the hindsight of modern science, it seems unlikely that Crosse actually created life during his experiments. It is currently possible to artificially create the building blocks of life (amino acids and other complex organic molecules) but it will be hundreds of years before it is possible to construct a single working cell in the laboratory, let alone a complex organism. The descriptions and illustrations of the *Acari*, however, suggest that they were fully functioning metazoan (multi-celled) animals that were either crustaceans (lobsters, crabs, etc.) or closely related to them. If Crosse had created a new form of life, then one would expect it to have been a very primitive single-celled organism (such as a bacterium) built from the raw materials around it. For Crosse to have grown a fully functioning creature that fits into a known group of animals is improbable in the extreme.

This might sound harsh, but it should be borne in mind that the first single-celled organisms on earth are found in rocks over 3,600 million years old, while the first multicelled life is thought to have evolved approximately 600 million years ago. If it took nature over 2,900 million years to evolve complex life, then it is unlikely that Crosse could have bypassed this period of evolution to 'grow' new life in 30 days.

If, then, Crosse's animals were not a new form of life, what were they? The most likely explanation is that his samples were indeed contaminated with the dried eggs of a crustacean before the experiment began. There are many types of crustacean on the earth that are capable of surviving the harshest of conditions and still live. One such group are the ostracods. These minute animals are generally less than a millimetre long and resemble a shelled pistachio nut with dangling legs. They currently occur wherever there is water – rivers, seas, sulphurous springs, desert pools, raindrops on leaves. Some species can survive several years without water. There are many similar crustacean groups, including, for example, the brine shrimps, which are sold commercially in dehydrated form as sea monkeys.

The *Acari* probably belonged to one such group and the poor quality of microscopes at the time did not permit Crosse to see the growth stages of the animals. He did not specify the amount of current that he ran through the rock or the nature of the solution that he dripped on to it. It can only be assumed that the solution was not toxic and that the current was minimal enough to permit the growth of the *Acari*. It is probable that their eggs were either in the water (which would be rainwater) or attached to the rock in the first place. Whatever the real answer, it is certain that the *Acari* do not represent created life, although they could well have been new to science at the time.

Mrs Pett, Bailey
and Mr Angel

❖

SPONTANEOUS HUMAN COMBUSTION

SPONTANEOUS HUMAN COMBUSTION (SHC) is one of those rare areas in the paranormal where there is well-documented and investigated evidence. Despite this,
science has devoted little time to the subject, suggesting that, as an identifiable
phenomenon, it does not exist. Yet there do seem to be too many similarities between
described cases to ignore the subject altogether. I will here present three cases that
illustrate the topic well and possibly give clues to what is behind the phenomenon.

The first case is one of the earliest detailed historical recordings of SHC,
although it was not recognized as such until some time afterwards. It concerns a
Mrs Grace Pett, a fisherman's wife, who lived in the eighteenth century in
Ipswich. She had welcomed a daughter of hers back from Gibraltar and both
women had got drunk on gin. They went to bed, but later Mrs Pett went downstairs to smoke her pipe. The daughter testified that her mother did this at 10 p.m.,
8 April 1744, taking a candle with her. At 5 the next morning, some passing ship's
carpenters saw a fire in a downstairs room of the house and broke in. They found
the body of Mrs Pett fully ablaze in the living room. When they quenched the
flames, the body apparently hissed as if it were red hot. A quote from one of the
witnesses at the coroner's inquest describes the state the body was found in:

> The feet and the lower part of the legs were not burnt, with the stockings
> on the parts remaining not singed; very little of the parts of the legs that
> were burnt lay on the wood floor, the rest of the body on a brick hearth
> in the chimney; part of the head was not burnt; a body of fire in her
> breast...was quenched with water, her bone was calcified and the whole so
> far reduced to ashes as to be put in the coffin with a shovel.
>
> The matter extraordinary seems to be the burning in such a manner
> without any other fuel but the clothes on her back, though there was a
> long time to do it in. It seems the legs were burnt so far only as were
> covered by her petty coats, as she lay on the floor.

This description describes all the typical features of SHC. The body, including the bones, was reduced to ashes yet the floor underneath and nearby combustible material (including the clothes on her unburnt body) were untouched by the heat.

The inquest verdict was accidental death, but as the inquest notes show even then the circumstances were unusual enough to warrant considerable comment. The death was the talk of the town and before long the incident was being linked to witchcraft. Mrs Pett was apparently thought of as a witch and a local farmer was blaming her for an outbreak of disease among his sheep. In order to remove the curse, the farmer's wife burnt one of the diseased sheep alive. This was then linked to Mrs Pett's mysterious death and used as proof of her status as a witch.

Mrs Pett was still on fire when she was found, although no detailed description was given about this. It is quite rare for SHC victims to still be on fire when discovered.

The next case describes a classic case of SHC in which the victim was actually on fire when discovered.

On the morning of 13 September 1967, the London Fire Brigade was called out to a reported house fire in Auckland Street, south London. The house had been derelict for some time and when the fire fighters arrived they saw a blue flame flickering at the first-floor window. After breaking in they found the body of a middle-aged tramp, called Bailey, lying face down on the first-floor landing, his chest and head resting on the bottom two steps of the stairs. His head was resting against the bottom rung of the banister, with his teeth sunk into the wood so deeply that they could only be prised off with a crowbar, suggesting that Bailey had been in excruciating pain when he died.

What amazed the firemen was that there appeared to be a four-inch slit in Bailey's abdomen from which a blue flame was 'issuing at force'. The flame could be extinguished only by placing a hose in the abdominal cavity of the body. The only other damage appeared to be a burnt section of floorboards corresponding to where the flame was issuing from the body. No source for the fire, such as matches, cigarettes, etc., could be found nearby.

The pathology report confirmed that Bailey had been alive when he started burning and determined that he died not from burns but from suffocation after inhaling the smoke from his own fire! The coroner's report recorded an open verdict.

If finding a SHC victim on fire is rare, then cases where a victim has survived are almost non-existent. The strange experience that occurred to Jack Angel may be one such example.

On the night of 12 November 1974 travelling salesman Jack Angel parked his caravan at a roadside motel in Savannah, Georgia. Exhausted from driving, he retired for the night, thinking that nothing was out of the ordinary. He did not wake up for four days (until noon on the 16th) and was shocked to find his right hand burnt and blistered from the fingers to the wrist. He also described having 'this big explosion' in his chest which left a hole there and he had burnt patches on his legs, groin, back and ankle. His nightclothes and the sheet he had been lying on were unscorched. Unaware of being so badly injured, he dressed and went to the motel to eat. Here he collapsed and was taken to hospital.

Angel awoke to find himself surrounded by baffled doctors, who explained to him that his burns were all internal and his skin was little affected. He was transferred to a specialist burns centre, where it was found that Angel had third-degree internal burns in his right hand and the nerves had been burnt some distance into his forearm. The damage was severe and a few weeks later his hand and lower forearm were amputated. After an abnormally fast recovery, Angel was discharged from hospital in January 1975.

The cause of his misfortune was still a mystery. However, a local law firm thought that a design fault in Angel's caravan must have been responsible and asked Angel if they could investigate with a view to suing the caravan manufacturer for $3 million. A top specialist technical firm was called in and they stripped the caravan down to its constituent components. No explanation could be found and the legal firm withdrew the case from court. The mystery was never solved.

❖

SHC remains in that shadowy world known as pseudo-science. Is it, as many scientists claim, simply a series of similar fire-related deaths that have been collected together by amateur parapsychologists? Or is it a genuine phenomenon with a consistent cause and a predictable set of results?

Cases of death attributed to SHC do seem to share a number of features. The victim usually appears to have burnt from the centre of the body outwards, so all that is normally found are the remains of the arms or legs. The burnt sections of the body, including the bones, are reduced to ashes, although the skull can sometimes remain intact or even shrunk by the heat. Nearby combustible objects, including wooden floors, furniture, clothes on the unburnt body, candles, etc., remain intact except where they come into contact with the body itself. If the body is lying face down, then considerable damage can be done to floorboards or carpets underneath, suggesting that the fire originates from the chest cavity. In some recent post-mortems of SHC victims, it has been found that the victims were alive when the burning started and that some (including Bailey the tramp) died after suffocating on their own burning fumes. At SHC sites, there is often a thick covering of grease (vaporized from the burning body) covering the windows, walls, light bulbs, etc.

In addition to the physical features associated with the death, there seem to be common traits in the lifestyles and personalities of the victims themselves. Most live on their own or are on their own when the fire starts. Many of the victims, but not all, are alcoholics (Mrs Pett and Bailey were) and seem to have been awake when the burning started. Very few cases seem to occur while the victim is in bed. Most of the cases seem to take place at night and the body can be reduced to ashes in only a few hours.

The truly perplexing aspect of SHC is how a human body, bones and all, can be reduced to ashes while nearby objects remain intact. Dr Wilton Krogman observed that when a body is cremated industrially, it is burnt at 1,100°C for eight hours. At the end of this, the flesh may have burnt away, but the bones still remain (these are later reduced to powder mechanically). He found out that a temperature of 1,650°C is needed to reduce the bones to ashes. How, then, could heat probably considerably greater than this be generated without affecting the surrounding area?

The most common scientific theory put forward is known as the 'human candle' effect. This states that the clothes catch fire and this then melts and becomes entwined in the human body fat. The clothes then act as a wick, slowly burning away the body's fat reserves until eventually only the limbs remain and the fire goes out.

Although this theory is physically possible and could explain some aspects of SHC, it cannot explain the reduction to ashes of the bones, as the temperatures generated are far too low, being approximately 250°C. It has also been suggested that, in the case of drunk or alcoholic people, the flesh becomes saturated with alcohol and then burns as a result. This too is impossible, for the amount of alcohol needed would poison the drinker, and again burning spirits would not generate the heat necessary to burn the bones.

Three more unusual theories also exist. The first, put forward by Livingstone Gearhart (in the magazine *Pursuit*, 1975), links a number of reported SHC cases to rises in the earth's geomagnetic field. No positive proof exists for this at all and SHC is only one of a number of paranormal phenomena (including earth lights, UFO abductions, ghosts, ball lightning and crop circles) that have been linked to geomagnetic/geophysical processes.

The second theory, put forward by John Heymer (in *The Entrancing Flame*, 1996), suggests that electrolysis within the human body could separate out the hydrogen from the oxygen in water and this then burns. From a biochemical point of view, this theory is highly improbable and, if hydrogen were loose in the body cavity, it would be more likely to cause an explosion when ignited than a steady burning flame.

The third theory, put forward by Michael Harrison (in *Fire from Heaven*, 1977), suggests that SHC is a form of psychic suicide. In this scenario a depressed, lonely person gets so fed up that there is a sudden release of psychic energy, causing the victim's body to burn in the way it does. This theory would certainly explain the large number of SHC victims who live alone or have led wretched lives, but again there is no solid proof and the term 'psychic energy' is used as an abstract concept to explain the theory.

I must admit that I do not know where the truth behind SHC lies. From the case histories and perhaps from Jack Angel's experience, it would appear that if the phenomenon does exist, then the fire originates from within the chest cavity. It would then seem to progress outwards in all directions and must burn at a fierce but controlled heat, vaporizing the flesh and reducing the bones to ash but keeping the heat localized enough not to affect surrounding objects.

It has been noted that some of the SHC sites have had very poor ventilation, thus preventing plentiful supplies of oxygen from reaching them. Under such conditions it has been suggested that a person accidentally setting fire to themselves would burn slowly, consistently and thoroughly, rather like a lesser version of the process used to create charcoal. Such an environment would prevent high flames, which could burn down a house, from forming and would lead to the thick, grease-laden atmosphere that is often reported with SHC cases. However, some cases of SHC have occurred in well-ventilated rooms, although the bodies involved are not usually as completely burnt as in other SHC cases. Using this theory, it is possible to create a scenario where a person accidentally sets fire to themselves in a poorly ventilated room and then falls over on to a hard non-combustible surface, such as a tiled floor or treated floorboards. This is the opposite of what happens to people who set fire to themselves in beds or chairs or who fall on to carpets and generally also set fire to the whole house. Once alight and on a non-combustible surface, the body could initially burn fast until the oxygen was used up and thereafter burn slowly like a cigarette left in an ashtray. If on their own, the person would not be missed and would be left to burn until the fire is stifled or burns itself out naturally.

It must be admitted that this theory does not fit all the cases any better than some of the others. I do, however, feel that the most likely explanation is to be found firmly within the bounds of known physics or chemistry, rather than in parapsychology. Whether the phenomenon exists or not, it needs to be investigated properly so that, if necessary, it can be used as a verdict in inquests rather than the accidental-death verdict that is currently assigned to most of these cases.

RELIGIOUS PEOPLE

INTRODUCTION

WHETHER IT IS welcome or not, religion permeates its way into every aspect of the paranormal and many areas of the paranormal overlap with or are reliant upon organized religion.

There is a large range of phenomena associated with the Jewish and Christian religions. In the Old Testament there are many prophets who use dreams, astrology, symbolism and precognition to predict the future, while the New Testament gives us examples of levitation, spirit possession, psychic healing and remote-viewing. It is therefore perhaps no surprise that so many members of the Christian Church report examples of these phenomena themselves with virtually all the documented cases of levitation, stigmata and miraculous healing coming from devoutly religious Christians. After centuries of such phenomena being reported from within its ranks, the Catholic Church has set up a rigorous set of criteria for investigating paranormal claims, very few of which actually get validated. In fact, considering the supernatural content of the Bible, the Church is very anti-paranormal indeed and refuses to recognize many types of phenomena, including ghosts, telepathy, life on other planets (whether they have visited us or not) and clairvoyance. This is partly because explanations for them are not covered in the Bible and partly because of the control that the Church of old required over its congregation.

In the late nineteenth century, frustration at the Church's refusal to recognize paranormal phenomena led to large numbers of people deserting it to join the newly formed esoteric religions of Spiritualism and Theosophy (see pages 122, 127). These religions did recognize, and indeed relied upon, the existence of many types of paranormal phenomena and were prepared to demonstrate them to an eager public. More crucially, the spiritualist religions also recognized important aspects of the Christian Church, so their followers did not feel that they had deserted Christianity altogether.

Although this chapter concentrates on Christianity, it is not the only religion to recognize paranormal events. In September 1995 the world's Hindus were in great excitement as statues of the elephant god Ganesh began drinking spoonfuls of milk that were offered to it. Supermarkets ran out of milk as the phenomenon was reported worldwide. Some statues were reported to have drunk gallons of milk in a single day. Scientists put forward theories that the milk was either absorbed into the porous stone of the statues or subconsciously tipped down the front of it. Other Indian religions accept reincarnation, levitation and psychic-healing. In other areas of the world many animist religions, including the much misunderstood Voodoo, believe in ghosts and out-of-body experiences and even try to induce such phenomena. Many of the reported phenomena from these religions are, however, not as clearly documented as the Christian ones and are therefore more difficult to research.

It is hoped that the people discussed in this chapter will illustrate both the type of phenomenon accepted and promoted by the Church, such as levitation, and some of the more loosely connected phenomena that have become attached to the Church, such as those surrounding Comyns Beaumont (see page 00).

Berenger Saunière

❖

SECRET SOCIETIES

THE STORY OF Berenger Saunière has sparked many different investigations into his life and the village with which he is most associated, Rennes-le-Château. The book that sparked the widespread interest in this story (*The Holy Blood and the Holy Grail* by Baigent, Leigh and Lincoln) is now an occult classic and huge debate still exists as to its findings. Here we will deal simply with the story of Berenger Saunière and some of the basic theories associated with it.

Berenger Saunière was born in 1852 in the Pyrenean foothill village of Montazels. He was the eldest of 11 children and, faced with the alternative of life in a mountain backwater, he joined the priesthood. It seems that he excelled himself in the seminary and was destined for a promising clerical career when he managed to upset people in high places, so on 1 June 1885 he took up his post as priest in a quiet village within walking distance of his birthplace. Rennes-le-Château is located on top of a steep hill about 25 miles south of Carcassonne, in the Languedoc region of south-west France.

Rather than regret his posting to such a remote place, Saunière seems to have made the most of his situation by taking advantage of the beautiful countryside and immersing himself in the study of languages and local history, for which he had a particular passion. Soon after his arrival in the village he enlisted an 18-year-old housekeeper, Marie Denarnaud, who was to play a vital role in the later stages of this story. In 1892 Saunière learned of a legacy that had been specifically to help in the upkeep of the village church and decided to remove and restore the altar. The altar had one end embedded into the church wall and the other supported by two ancient stone pillars. After removing the top of the altar, Saunière found that one of these columns was hollow and there were three sealed tubes inside. These tubes contained four parchments between them. Two were said to be dated 1244 and 1644 respectively and to contain family trees; the other two were Latin transcriptions of New Testament texts written by a previous priest of the church, Abbé Antoine Bigou, in the 1780s.

Although the Latin parchments looked normal at first glance, there were definite signs that the text was in some way ciphered. For example, some letters and words had been run together, while others had been marked with dots or were displaced. One manuscript contained a number of raised letters which spell out the message, 'To Dagobert II, King, and to Sion belongs this Treasure and he is there Dead.' The meaning of most of the ciphers remains hidden.

In 1893 Saunière took the manuscripts to his superior, the Bishop of Carcassonne, and was immediately dispatched to Paris, where he was instructed to show the documents to Abbé Biele and his grand-nephew Emile Hoffet, an up-and-coming expert on handwriting and cryptography, and also dabbler in esoteric matters. Saunière spent only three weeks in Paris, during which time he was introduced to and accepted into Hoffet's circle of highbrow friends. It was even rumoured that Saunière had an affair with the then famous singer Emma Calve, although this was never proved. However, the most interesting aspect of Saunière's visit was his purchasing of three seemingly unrelated copies of paintings from the Louvre. One was by David Teniers and depicted Saint Anthony, another was a portrait of Pope Celestin V and the third was Nicolas Poussin's *The Shepherds of Arcadia*.

On his return to Rennes-le-Château Saunière enlisted some young men to help him continue work on the restoration of the church. In front of the altar they lifted a stone slab and found that the underneath of it was engraved with two scenes. One depicted a knight on a horse blowing a hunting horn and the other a knight with a staff in one hand and a child in the other. The carvings were dated as seventh or eighth century AD. Saunière then ordered the youths to dig further and it is reported that they uncovered two skeletons and a pot full of shiny objects that Saunière declared worthless. After this the church renovations ceased. Instead, Saunière and Marie, his housekeeper, would wander the countryside collecting bags full of pebbles for their garden. He also showed an unusual interest in two memorial stones that marked the grave of Marie de Negri d'Ables, the wife of the Seigneur of Rennes, who died in 1781. This memorial had been designed and installed by Abbé Antoine Bigou, the same priest who had written the cryptic manuscript hidden in the alter. Saunière eventually obliterated the inscriptions on the memorial, although he was unaware that they had been copied previously by archaeologists. Along with his other eccentricities, villagers were beginning to notice that his expenditure was extremely high in comparison with his known income.

As a priest, Saunière was paid the equivalent of six pounds a year and yet, by 1896, he was spending more than this in postage alone. He was also travelling extensively across Europe and was known to have opened at least four bank accounts. Money orders, some from obscure religious orders, poured into the village. After 1896, Saunière started spending outrageous sums of money on both his church and his village. He built a road for the village and restored his church so sumptuously that it is still impressive when seen today. He placed a large statue of the demon Asmodeus (guardian of secrets and treasures) inside the entrance, paved the floor in a chequered pattern of black and white marble slabs, renovated the altar and covered the walls in unconventional representations of the stations of the cross. Most strange was his carving on the church porch of the phrase 'Terribilis est locus iste' (Your place is fearful).

When the renovation was finished, Saunière could not rest and moved on to build a large stone tower on a sheer hill face at one end of the village. He also had built a luxurious country house called Villa Bethania, which he never occupied. By the time he finished spending, he had also accumulated for himself rare books, china, stamps and fabrics. He had built himself an orangery and zoo and gave magnificent banquets for his parishioners and the many noble guests who visited. According to Baigent et al., by his death Saunière had spent more than the equivalent of seven million pounds.

At first the Church pretended not to notice these goings-on, but the newly installed Bishop of Carcassonne attempted to force an explanation out of Saunière. When he refused, the Bishop tried to transfer him, but Saunière would not go and he was suspended. When the Vatican heard of this, Saunière was reinstated immediately.

Saunière's death too was unusual. On 12 January 1917, despite his good health, his housekeeper ordered him a coffin. Five days later he suffered a stroke and a priest was called to hear his confession and administer the last rites. The priest emerged looking very shaken and was reputedly depressed for some months afterwards. When Saunière died, on 22 January, his body was placed upright in a chair and was visited by a large number of unidentified mourners. Marie, the housekeeper, continued to live in some luxury in the Villa Bethania until a post-World War II declaration that all old francs should be exchanged for new francs. She was then seen burning bundles of old francs in her garden. She lived from then until her death on the proceeds of selling the Villa Bethania. Despite promising to reveal a secret that would make the villa's new owner rich and powerful, Marie had a sudden stroke and died on 29 January 1953.

❖

The theories regarding what exactly it was that turned Berenger Saunière from a humble village priest in a remote backwater to a very rich and powerful man with connections in high places are numerous. Whether by coincidence or not, Rennes-le-Château is at the centre of a region that has undergone extraordinary political and religious upheaval since the times of Christ. It has been inhabited by Gauls, Celts, Visigoths, Cathars and Catholics and has had a very bloody past, including the infamous Albigensian Crusade, during which local Cathars were massacred at the hands of Vatican forces in the thirteenth century. The area has also been associated with organizations such as the Knights Templar.

Opinion tends to divide around whether Saunière had in fact discovered some great hidden treasure buried in the local countryside or found some secret that powerful organizations, including the Vatican, were prepared to pay to keep secret.

On the treasure front, there could be endless possibilities. All the historical comings and goings in the area have left a large number of legends concerning buried wealth. Treasure is still thought to be buried from Roman times, from the Visigoth King Dagobert II, from the Knights Templar and the Cathars themselves – the list is endless. If, however, Saunière had indeed discovered a treasure trove, why did he keep so secret about it while at the same time obviously splashing enormous amounts of cash around? If he was worried about people stealing it, then could he not have put it in a bank, as he did with so much of his other cash and possessions?

The main opposing opinion is that Saunière found out about something that was supposed to be a secret and was being paid to keep quiet. All the cryptic messages he uncovered and later tried to destroy suggest the conveyance of a message through code. This option has been explored fully in a number of different books. *The Holy Blood and the Holy Grail* follows a whole series of different clues and trails associated with the Saunière mystery and comes to the conclusion that he had stumbled on to the proof that Christ did not die on the cross but escaped to the south of France with his wife (Mary Magdalene) and family, and that Christ's bloodline, and the organizations set up to protect it, including the Knights Templar, were responsible for Saunière's upkeep.

Perhaps the truth is more mundane. Recent research by the BBC has been able to find no trace of Saunière's visit to Paris or of him buying any replica paintings, and concludes that a lot of the links to secret organizations were a clever practical joke by the eccentric Frenchman Pierre Plantard de Saint-Claire. Although this may bring into doubt any secret-society connections, there is still the very real question of where the wealth came from.

Was Saunière blackmailing somebody in a very high position? It seems unlikely, for, if anything, he would seem to have been the one capable of being blackmailed for his very close association with Emma Calve and his housekeeper. I have visited Rennes-le-Château, which, much to my surprise, has become a minor mecca for occultists. When one sees the wealth that Saunière bestowed upon his church and, in the form of buildings, upon his village, one cannot but wonder at the source of his wealth.

María de Jesus

❖

TELEPORTATION

MARÍA DE JESUS was born on 2 April 1602 in the town of Agreda, in the mountainous Spanish province of Castile. Her childhood was an unhappy one, largely due to the extreme religiousness of her parents, both of whom believed that physical suffering was a means of being closer to God. By the time María reached puberty she had been verbally abused, starved, ignored and brought up as though she were in a convent. She was both physically and mentally unwell. Probably as a result of her parents, she joined a convent at an early age and was apt to spend many hours meditating.

When she was 18, the meditations began to give way to frequent fits of hallucinations, visions and religious ecstasies. She also seems to have exhibited a form of what today could possibly be diagnosed as multiple personality disorder (see page 63) with lightning changes in personality and periods of verbal abuse and horrific hallucinations. In addition she had ecstatic visions in which, she claimed, she met with angels and even God himself. She tried to overcome these problems by resorting to self-abuse which involved refusing food, beating herself and wearing coarse hair shirts and chain mail. Soon after this, she began to levitate.

This first occasion was in May 1620, when María was alone. The second time, however, in July, she remained airborne for two to three hours. After this the levitations started to occur regularly and, as with Joseph of Copertino (see page 166), seemed to be particularly common during moments of religious concentration such as Holy Communion. At first her fellow sisters were annoyed and angry at María, but before long they started to exploit her trances by showing her off to visitors to the convent. This situation continued until 1623, when the provincial father stepped in and ordered María to ask God to stop the trances. She did as she was told and they stopped instantly.

The most unusual aspects of the trances that María experienced were not the meditation or even the levitation, but the descriptions that she would give about travelling to 'the New Lands' (the Americas) and there meeting with undiscovered tribes and educating them in the ways of Christianity. She said that she had vivid visions of visiting these peoples and of talking to them (although she could not remember in what language), telling them about Christianity and that other priests would soon call on them. She is later reported to have said of the visions:

I have always doubted that it was my actual body that went...I cannot comprehend the manner in which I travelled or was bourne there...yet sometimes I seemed to see the earth beneath me and to recognize that parts of it were in the darkness or night and other parts in daylight.

These visions might not seem to be unusual, given María's mental state at the time, but they later became connected with an unusual event that occurred on the other side of the world in the Spanish colonies in north Mexico. In 1625 Father Alonso de Benavides, who was a Franciscan priest in charge of the trading posts and missionaries around Santa Fe, arrived there. Shortly after, he heard about the Jumanos, a group of Indians who, although they lived 300 miles east of a trading town just outside Albuquerque, would regularly make the journey to beg for a priest to be sent to their tribe so that he could baptize them. This was a source of great mystery, for no priests had been anywhere near the tribe at the time, yet the Indians seemed to have a good knowledge of Christianity. As the missionaries did not have any priests to spare, the tribe's wishes were not granted.

In 1629 a letter arrived in Mexico that described María's claims of having visited New World Indians between the years 1620 and 1623. The odd case of the Jumanos tribe was remembered and Father Benavides was sent to investigate. When he met with the Jumano, he discovered that the reason they were so keen to be baptized was that they had regularly been visited by a white woman, dressed in blue, who would appear to them, preaching and promising that priests would arrive. When shown a picture of a nun, they said that the woman who had visited them was dressed similarly but was much younger, being a girl. They said that she still appeared to them and so two priests were dispatched to return with the Jumanos to their homeland.

When they approached the tribal village, the priests were surprised to discover that the 'nun' had appeared in advance to the villagers, telling them that the priests were on their way and that they should be prepared to be baptized. The priests stayed for only a week, but a mission was set up in the village the next year, although the harsh environment meant that it did not become permanent for 20 years. Father Benavides wrote an account of the history of New Mexico called *Memorial* which included the dealings with the Jumanos but did not give a name to the mysterious blue nun.

After his arrival back in Spain in 1631, Father Benavides was asked to interview María to see if the two stories were related. María was by this time in a better mental state and very popular in the convent, having risen quickly to become an abbess. Sadly, it seems that Benavides was rather liberal with the truth when it came to writing up the results of his interview with María. She claimed that the two events were not connected and that it was a heresy to suggest that they were. This did not stop Benavides telling some outrageous lies, including the claim that saints would fly María across the Atlantic and that María had donated to him the habit she wore for the journeys. Under pressure from her superiors, María was forced to sign a statement against her will agreeing that she had flown across the Atlantic to meet the Jumanos tribe.

Memorial was selling extremely well and although no formal connection was made between María and the Jumanos tribe in the book, the public made the connection themselves. These claims were not formally denied by either Benavides or the Catholic Church.

María continued to deny any connection and had to face three inquisitions, during which she recanted the signed statement. After Benavides's death in 1647 she sought out and destroyed some of the copies of the 1631 testimony. She continued to deny that she had ever bodily teleported to the New World until her death, on 24 May 1665.

❖

Teleportation is a rarely reported phenomenon that has occasioned little if any serious research. The majority of reported cases occur in association with physical mediumship or poltergeist activity. For example, in 1871 a small spiritualist meeting in London was undertaking a seance at which people asked the spirits to provide them with a physical object. There followed an almighty crash and when the lights were turned on the group was surprised to see the vastly overweight medium Agnes Guppy sitting in the middle of the table clutching her account book. According to Mrs Guppy, she had been sitting at a table doing her accounts when she suddenly found herself inadvertently attending somebody else's seance. Similarly, in the Enfield Poltergeist case (see page 38), Janet Harper was alleged to have teleported into a next-door house, leaving a book behind as proof of having been there. Related to teleportation is the phenomenon of apports, defined as when an object spontaneously appears apparently from nowhere. Apports are again chiefly associated with physical mediumship and poltergeists, when nails, coins, flowers and other objects reportedly dematerialize in midair.

Other than outright fakery, there is no current scientific explanation that can even come close to giving an explanation for either teleportation or apports. Every visible object is made of billions of atoms interacting with each other. The dematerialization of a solid object would first involve the dissipation of all these atoms – something that would involve the release of energy many times greater than that of all the nuclear weapons on earth combined. In order to rematerialize the object, the location of every atom in the original would have to be known and then identical atoms would have to be assembled in their place. The logistics of this are currently, and will probably remain, impossible. So, if this is how the teleportation process works, then it breaks the known laws of physics. Even the great physical medium Daniel Dunglas Home (see page 81) did not believe in teleportation, exclaiming, 'Matter cannot go through matter!'

The teleportation claimed for María de Jesus differs considerably from that reported in modern seances. Most recent reports of teleportation and apports involve travel over very short distances of, at most, a few miles. María de Jesus was supposed to have teleported several thousand miles from Spain to the Americas. It was also claimed that she could see the ground below while she crossed the Atlantic, suggesting that she was in some way flying. However, objects (and the few cases of people) that have teleported do so instantly, disappearing from one place and reappearing instantly in another. There are also other inconsistencies in the de Jesus case that make a paranormal connection unlikely.

The first is that the majority of facts comes from de Benavides's book *Memorial*. It has already been proved that his and the Church's motives for including an embellished version of the story in *Memorial* were less than honourable. The fact that María herself completely denied any paranormal activity also indicates that the alleged teleportation never took place. It is therefore likely that the case is an example of somebody putting two and two together and making five. The original flying visions of María de Jesus, which were probably just hallucinations related to her poor mental state at the time, were linked to the stories of the Jumanos Indians. Later, when María denied the link between the two, the Church simply disregarded this and created its own version of events. As such, it is very likely that the account from *Memorial*, from where all the others have been taken, is highly exaggerated.

St Thérèse de Lisieux

❖

MIRACLE CURES

THÉRÈSE MARTIN WAS born in 1873 in Alençon, France. She was the youngest of nine children born to Zelie and Louis Martin. The family were devoutly Catholic and, even after Zelie's death in 1877, Thérèse and her brothers and sisters were brought up in a happy and relaxed atmosphere.

All of Thérèse's older sisters became nuns in the Carmelite convent of Lisieux and, by the age of 14, Thérèse was desperate to join them. Her approaches were continually turned down because of her age, but Thérèse was strong-willed and, on an official visit to the Vatican, she grabbed Pope Leo XIII's hand and explained her situation to him. Despite disapproval of her actions she was admitted into the convent the next year.

The Carmelites were a harsh order, believing that physical suffering was an aid to cleansing the soul. Thérèse devoted herself wholeheartedly to convent life and quickly became an important member of the community. Her life of devotion started to draw to an early end when, aged 23, she had a sudden stroke and was diagnosed as suffering from tuberculosis. As she degenerated over the next year, she promised her fellow nuns that she would use the freedom of death to return to earth and use God's love to help people. She specifically said that she would let fall a shower of roses as a sign that she was alive and watching over the convent. Her death was slow and painful and in the final hours she requested that roses be brought to her bed. She plucked and individually blessed each rose petal and said to those by her bed, 'Gather them carefully! One day they will give comfort to other people. Do not lose a single one of them!' She died shortly afterwards.

The year of her death was 1897, but in the following years she was associated with a number of miracles that eventually led to her canonization by the Vatican in 1925.

One of the first testifiable miracles occurred in 1906, when Charles Ann, a student priest from Bayeux, contracted tuberculosis. The disease had progressed to an almost terminal phase when Charles was persuaded to wear a purse containing a locket of Thérèse's hair around his neck. He then prayed to Thérèse to cure him in order that he might carry on God's work on earth. The next day he awoke to find all trace of the disease gone. The doctors treating him were amazed and wrote testimonies as to the extraordinary nature of this miracle.

In 1910, in Lisieux itself, Ferdinand Aubry contracted violent gangrene in his tongue and was subsequently only given a matter of days to live. One of the sisters looking after him managed to beg one of Thérèse's deathbed rose petals and persuaded Aubry to swallow it. Again, the next day the gangrene had gone and within a few days the missing pieces of his tongue had grown back.

One of the cases that was rigorously investigated as part of Thérèse's canonization involved a nun, Sister Louise de St Germain, who lay dying from a stomach ulcer. On the night of 10 September 1915 Sister Louise had a vision of Thérèse, who promised the nun that she would be cured. The next morning she awoke to find her bed surrounded by rose petals, which no one admitted to having put there. Within 15 days she too was cured, a fact that her doctors were able to confirm using X-rays taken before and after the vision.

This testified incident and three others were pronounced by the Vatican to be genuinely miraculous and attributable to Thérèse Martin. She passed the strict guidelines required and was canonized St Thérèse of Lisieux in 1925.

❖

Much of the Christian faith is based on the large number of supernatural effects and miracles associated with Jesus's life, including many miraculous cures and even raising the dead. In this respect the Christian faith is unusual, as most other religions do not require belief in supernatural events as part of their creed. However, despite the modern Church's devout belief in the biblical healing miracles, there is much resistance to the acceptance of modern miracles. The Catholic Church has a special committee which rigorously investigates all claims of miraculous cures and other paranormal events. For cures to be accepted as miraculous, testimonies, doctors' reports, X-rays and other evidence have to be absolutely watertight, so as a result very few pass the test. In this respect the Church does much of the work of parapsychologists for them. In the eighteenth century the Vatican's chief inspector of miracles, Prospero Lambertini, noted that miracles and other psychic phenomena were just as common in the non-religious as in devotees. He also noted the prominence of dreams in religious miracles and eventually concluded that much of what he saw was more a product of the mind than of God.

Where the established Church has been cautious and sceptical, the new Evangelical Churches have stepped in. Many of these young churches base their services around providing physical evidence of God's presence and many types of phenomena may be displayed including speaking in tongues, religious ecstasy and miraculous cures. Huge controversy rages over the validity of miraculous cures performed at Evangelical

Christian gatherings, and the initial enthusiasm of the public has been tempered by a number of public exposures of Evangelical religious leaders.

Geographical areas associated with miracles, such as Lourdes, are equally controversial. François Leuret and Henri Bon (in *Miraculous Modern Cures*, 1957) studied a number of Lourdes miracles and found them all to be genuine. However, D. West (in *Eleven Lourdes Miracles*, 1957) could not find any evidence at all. Many of these cures are reported by people who suffer from diseases which are known to have remission phases. Initial miraculous relief from the symptoms of arthritis, certain cancers and multiple sclerosis has, unfortunately, been found to be short-lived when followed up by investigators. However, there are some cures that have been thoroughly researched and still manage to defy explanation, such as the miracle of Ferdinand Aubry's gangrenous tongue. Such cases are generally explained in one of two ways.

The first explanation is that they are a genuine supernatural phenomenon. The religiously minded believe that it is the hand of God at work. Faith-healers believe that it is to do with an inner power within the body or with healing a body's damaged aura. There are even those who claim to be able to channel the spirits of dead doctors and utilize their power and knowledge to cure people. José Arigo (see page 92) is an example of the related phenomenon of psychic surgery.

The second theory is that such miracles are related to the power of the subconscious. A large number of modern miraculous cures involve terminal cancer cases where the cancer or tumour has disappeared overnight. This has often been explained in terms of the subconscious mind's control over the body being able to repair the body using conventional defence systems rather than supernatural ones. In addition to this, some authors suggest that miracle cures are only pronounced when people are not in possession of all the medical facts in a case. For example, it has been suggested that tumours can sometimes 'disappear' as a result of their becoming infected after surgery or that what were earlier diagnosed as tumours were in fact fluid- or fat-filled cysts that have been reabsorbed by the body. Some of the miracles associated with St Thérèse de Lisieux are hard to fit into the subconscious-mind category, as they involve factors over which the mind has no recognized control, such as the regeneration of missing tongue tissue.

There is an undeniable link between Christianity and claims of cures. Traditionally this has been based on the Christian belief that God and Jesus performed miracles in the past and are therefore capable of doing so again. As with the Angel of Mons case (see page 176), people with strong religious convictions try to make events fit the pattern of their belief, and this includes the majority of miraculous cures. However, as with many areas of the paranormal, once the unreliable and explicable cases are stripped away, there remains a hardcore of currently inexplicable cases.

St Joseph of Copertino

❖

LEVITATION

JOSEPH WAS BORN in 1603 in northern Italy and spent his youth devoutly starving, flagellating and punishing himself in preparation for life as a monastery priest. He was refused from his initial choice of order, the Capuchins, and at the age of 22 joined a Franciscan order in the town of Copertino. It is said that he was able to read people's minds and was noted for knowing when parishioners were holding back confessions. However, soon after his arrival at the monastery his psychic powers blossomed and he began to experience periods of levitation.

It would appear that he had no control over the timing or nature of his levitations and as a result they sometimes occurred at the most embarrassing times. For example, a member of a congregation at the service of the Feast of the Nativity testified that Joseph, who was seated in the middle of the church, suddenly gave out a cry and flew to the high altar, where he embraced the tabernacle. He remained airborne for a quarter of an hour before gently floating down to earth again.

Rather than accepting this miraculous behaviour, the Church authorities found it exceedingly embarrassing and he was more or less banned from participating in public services for 35 years. Although he had no conscious control over his levitations, they do seem to have been related to his devout faith. He was particularly apt to take to the air when in front of an image of the Virgin Mary or during prayers. Joseph's strange ability was witnessed by Pope Urban VIII, who, during an audience at which Joseph was present, saw him take off and remain suspended in the air for several minutes. Testimonies were also given by the High Admiral of Castile, the Duke of Brunswick (who was actually dragged into the air with Joseph) and countless members of the order and the public.

One of Joseph's best-known incidents occurred while he was out walking in the gardens with a fellow priest. The priest said to him, Brother Joseph, what a beautiful heaven God hath made!' At this, Joseph took to the air and came to rest on the thin branch of an olive tree. Despite his weight, the branch did not bend and ladders had to be fetched to retrieve him.

Joseph never offered an explanation as to the nature of his levitations, describing them as fits of 'giddiness'. Some descriptions of the events seem to suggest he was in some sort of trance when aloft.

Joseph died in 1663 and although an embarrassment during his lifetime, he was later canonized when his levitations were seen as a sign of his sanctity.

❖

There has always been a strong link between religion and periods of levitation, so much so that the Catholic Church has recognized its existence and has even given the phenomenon the name of transvection. The prime time for levitating priests was the Middle Ages, from when there are a number of testimonies describing the phenomenon. Practitioners include St Philip of Neri, who would become airborne during prayers, and St Ignatius Loyola who would, in addition to levitating, apparently become luminous as well. Unfortunately, St Robert of Palentin could only manage to rise 18 inches from the ground during his religious trances. It should also be remembered that Jesus was reported to have levitated upwards on Ascension day and also walk on water, something else that would require a defiance of gravity.

Among the reported cases of levitation in the Church, there is a strong correlation between religious devotion and the timing of the phenomenon. The commonest reported time for levitations to occur was during prayers or religious meditation, when the priests were concentrating their hardest on their faith. This suggests that perhaps there is a link between religious ecstasy and psychic phenomena – something borne out by Joseph of Copertino's levitation after being reminded of the beauty of God's world. Another commonly reported feature in levitations is the trance that the person seems to go into before and during their airborne time. This is suggestive of the trances that many physical mediums must descend into before they can perform publicly. Indeed, the so-called greatest medium of them all, Daniel Dunglas Home (see page 81) was renowned for his acts of levitation, including a very famous occasion when he was reported to have floated out of a third-floor window. Levitations have also been reported as part of poltergeist cases (see the Enfield Poltergeist, page 38), when objects and people have been seen to levitate and move of their own accord across rooms and other open areas. Then there is perhaps a link between the religious levitations of the Middle Ages and more modern psychic phenomena such as physical mediumship and poltergeists. This could perhaps give us a clue as to the nature of this phenomenon.

The first thing to note about levitation episodes is that they are directly related to specific individuals. There are no reliable reports of groups of people simultaneously levitating and those who have tried to physically drag individuals down have instead been pulled into the air with them. This happened with both Home and St Joseph. In nature, it would appear that levitation is essentially an anti-gravity process. People of considerable weight rise vertically into the air without any artificial aid, as if they were attached to a hot-air balloon or were being hauled up by a rope, which, according to the witness testimonies, they are not. Such a direct defiance of gravity is deemed to be impossible under the laws of physics, where in order to become vertically airborne, a considerable amount of energy is needed to force an object away from the earth's gravitational pull. Think of the energy needed to get a rocket into space. A rocket on a launch pad is dwarfed by the size of the fuel tanks attached to it. St Joseph was obviously not the same size as a rocket, but the energy needed for him to leave the ground would still be phenomenal, yet there are no reports giving any suggestion of where the energy could come from. People levitating are also reported to have a degree of control over their actions and are not out of control. Home levitated out of a window, while St Joseph came to rest on a delicate branch. This amount of control again indicates a mental input into the process and also that the person is literally floating in the air as opposed to being propelled from underneath or held up from above.

The nature of anti-gravity is complex. Using magnets and superconductors, it is possible to get trains and other objects floating above the ground, but again this requires considerable energy. Claims have been made for various anti-gravity devices over the years, mostly linked to UFO propulsion units, but none of them has either been proved to work or would be capable of producing effects like those reported for St Joseph. Modern physics does not allow for a direct defiance of the earth's gravitational pull in such a way, so if one accepts the validity of levitation, the explanation can only be guessed at.

There are also more down-to-earth (no pun intended) explanations for the phenomenon of levitation. It has been pointed out that the majority of reported levitations come from the religious environments of the Middle Ages and that some of the testimonies are either second-hand or were written on behalf of the people signing them. There is therefore a danger that, as with the case of María de Jesus (see page 159), the Church may have embellished rumours for the purpose of publicity and finance. The well-witnessed levitation of Home is more difficult to explain away, but criticism does exist about some of the people who claimed to watch him fly out the window.

Other groups of people have claimed similar effects to levitation, but these are almost certainly false. In the 1992 British general election, the Transcendental Meditation Natural Law Party claimed, as part of their manifesto, that those joining their party would be capable of achieving levitation, or Yogic Flying, as they termed it, through meditation. There are also the examples of medieval witches who reported sensations of flying, of animal transformation and of leaving their bodies, much of which has been blamed on taking hallucinogenic drugs such as belladonna and mandrake. Perhaps the priests experiencing religious ecstasies (a psychological state of mind related to hysteria and close to the trance-like state reported during levitations) may also have believed that they were flying and it was the rumours of these episodes that eventually became incorporated into fact. Mass hysteria has also been blamed as the reason for people believing in the Indian rope trick, where a rope apparently levitates by itself while a boy climbs it. Various photographs exist of people apparently levitating, but on examination most are proved to be fraudulent, with stepladders or wires being conveniently painted out of the photographs.

FRAUDS AND MISCONCEPTIONS

INTRODUCTION

FRAUDS, HOAXES AND MISCONCEPTIONS are the bugbear of the paranormal world. Each case or phenomenon that is debunked or proved to be wrong causes embarrassment and humiliation among occultists and jubilation and 'I told you so' from sceptics.

The majority of frauds are carried out for personal profit, publicity or to ridicule believers in the paranormal. Misconceptions and misunderstandings usually arise from people's over-eagerness to believe in a phenomenon without questioning it. Sadly, examples of both are abundant in the history of the paranormal.

The first recorded paranormal frauds are the scare stories spread by seventeenth-century pirates to keep people away from their activities. Many traditional ghost stories which involve phantom dogs, headless horsemen and spectral processions are originally smugglers' tales. In order to re-enforce these tales, the smugglers would sometimes move their booty around in hearses with headless dummies placed on them. Similarly, superstition in the sixteenth and seventeenth centuries led to everyday events, such as epileptic fits or livestock dying, being blamed on black magic or witchcraft for which many innocent people were executed (see the Salem Witch Trials, page 52).

From the eighteenth century onwards, more unconventional phenomena started to be recorded. Franz Mesmer discovered hypnotism and the first accounts of mass hysteria, precognition and extrasensory perception were given. It was from this time that individual frauds and misunderstandings start to appear, many of them centred around the subjects of healing, alchemy, hypnotism, fortune-telling and religion. It was in the mid-nineteenth century, with the rise of Spiritualism and the decline of the Church, that widespread frauds were perpetuated. The public's insatiable desire for psychic phenomena led to a large number of conjurors and charlatans setting themselves up as mediums, clairvoyants, hypnotists and other psychics whose services the public were prepared to pay for. Scientists were still revelling in their freedom from the church and wanted nothing to do with Spiritualism. When, in the late nineteenth century, a series of spectacular hoaxes and scandals was revealed, scientists took a firmly sceptical stance and devoted what little time it spent on the paranormal to negative research. Even the Society of Psychical Research (SPR) switched from investigating phenomena to trying to disprove them.

Between the two world wars there was a drop in public interest in the paranormal and it was not until the 1950s, with the advent of B horror movies and UFOs, that interest surged again. This wave of interest, which has continued patchily to this day, brought with it a whole new series of frauds and unintentional problems.

In the 1950s and 1960s most frauds and falsehoods revolved around the UFO phenomenon. These were mostly faked photographs, but there were also many more subjective claims involving stories of aliens contacting or abducting people or of collusion between world governments and alien races. Although few of these claims have been proved false, there are undoubtedly some people who have been making extraordinary amounts of money out of flimsy claims.

The 1970s saw interest spread to other supernatural areas, including the yeti, the Loch Ness Monster, astrology, Uri Geller, the Bermuda Triangle and ancient astronauts. Each topic spawned a series of fanatics who would distort or use evidence to construct rather far-fetched theories which would then get published. The advent of television shows and films with a supernatural theme, including The Invaders, Bewitched, Close Encounters of the Third Kind, ET and Poltergeist, perpetuated and fed the public's appetite for the paranormal. Indeed, after a lull in interest in the 1980s, the cult 1990s science fiction series The X Files was responsible for the largest upsurge in paranormal interest seen since the 1950s.

Generally, wherever there is money to be made, then unscrupulous people will be around to take advantage of the situation. This would include any publication, lecture or claim by any person or organization that has not been fully researched or which panders to people's gullibility. The amount of literature available that involves no research at all never ceases to amaze.

The possibility of fraud and mistake has hampered the scientific study of the paranormal more than anything else. Fraud nearly brought down the SPR in the late nineteenth century, leading it to become more sceptical in order to still be taken seriously. Many smaller modern organizations are founded on the unsound basis that the phenomena they study exist and that all they need to do is record testimonies from witnesses in the way a bird-watcher will record sightings of birds they know to exist. Others, such as the Association for the Scientific Study of Anomalous Phenomena (ASSAP), were founded with the better objective of painstakingly studying specific areas of the paranormal with a neutral attitude and then assessing the results afterwards.

Unfortunately, frauds, far-out theories and mistakes are so common in the paranormal that anyone researching a topic must start off being a hard-nosed sceptic, especially where second-hand testimonies are involved. This upsets the more optimistic people, who want only to hear positive evidence and will generally disbelieve negative findings. None the less, it is the objective of any individual researcher to say when findings are negative (which upsets the believers) and, conversely, to say when they are positive (which upsets the sceptics). Most open-minded researchers find themselves being attacked from both sides at once – which is normally a sign that a decent job is being made of the research! It can certainly be a 'heads I win, tails you lose' situation in which, at the end of the day, any findings you have are unlikely to persuade fanatical believers or sceptics away from their positions.

The Cottingley
Fairies

❖

FAKE PHOTOGRAPHS

THE COTTINGLEY FAIRY photographs have been described as the most obviously faked pictures in the history of supernatural photography. Despite this, the case has had (and still has) supporters over the 66 years that it took the two photographers to come clean about their trickery.

In the early part of this century, Cottingley was a small village located between the Yorkshire towns of Bradford and Bingley. The story begins in early July 1917 when engineer Arthur Wright lent his camera to his 16-year-old daughter Elsie and her 10-year-old cousin Frances Griffiths. When the girls returned the camera to their father, he set about developing the plate and was shocked at the result. The developed plate clearly showed Frances resting her elbows on a bush in front of a waterfall, while a ring of clearly definable fairies, complete with wings and musical instruments, danced in front of her. When Mr Wright asked for an explanation, Elsie replied coolly that the figures were indeed fairies. He must have been quite a reasonable father, as he pressed for no further explanation and was also prepared to lend his camera to the girls for a second time the following month.

This time the camera was taken by the girls to a well-known stretch of oak wood (called the Dell) that lay across a stream (the Beck) to the south of the Wrights' house. When this second plate was developed, it showed Elsie sitting on a patch of grass holding out her hand to a tiny gnome-like creature. Mr Wright and his wife, Polly, again questioned the girls, but they still insisted that there were fairies and that the photographs were genuine. The parents searched the girls' bedrooms in the hope of finding cardboard cutouts or pictures that may have been used in the photographs, but to no avail. The girls were banned from using the camera.

In November 1917, Frances wrote to a South African friend enclosing a copy of the first photograph and saying casually that the photo was 'me with some fairies up the Beck'. On the back of the photograph she wrote, 'Elsie and I are very friendly with the Beck fairies. It is funny, I never used to see them in Africa. It must be too hot for them there.'

The photographs were nothing more than a local curiosity until, in the summer of 1919, Elsie's mother visited a meeting on fairies at the Theosophical Society in Bradford. This resulted in copies of the girls' photographs circulating through the Theosophical Society until they finally came to the attention of Edward Gardener (a senior Theosophist) in early 1920. Gardener sharpened the prints and studied the original plates closely. He eventually proclaimed that no trickery was involved and he passed the negatives on to a photographic expert called Mr Snelling, who also declared that there was no double exposure and that the fairies were not made from paper or painted on to glass. Sir Arthur Conan Doyle, a keen spiritualist, heard of the photographs and persuaded Gardener to go to Cottingley to interview the girls in July 1920. He took with him two new cameras with several sealed plates and gave them to the girls to use. When the still-sealed plates were developed there were three more astounding photographs of fairies. One shows Elsie looking quizzically at a female fairy standing on a bush holding a tiny bunch of flowers. Another shows Frances in some foliage, flinging her head out of the way of a vigorously leaping fairy. The final and most impressive photograph shows two female fairies standing in the middle of a bush. Again, the photographic evidence was vindicated by experts.

During Christmas 1920 Conan Doyle published the first two photographs in an article on fairies he had written for the *Strand Magazine*. A sensation was caused and many explanations were put forward to explain how the photographs were faked (few members of the public believed that they were genuine). Arthur Wright was bemused at all the attention, as he himself was still convinced the girls had faked the photographs. Polly Wright, being more interested in spiritualist matters, does seem to have believed the girls.

The final three fairy photographs were published in the *Strand Magazine* in 1921 and the following year Conan Doyle wrote a book on the subject entitled *The Coming of the Fairies*. After this, interest seems to have waned considerably, although Conan Doyle's reputation never quite recovered from the blow it had been dealt by the affair.

A final attempt was made to photograph the fairies in August 1921, when psychic Geoffrey Hodson accompanied Elsie and Frances to the Beck. Although Hodson and Elsie claimed to have seen the fairies, they apparently refused to be photographed. No more fairy photographs were ever to be taken and the girls, now thoroughly bored with the whole business, claimed never to have seen them again.

❖

Although both girls have since come clean about the faking, there were numerous clues and hints that should have been picked up on sooner.

The first concerns the photographs themselves. The first photograph shows the dancing fairies with clear, sharp outlines even though they are apparently moving. This indicates that a fast shutter speed would be needed to freeze their movements. Yet, the waterfall in the background shows the falling water as blurred streaks, indicating that a slow shutter speed was used (probably a third of a second or more). The only explanation for the discrepancy in shutter speeds is that a slow shutter speed was in fact used (causing the blurred water) but the fairies were in fact stationary (not dancing) and were therefore probably cardboard cutouts. This also applies to the 'leaping fairy' who is pin-sharp, while Frances's head is blurred through jerking backward. The second point is that the fairies (though not the gnome!) all have fashionable bob hairstyles and Charleston-type dresses. This has been used to suggest that the girls either drew them or cut them out of magazines. In 1978, James Randi computer-enhanced the photographs and claimed to have seen strings attached to the fairies.

A further major reason for doubting the photographs concerns the girls themselves. Both had grown up together, shared an attic bedroom and, from an early age, were obsessed with fairies. Elsie was a talented artist who had long been fascinated with photography and had even worked in a photographer's shop for six months. Frances is said to have been highly energetic, with a keen sense of humour. Both girls were also reportedly highly intelligent.

In the 1970s (before their confession in 1983), the 'girls' gave a series of interviews to the press and television. In an interview for *Woman* magazine in 1975, Elsie said that on the day of the first photograph Frances had fallen into the Beck and had been scolded for later lying about the incident. Elsie had borrowed the camera to try and cheer her up and the girls had apparently got into a discussion about the nature of lying. They decided that if grown-ups could lie about Father Christmas, then they would fake some fairy photographs and if anyone took them seriously then they would say, 'But you know fairies don't exist'. Despite this semi-confession, Elsie still insisted that the photographs were genuine.

Both 'girls' were interviewed on BBC1's *Nationwide* programme in 1971. Here they admitted fooling Geoffrey Hodson and refused to swear on the Bible that they had not faked the photographs. They again denied faking the photographs when asked in 1976 and 1980. However, in the early 1980s a private letter written by Elsie in the 1970s came to light. In it she stated that the whole affair was a hoax and, in 1981, Frances finally said to researcher Joe Cooper, 'How on earth anyone could be so gullible as to believe the fairies were real is a mystery to me!' The whole matter was finally laid to rest when, in 1983, both Elsie and Frances publicly confessed to the whole affair being a hoax, although to this day there are those who still support the validity of the photographs.

Arthur Machen

❖

THE WILL TO BELIEVE

LITTLE DID ARTHUR MACHEN know that when he settled down to write a patriotic war story he would be starting a controversy that continues to run to this day.

From 26 to 28 August 1914 the first significant battle of World War I, between the combined British and French troops and the Germans, took place near Mons in Flanders. Instead of the expected quick victory, over 15,000 Allied troops were killed, forcing them to retreat rapidly. The German army followed behind, but thanks to luck and good tactics remarkably few of the retreating Allies were killed.

A few weeks after the retreat a British journalist, Arthur Machen, was sufficiently moved by the stories coming from the front to write a short story entitled 'The Bowmen'. It told of a group of retreating British soldiers who were about to be overrun by the pursuing Germans. Just as all seemed lost, one young soldier remembered pictures of St George that he had seen in a restaurant and shouted loudly for him to come to the aid of the British. Within seconds the ground started to vibrate and a line of phantom archers or bowmen from the fifteenth-century battle of Agincourt (which had taken place near Mons) appeared between the British and German lines. The archers let loose volleys of arrows into the German ranks, killing thousands of them but without leaving any wounds on the bodies. Taking their chance, the British troops escaped, determined to return another day to exact their revenge.

The story was printed by the *London Evening News* on 29 September 1914. Within a week or so, Machen was surprised to receive a letter from the editor of the *Occult Review* asking whether the story was based on fact. A few days later an identical letter arrived from the editor of *Light* magazine. In both cases Machen replied that he had made up the story himself.

In late October a vicar wrote to him to ask permission to release the story as a pamphlet. After agreeing, Machen was asked to write a short introduction to it, listing his original sources and interviewees. He again replied that he had made the story up, but the vicar refused to believe him and pointed to a number of other reproductions of the story in parish magazines that claimed the story as fact. Machen was stunned and realized that he had created a modern myth.

By the spring of 1915 a number of variations on Machen's story were circulating in a number of small publications. In true urban-myth style, most of them revolved around the testimony of an unnamed friend of the author who claimed to have witnessed the events. In some accounts the line of archers had been replaced by the figure of St George on his white steed accompanying a group of trapped soldiers who were making a suicide charge on the enemy. Versions of Machen's tale, using the St. George figure, appeared in publications by the Catholic, Protestant and Spiritualist Churches. All of them portrayed the stories as being the second-hand testimonies of soldiers.

Wide-scale publicity for the story started when the 24 April 1915 edition of *Light* carried an article entitled 'The Invisible Allies: Strange Story from the Front'. This claimed that an army officer had visited their headquarters stating that a supernatural cloud had descended between the retreating British and the advancing Germans, allowing the former to escape certain death. Most significantly, reference was made to Machen's story, implying that it might be true.

In the 15 May 1915 issue of *Light*, there appeared a poem based on 'The Bowmen' which, as far as is known, is the first reference to mention the appearance of angels on the battlefield. The relevant section of the poem ran:

> *Our foes, their horses, saw; they turned and fled,*
> *As troops of silent angels filed between*
> *Our broken ranks and theirs, and stilled our dread.*

The angels theme was rapidly picked up by vicars for their sermons and before long tales of divine intervention were sweeping the country, both by word of mouth and in print.

Even Machen could not resist this opportunity to make money and in August 1915 he published the original story, plus three other tales, in *The Bowmen and Other Legends of War*. In a lengthy introduction, he was at pains to point out that the story was not based on any known incident. The book was an immediate best-seller.

When people read this denial, they accused Machen of being arrogant and wanting to keep the glory of the story to himself. Very quickly a pamphlet entitled 'The Angel Warriors at Mons' was published by Ralph Shirley, listing a number of testimonies by returning soldiers of the miraculous angelic intervention at Mons. To overcome Machen's denials, Shirley claimed that Machen had picked up the story telepathically from the soldiers at the front! A more direct rebuttal of Machen came in the form of Harold Begbie's *On the Side of the Angels – An Answer to 'The Bowmen'*, which accused Machen of being an egotist who had sought to cause confusion by denying the truth of the tales. Yet more versions of the original story were published in small pamphlets.

Amid all the controversy, named testimonies were at last published, three of which are most noteworthy.

The first is from the daughter of Canon Marrable, known only as Miss Marrable. In it she allegedly tells a Reverend Gillson that she had spoken to two officers who had witnessed the angels. One of the officers is quoted as saying to Miss Marrable, 'They turned around to face the enemy expecting instant death when, to their wonder they saw between them and the enemy a whole troop of angels, and the horses of the Germans turned round terrified.'

This was widely published and used as absolute evidence of the angels' existence. In September 1915 Miss Marrable wrote to the *London Evening News* saying that she had no knowledge of the angels and that she had no idea how she had become linked to the stories in the first place.

A second first-hand testimony was provided by Private Cleaver of the 1st Cheshire Regiment, who swore an affidavit before a Justice of the Peace, George Hazelhurst. In this Private Cleaver claimed to have been at Mons and to have witnessed the angelic intervention. The story was widely published as first-hand evidence. However, in late 1915 Hazelhurst wrote a letter to the *Daily Mail*, stating that he had looked into Private Cleaver's war record and had found that he was stationed in England during the whole of the battle of Mons and the subsequent retreat.

The third testimony comes from Phyllis Campbell, the daughter of an English novelist. When war broke out she volunteered as a nurse. She was soon at the front and was unquestionably working in an area that received casualties from Mons. She claimed to have met a number of injured men who had seen both St George and the angels. She also said that French soldiers had seen a vision of Joan of Arc and that, on the Russian front, St Michael had appeared to fight the Germans. Here at last seemed to be the proof that people wanted to see – first-hand testimonies from somebody who had both been in the area and was also prepared to talk about it.

However, research done into the background of Miss Campbell revealed that she came from an occultist background (her aunt was a medium) and had written a number of occult articles before World War I. She absolutely refused to name any of the soldiers in her accounts and, when asked why no other soldiers had come forward, she replied that all the witnesses to the visions had been sworn to secrecy by the army! Although she never wrote a book about her war experiences, after the war she wrote *Back to the Front*, which promoted numerous false stories about so-called atrocities committed by the Germans. In the book she resorts to such outrageous patriotism and hatred of the Germans that her original story about Mons must be called into doubt.

Although disproved, the stories still circulated (often with the authors' names removed) until the end of the war. There were songs written about the incident and numerous pleas were issued for soldiers who had witnessed the events to come forward. No one ever did. Despite a number of ferocious attacks on him by Campbell, Machen remained calm and refused to resort to her aggressive tactics. Although the fervour died down after the end of the war, differing varieties of the story still circulate today. In 1994 there was an enormous upsurge of interest in the angels in America, allowing a whole new generation of books to be published which portrayed the angels of Mons as a fact. A 1994 survey by *Time* magazine found that 69 per cent of Americans believed in the existence of angels and that many people claimed to have seen them.

In 1930 Friedrich Herzenwirth, the director of German espionage, claimed that angels had been projected on the clouds by pilots in planes. Another theory says that the angels could have been the ghosts of recently dead soldiers who had reappeared to help out their living colleagues.

❖

Despite the claims of even recent writers, the various 'angels of Mons' incidents are unquestionably all traceable back to Machen's original story. It is, however, an interesting insight into the creation of a pseudo-urban myth. It started off as a rather poor story that appealed to people's patriotism and sense of pride, convincing them that God was on the side of the British during the war. The story was picked up by the Church, which must have been desperate to tell congregations the encouraging news that God would be fighting alongside their sons, husbands and brothers at the front. It might also have helped lessen the humiliation felt by the British and French at having to withdraw from the battle so hastily.

Once in circulation, the story was repeated as an abstract tale told without any reference to its original publication. It very soon got distorted, with each successive teller personalizing it in their own way. Thus the archers become St George, who becomes a troop of angels, who become Joan of Arc, St Michael, etc. The soldiers themselves went from being a whole retreating army to a patriotic pocket of trapped men making a suicide charge at the enemy. The enemy themselves went from dying in their thousands without being marked (for which there was no battlefield evidence) to a more plausible retreat at the sight of the visions. In common with urban myths, the witnesses to the events are either fictitious or mysterious 'friends of friends'.

For those still not convinced, it is worth bearing in mind that the only vaguely credible testimony was that of Miss Campbell. However, she could not name any soldiers or produce letters or written testimonies to back up her stories. The visions were not reported from any other battles in the war, although their help would have been more needed in the horrific carnage at the Somme and other such battles, where hundreds of thousands were slaughtered on both sides. Even so, 'The Bowmen' will continue to be quoted as a true story. It continues to be used in religious and occult books, often only in abbreviated form, with no reference to Arthur Machen at all. The last time I saw it mentioned as such was in a television special on angels in December 1995. By using this story as an example of a genuine angel phenomenon serious doubt was immediately cast upon the research done for the whole programme.

A modern case illustrates that the Machen phenomenon is not an isolated incident. In 1979 science fiction writer David Langford wrote a book entitled *An Account of a Meeting with Denizens of Another World, 1871, by William Robert Loosley*. In this book, an undertaker named William Loosley was kidnapped by a flying disc in 1871. Strange beings took samples of his clothes and body and showed him their extraordinary technology. He wrote down his experiences and sealed the documents in the drawer of his desk. The drawer was not opened until the 1970s, when the documents were found again. Langford then used the documents to write the aforementioned book.

In reality, what Langford did was to use real historical figures in his book, creating around them a completely false alien abduction story. Although William Loosley had once existed, the abduction and documents did not. However, Langford did not state this at the time his book was published. The story was immediately picked up by UFO investigators and became incorporated into a number of books, including *The World's Greatest UFO Mysteries* and other similar publications. In the 26 May 1988 issue of *New Scientist* Langford came clean and confessed to the hoax. Authors and UFO investigators were disbelieving and he immediately received letters insulting him and even accusing him of being paid by the CIA to cover up the story. Despite his widely published confession and further denials, the story still continues to be published as genuine. It was included in Whitley Schrieber's *Majestic* as part of a supposed 1947 CIA file of proven flying saucer cases and was last spotted in the *Bucks Free Press* in 1995.

Blackburn
and Smith

❖

HOAXING THE SPR

ALTHOUGH NOT MENTIONED widely by occultists and parapsychologists, the case of Blackburn and Smith has often been used by those sceptical of psychic powers to instance the non-objectivity of parapsychologists and the power of deceit practised by some conjurors posing as psychics.

In 1882 Douglas Blackburn was a journalist on a small Brighton newspaper when he chanced upon a young 19-year-old stage hypnotist named George Albert Smith. A strong friendship developed between the two and before long they began performing a stage mind-reading act in which Smith would receive messages sent by Blackburn. Local reaction was good and Blackburn wrote a letter to the spiritualist magazine *Light*, claiming that he and Smith were capable of the most extraordinary telepathic feats. The letter was published on 26 August 1882 and in it Douglas describes how:

> Mr Smith...places himself *en rapport* with myself by taking my hands...Not only can he read numbers, words and even whole sentences which I alone have seen but...he rarely fails to experience the taste of any liquid or solid I choose to imagine.

The publication of the letter had the desired effect and before long one of the founder members of the Society for Psychical Research (SPR), Edmund Gurney, had contacted the duo, requesting a private demonstration.

Blackburn and Smith willingly performed for Gurney and other SPR members on a number of occasions. These demonstrations were very impressive, with Smith, frequently blindfolded, being able to reproduce identical drawings to those shown to Blackburn. However, what really impressed Gurney and his colleagues was one particular demonstration where there seemed to be no conceivable means of cheating. In this experiment, Smith sat in a chair in front of a desk and had cotton wool and bandages applied to his eyes. His ears were filled with cotton wool and then putty. His chair was placed on a heavy rug to prevent any vibrations from coming through the floor. As a final precaution, both Smith and the chair he was sitting on were covered in two heavy blankets. At the far end of the room Blackburn was shown a drawing made of completely random squiggles and lines. After a few minutes of Blackburn redrawing the picture (in order to familiarize himself with it), Smith would suddenly announce that he had received the picture and a couple of minutes after that came out from underneath the blankets with an exact reproduction of the random drawing shown to Blackburn. The SPR were totally convinced that the demonstration was genuine and that at last they had evidence of the hidden powers of the human mind. The experiments were published in the first volume of the *Proceedings of the Society for Psychical Research* and were subsequently quoted in reply to sceptical articles about thought-transference.

Shortly after this Blackburn became implicated in a divorce scandal and hastily moved to South Africa, where he became a successful novelist. Smith joined the SPR and stayed in contact with Gurney, eventually being hired as his private secretary.

The validity of the experiments was never questioned by the SPR until 20 years later, when, on 8 September 1908, Blackburn wrote a letter from South Africa to the popular magazine *John Bull* in which, under the impression that all the other people involved with the experiments were now dead, he confessed that he and Smith had fooled the SPR.

He wrote at length about how he and Smith had both had an interest in the occult and how it was their belief that the majority of mediums, thought-readers, hypnotists and suchlike were nothing more than fraudsters and the so-called scientific investigators were too willing to rely on people's good character when checking these claims. The two of them decided to work out the mind-reading act with the sole aim of deceiving the scientific community and exposing them for the gullible people they were. It was therefore with some delight that they agreed to be examined by the SPR.

The mind-reading act worked chiefly on a series of hidden codes which Blackburn would transmit to Smith. These codes could be anything from a change in his breathing pattern to jingling his cufflinks or blowing on to Smith's cheek. Using this, Smith could receive descriptions of most regular and familiar objects or phrases, although the pair stumbled when it came to trying to describe anything that was random or irregular in nature. Using this system, though, they initially managed to fool the SPR's committee totally. However, eventually, their lack of success at being able to reproduce random drawings began to draw suspicion and it was then that their greatest demonstration, the one in which Smith was covered in the blankets, was performed. After this they were above suspicion – although in his first letter Blackburn refused to say how the trick was done.

Blackburn also described how he and Smith soon realized that they had made a mistake in trying to con the SPR. He describes the SPR committee as being genuine men of scientific standing who were earnest in their pursuit of the paranormal. Both men got on well with the SPR members and decided that it would be unsporting and cruel to deliberately expose them for being naïve. At the same time, they also felt duty-bound to finish the experiments they had started.

Blackburn was wrong when he thought that all concerned in the matter were dead. In fact, Smith was still very much alive and still working for the SPR! Interviewed by the *Daily News* (published on 1 September 1911), he denied that any trickery had occurred and said that he had the full backing of the SPR. He publicly accused Blackburn of lying.

Blackburn's reply to this came in the form of a long letter published on 5 September 1911 in the *Daily News*. In this he at last explained how the random drawing trick had been done.

After all the precautions of blindfolding, deafening and covering Smith with blankets were complete, Blackburn was shown the random drawing as far away from Smith as was possible. The figure was described by Blackburn as being 'a tangle of heavy black lines, interlaced, some curved, some straight, the sort of thing an infant playing with a pen or pencil might produce'.

Blackburn looked at the picture, paced around the room, stared at it, pretending to absorb the mental image ready for transference. He then openly drew and redrew the figure many times. During this time he also made a copy of the drawing on a cigarette paper which he then inserted into the brass tube surrounding the pencil he was using. This done, Blackburn purposefully tripped against the rug on which Smith's chair was resting – this was the signal that he was ready. Smith then cried out 'I have it!' and put his right hand out from underneath the blanket, saying, 'Where's my pencil!' Blackburn immediately thrust his pencil, with the concealed cigarette paper in it, into his hand. Underneath the blanket Smith used light from a small luminous slate to copy the figure down before emerging triumphant from underneath the blanket. The truth was out and there were now few in the SPR who believed that Blackburn and Smith had shown genuine acts of telepathy.

❖

The case of Blackburn and Smith is an ironic one in the sense that what had once been a *cause célèbre* for parapsychologists now became a stick with which sceptics could beat them. Perhaps the worst legacy of the saga (apart from Gurney's possible suicide) is that Smith's later work on levels of consciousness associated with hypnotic states must also be regarded with some suspicion. It was possibly to safe-guard this work, as well as his reputation in the SPR, that he denied cheating during his time with Blackburn.

There is not really much further comment that can be made about this case, for it is now clearly accepted as false. It has been pointed out that the real prob-lem was not the trickery but the willingness, even desire, of the SPR committee to believe what they were seeing. They allowed Blackburn and Smith partially to dictate the conditions of experimentation and also believed some of their expla-nations when the thought-reading failed. Perhaps worst of all, they clearly did not pick up on the pencil-swapping incident and also did not find the luminous slate hidden in Smith's clothes. These actions were the result of bad scientific condi-tions, but then it must be remembered that Blackburn and Smith were some of the first people claiming psychic powers ever to be tested by scientists. It is easy with the aid of hindsight to criticize, but at the time parapsychology was in its absolute infancy, with little previous work on which to base the new field of research.

These days the science of parapsychology does not rely so much on mediums or psychics coming forward with strong psychic powers that can give spectacular results. Instead, it bases its work on the collection of volumes of information by performing repeated experiments on ordinary people under laboratory condi-tions. People like the late Charles Honorton devoted their lives to repeating experiments, relying on statistical significance to test the existence of psychic powers. Some of these experiments have found their way into standard psychology textbooks.

In the same way that Harry Houdini's attempt to plant false evidence at a seance (see page 210) does not mean that all his previous exposés of mediums are invalid, the exposé of one set of badly tested showmen does not prove the non-existence of all psychic powers. After all, in the words of Blackburn himself, 'The existence of a false coin does not prove the non-existence of a good one.'

Benjamin Bathurst and the Marquis of Dufferin and Ava

❖

AN HISTORICAL ERROR

THE FOLLOWING TWO cases are classic paranormal stories that occurred to real historical characters and are quoted in books as being documented examples of the phenomena they wish to illustrate when in fact historical research shows them to have no factual basis at all.

The first story concerns Frederick Temple Hamilton Temple Blackwood, the first Marquis of Dufferin and Ava, who lived from 1862 to 1902. Legend has it that in 1883 he was residing in a friend's mansion in the County of Offaly, Ireland. One night he was woken from a deep sleep by strange noises coming from the gardens below his first-floor bedroom. He went to his window and opened it fully, trying to see what was causing the fuss. After a few seconds he became aware of a man walking across the lawn carrying a heavy object on his back. The Marquis was horrified to see that the heavy object was a coffin and shouted at the man. The man looked up and presented such a hideous face that the Marquis recoiled backwards in horror. When he had recovered himself enough to look out of the window again, he discovered that the man and his coffin had disappeared.

The Marquis of Dufferin often thought back to the strange manifestation he saw that night, but the experience was not to assume any significance until ten years later, when he was on a visit to Paris. While attending a crowded diplomatic function at the Grand Hôtel in central Paris, he was invited to a reception in the upper rooms. As he was about to get into an already overcrowded lift, he noticed that the lift attendant was the same hideous man he had seen on the lawn all those years before. The Marquis quickly stepped out of the lift, mumbling an excuse about not feeling well. Less than a minute later the packed lift crashed down the lift shaft, killing everybody inside, including the attendant. When later questioned, the hotel said that the lift attendant had been employed only that morning and nobody had taken his details yet. It appeared that the Marquis had been saved from certain death by his vision.

Various versions of this case exist in books on the paranormal, but close investigation has revealed serious flaws in the case. A consultation of *Palmer's Index to The Times' Newspaper* reveals that there was no recorded lift accident in Paris during 1893. There was a lift accident, in which nobody was killed, in the Grand Hôtel of Paris in 1878, some five years before the original vision was supposed to have occurred. At the time of the real lift crash, the Marquis of Dufferin was on extended diplomatic duty in Canada and could therefore not have been in the hotel. Clearly there was something wrong with the story as it was originally told. Luckily, the Society for Psychical Research (SPR) has done some research on this case and the conclusions it reached go some way to explaining the story's origin.

In 1949 the SPR traced a relative of Dufferin who informed them that the late Marquis had indeed told a story similar to that of the legend. However, he used to tell it about somebody else and claimed to have read it in a magazine. After exhaustive research, the story was eventually traced to the 16 April 1893 edition of the occultist magazine *Light*. This version involved not a man on a lawn but the driver of a hearse who caused a woman not to step into a hotel lift. It was assumed that the Marquis had heard this tale, that he had recounted it as one of his famous after-dinner stories and that his telling of it and his eventual participation in it were the result of later confusion.

In fact, the first version of this story naming the Marquis of Dufferin can be found in the book *Death and Its Mystery*, written by Camille Flammarion in 1923. All subsequent repetitions of this tale are traceable back to this book, making it absolutely certain that the Marquis was not involved in any supernatural incident concerning a hideous man, a coffin or a fatal lift accident.

The second story is extremely short. It states that on 25 November 1809 another diplomat, Benjamin Bathurst, was about to board a coach outside an inn in the German town of Perleberg. He went to check the horses and, in front of witnesses, simply disappeared into thin air. This form of the story has been relayed since the middle of the nineteenth century, but it would appear that the story is not so mysterious after all.

Benjamin Bathurst was born in September 1784, the son of the Bishop of Norwich. He joined the British Diplomatic Service and, in early 1809, was ordered to Vienna to encourage the Austrian Emperor to form an alliance with Britain against the French. Aware that he would be a prime target for French agents, Bathurst disguised himself as a German merchant and his secretary as a courier. After delivering some letters in Berlin, he went west towards Hamburg and on 25 November arrived at Perleberg. The town was apparently very rough at the time, being overrun with troops, deserters and thieves. None the less, here Bathurst and his company rested for several hours during the day at the White Swan Inn. After dinner, at around 9 p.m., he stepped outside to take some air and was never seen alive again.

It would appear that the legend around his disappearing into thin air in front of witnesses may have originated from a misinterpretation of the account of the affair given by the Reverend Sabine Baring-Gould in 1889. Baring-Gould states that Bathurst 'stepped around to the heads of the horses – and was never seen again'. However, he follows this by saying that nobody was particularly observing the movements of Bathurst at the time of his disappearance.

After his disappearance a large-scale search was initiated and on 27 November his valuable coat was found in the outhouse of a family named Schmidt. It turned out that Auguste Schmidt had been working in the White Swan Inn on the night of the disappearance and had gone out after Bathurst had entered the courtyard. On 16 December Bathurst's pantaloons were found in nearby woodland. They looked to have been left there recently. There were two bullet holes in the pantaloons but no blood, adding to the suspicion that he had been murdered by locals who were now trying to place the blame on French soldiers. Despite a thorough investigation by Bathurst's wife, no one was ever formally charged with his murder. Several bodies found in the following decades were attributed to Bathurst but no confirmation was ever made and there the matter lies.

❖

These stories represent just two of several thousand historically inaccurate paranormal tales currently in circulation. It is a sad fact that, after careful analysis, many paranormal cases involving historical characters or locations turn out to be false. The way that innocent historical incidents become attributed to the paranormal varies from case to case, but the phenomenon as a whole resembles that of the urban myth.

Urban myths are modern-day fairy tales that get spread by word of mouth through entire communities. Although invariably false, an urban myth is told as a genuine story that has usually happened to a friend of a friend (some people actually call urban myths FOAFs) of the narrator. An example of a modern urban myth is the story of the person who has returned from abroad with a potted house plant. After some time, the person repots the plant, only to find a dead tarantula in the base of the plant. After consulting a local expert, it turns out that the dead spider was a pregnant female whose eggs have hatched and young tarantulas must now be wandering the house. This sounds plausible (although there are no recorded cases of it happening), but if a narrator is ever asked to give names and details, then it becomes rapidly apparent that the story did not occur to a friend of a friend but was told to him as a story that had occurred to somebody else's friend of a friend.

This repeating of a story from person to person without questioning its origins can be seen in both the Dufferin and Bathurst cases. Unlike urban myths, whose origins are unknown, the errors within these cases can be specifically traced to one source who made the initial error, with all subsequent reports being repetitions of this erroneous commentary. This is such a common situation that when a historical story involving the paranormal is investigated, there is invariably some discrepancy between the original facts and the modern version of the story. This underlines two points that need to be made about historical stories involving the paranormal.

The first is that all these cases need to be treated sceptically, no matter how plausible they may seem. The second is that adequate research must be done to prove their validity. This research is easier than people seem to think. Many regional libraries contain records of births and deaths, information about businesses and, most importantly, newspapers stretching back years. Although research is a painstaking enterprise, being able to prove or disprove that a person was alive or in the right place when an event supposedly occurred to them is very gratifying and essential if the case is to be taken seriously.

Count St Germain

❖

SELF-CREATED IMAGE

IF THE ACCOUNTS of him are true, Count St Germain was a charismatic, intellectual and artistically gifted member of eighteenth-century high society. He was adept at diplomacy, claimed to have perfected the art of alchemy and hinted that he had lived for over 2,000 years. Although now largely forgotten, in his time Count St Germain was the darling of Europe.

Despite a number of investigations into his life, including one commissioned by Napoleon, the exact origins of Count St Germain remain unknown. Legend has him born either in 1710, the son of a San Germano tax collector, or in the 1690s, the illegitimate son of a Bohemian nobleman.

However, his first definite appearance in history is in the early 1740s in Vienna, where he quickly made many friends among the aristocracy. Contemporary reports describe him as a handsome man in his thirties whose use of sombre black clothes made him stand out from those dressed in the brightly coloured fashions of the day. He also gave the impression of being quite wealthy and had a passion for jewellery, particularly diamonds.

Almost all those who commented on Count St Germain noted that he was an extraordinary conversationalist who was apparently capable of speaking eight languages and he had a reputation for being a faith-healer as well. While in Vienna, he was rumoured to have saved a friend of Madame de Pompador (the French king's mistress) from certain death after she had eaten some poisonous mushrooms and is on record as curing the French Maréchal de Belle Isle of an unknown long-term illness. In gratitude the Maréchal set him up in Paris with accommodation and the first of his many laboratories. It is from here that the mysteries surrounding Count St Germain really begin.

Around 1740, while attending a society function, he was remembered by the aged Countess von Gregory as being in Venice some 70 years previously. When she asked whether it could have been his father, Count St Germain replied negatively, saying that it was he himself who had been there. When Countess von Gregory said that this was impossible as the man she knew then was about the same age as Count St Germain was now, he replied, 'Madame, I am very old.' After further protestations, he went on to provide her with details of their

189

encounters 70 years earlier, after which she exclaimed, 'I am convinced. You are a devil of a man!'

It seems that the count was not the only one to have claimed extreme old age. When asked about his master, one valet commented, 'I know not if St Germain knew Christ for I have only been in his service for 100 years.'

From then onwards the count continually hinted at his old age, giving supposed eyewitness accounts of ancient historical events. He most famously claimed to have known Christ and his family intimately and said that he had been present at the wedding at Cana. To add to this enigma, he was never seen to eat or drink. He would sit at feasts and dinners refusing all food and drink, claiming that he lived on a personally developed magic food. He also told stories of his friends' intimate personal lives, claiming that he could become invisible and could therefore spy on his colleagues unseen. These stories delighted French society and he soon charmed the French king, Louis XV.

After a two-year period in Britain, he was arrested as a spy in London in 1743. His luck seemed to hold out here too and despite being in possession of anti-monarchy correspondence he was released. After this, Horace Walpole wrote of him to a friend:

> The other day they seized an odd man who goes by the name of Count St Germain. He has been here these two years, and will not tell us who he is or whence, but professes that he does not go by his right name. He sings and plays the violin wonderfully, is mad and not very sensible.

It seems that he may have been on a secret mission for the French king, for on his return he carried out several more overt diplomatic missions. After one such trip to The Hague in 1760, he fell out with both Casanova (a friend of his) and, more disastrously, Louis's foreign minister, the Duc de Choiseul. The minister discovered that the count had been having secret discussions about ending the Seven Years War between Britain and France. He was deemed a traitor in France and fled to Britain and then to Holland. The May issue of the 1760 *Gentleman's Magazine* records that 'an adventurer known by the name of Compte de St Germaine passed from France to England to Holland'. Although the *Gentleman's Magazine* was famous for recording unusual events of all sorts, no mention was made of his extraordinary claims to immortality.

While in Holland he found the money to build another one of his famous laboratories for staining clothes and perfecting the art of alchemy. In the case of the latter, he was reputedly successful and left for Belgium a very rich man. He then made appearances in various European royal courts under a number of different names. In 1768 he was General Welldone in the army of Catherine the Great and in 1774 he visited Nuremberg, where he found the funds to build another laboratory under the name of Prince Rakoczy. His last known resting place was with Prince Charles of Hesse-Cassel in Schleswig, Germany. Here he rested from 1779, suffering increasingly bad attacks of depression and rheumatism, until on 27 February 1784 he died suddenly of a heart attack. Buried locally, his tombstone reads: 'He who called himself the Compte de Saint-Germain and Welldone of whom there is no other information, has been buried in this church.'

This, however, is not the end of the mystery. Count St Germain's last patron, Charles of Hesse-Cassel, burned all of his papers 'lest they be misinterpreted', starting rumours that the count was not dead. Soon after this Marie Antoinette wrote in her diary of having met the count in Paris and of regretting that she did not take heed of his warning of the forthcoming revolution. He apparently visited the king of Sweden in 1789 and also a friend, Mademoiselle d'Adhemar, who noted in her diary that he still looked like a man of 46. He supposedly visited her on a further five occasions, the last time in 1820. He so intrigued Napoleon that a commission was set up to investigate his life. The findings were, unfortunately, destroyed in a hotel fire in 1871. The cause of the fire, needless to say, was attributed to the count himself. Madame Blavatsky (see page 127) announced that he was one of the Theosophical Society's hidden masters and the French singer Emma Calve autographed a photograph to him in 1897, saying, 'To Count St Germain, the great chiromancer, who has told me many truths.' Finally, a Parisian called Richard Chanfray claimed to be Count St Germain during a 1972 television programme. He apparently successfully transmuted lead to gold live on air.

❖

So who was Count St Germain? Was he really an immortal alchemist who had been friends with Jesus? The evidence suggests otherwise.

Although he appears to have been a highly intelligent and gifted individual, it is also apparent that he enjoyed being the centre of attention. Casanova noted that he was the most remarkable conversationalist he had ever met and the perfect ladies' man. He certainly seemed to be able to talk his way into the favours of not only French high society but also half the royal courts of Europe. However, his extrovert nature seems to have made him enemies as well. After their falling out in The Hague, Casanova revised his opinion of the count, deciding he was but a rather boastful impostor. He wrote of him:

This extraordinary man, intended by nature to be the king of impostors and quacks, would say in an easy, assured manner that he was three hundred years old, that he knew the secret of the Universal Medicine [alchemy], that he possessed mastership over nature, that he could melt diamonds... All this, he said, was a mere trifle to him. Notwithstanding his boasting, his barefaced lies, and his manifold eccentricities, I cannot say I found him offensive...I thought him an astounding man.

He did not much impress Count Warnstedt, who in 1779 described him as 'the completest charlatan, fool, rattle-pate, windbag and swindler'.

It would seem that virtually all of the count's activities, from his unusual clothes to his refusal of food, were designed to enhance his enigmatic image. His boasts of old age are likely to have derived from the initial evening with Countess von Gregory and the interest it clearly caused. His considerable charm and audacity, combined with his in-depth knowledge of history, would have enabled him to create scenarios surrounding his supposed involvement in historical events. Also, claims of longevity are a common factor within alchemy. The descriptions of his final years under the patronage of Charles of Hesse-Cassel do not convey the image of an eternally youthful 46-year-old but of the steady decline of a man in his old age. It is feasible that he survived his 'death' to warn Marie Antoinette and the king of Sweden, but very unlikely that he appeared to Mademoiselle d'Adhemar and certainly not as a man in his forties. It is suspected that the person to whom Emma Calve dedicated her photograph may have been something of an impostor himself. An occultist church, the Rosicrucians, still believe that the count is alive, that he was once Sir Francis Bacon and that he was the founder of Freemasonry.

So, then, it seems likely that the legend of Count St Germain is one of his own making that was believed, or at least tolerated, by gossip-ridden French society. However, before he is written off as a complete braggart, it should be remembered that, as his entry in this book confirms, his charisma and antics have achieved for him immortality as a legend, particularly in France, where his name lives on.

Comyns Beaumont

❖

WILD THEORIST

ALTHOUGH NOT STRICTLY a fraud, Comyns Beaumont has the dubious pleasure of being dubbed 'Britain's greatest crank'. He was certainly a religious fanatic and a fervent nationalist and these were probably the driving mechanisms behind his outlandish theories.

Comyns Beaumont was born into a respected English family. He worked in the Diplomatic Service and then made a moderate living as a journalist and newspaper editor. He showed no sign of insanity but does appear to have been remarkably patriotic and during the 1940s published three remarkable volumes in which he suggested that much of ancient and biblical history should be revised and relocated away from the Mediterranean and Middle East to north-west Europe in general and the United Kingdom in particular.

Although one can never be sure what drove an intelligent and educated man such as Beaumont to reach the conclusions he did, things seem to have started with his study of the legend of Atlantis. He worked out that the mythical continent must have been between northern Scotland and Scandinavia, with the Hebrides, Shetlands and Orkneys now all that was left. His next assumption was that the flooding of Atlantis was in fact the same event that caused Noah to build his ark. This suggestion had been made before, but Beaumont managed to add a new dimension to the tale by suggesting that Noah had settled in Britain and that all subsequent generations could be said to be British. His interpretations of Greek mythology were equally interesting. He proclaimed that the Scottish Isle of Skye was in fact the legendary Greek isle of Skyros. As Skyros supposedly lay across the River Styx, Beaumont decided that this must be the nearby Loch Alsh. By the same reasoning, the Greek Hades was placed in the Western Isles of Scotland.

As much of Beaumont's ancient world is mapped out in relation to Skyros, the Scottish Highlands became a veritable hotbed of famous ancient locations. Beaumont even claimed that the popularity in Scotland of the name Alexander was evidence that Alexander the Great had ruled over Britain. The same logic dictated that the Faroe Islands were the ancient seat of power of the Egyptian Pharaohs. Other relocations include placing Athens in Bath (deduced by removing the 'B' and adding 'ens' to the town's name), Sodom to Bristol, the River Nile to the Severn and, finally, Jerusalem and all the events associated with it to Edinburgh. Needless to say, Beaumont was not taken seriously. Although his books were widely circulated, his theories were dismissed as cranky and illogical.

❖

The surprising thing about Comyns Beaumont was not particularly his revelations, for there have been more irrational theories than his, but that such a highly educated person should really believe such things. He is, however, only one of a large number of similar religious zealots, all of whom were convinced that western Europe was the real location for biblical stories.

Another example is John Wilsen, a London phrenologist, who published a book entitled *Our Israelitist Origin* in 1840. He advocated that the Israelites were the ancestors of the Scythions, who in turn were the ancestors of the Saxons. According to his lineage, the Britons are direct descendants of the Israelite tribe of Ephraim and the name Saxon is an abbreviation of 'Isaac's son'. In 1861 the Reverend Glover proposed the same theory, except that the Scottish and Welsh could be related to the tribe of Manasseh.

In contrast, in 1870 Edward Hine identified Britain with all 12 tribes of Israel and said that the common use of the word 'dun' in Irish town names could be linked with the tribe of Dan. *Dun* is actually Gaelic for a hillfort.

It seems probable that the ultra-nationalism of these individuals gave them an overwhelming desire to locate the cradle of civilization within north-west Europe. In order to remove this privilege from Africa and the Middle East, inconvenient facts had to be altered. This same closed-mind attitude towards known facts has become prevalent among the group of fundamental Christians known as Creationists.

Creationists believe that the world was created by God in six days in 4004 BC. Modern isotope dating techniques suggest that the earth is over 4,800 million years old, with the oldest known fossils (simple bacteria) 3,800 million years old. Although the Creationists are entitled to believe what they choose, in some areas in eastern Australia and the southern USA their lobbying has ensured that the Creationist version of events is taught in schools in place of the geological and evolutionary ones. As with Beaumont and his allies, twisting (or suppressing) facts to fit personal pet theories leads to a very distorted view of the truth.

Not that science is entirely free of guilt in this area. It was desires similar to those of Beaumont that led a group of scientists to perpetrate the famous Piltdown Man hoax.

In 1912 they announced that they had discovered skull fragments from a new species of prehistoric human in a Sussex gravel pit. They dated the bones as being the earliest known hominid fossils and concluded that mankind must have evolved in Britain and not East Africa or Germany, as was previously thought. The British scientific community lapped it up and the textbooks were duly rewritten. The validity of the claim was never doubted and when a fossil cricket bat, fashioned out of deer antler, was found in the pit, it was taken to mean that the fossil was the earliest living Englishman. As palaeontological techniques improved through the early part of this century, people began to suspect that the bones had been interfered with or at least wrongly dated. As scientist after scientist found problems with the case, so the doubts grew until finally, in November 1953, the affair was denounced in the House of Commons as a hoax. It turned out that the skull fragments were cleverly altered pieces of human skull (carbon dated at 650 years old) and the fashioned jaw of an ape. The cricket bat was a carved piece of fossil bone. All the fragments had been stained to give them the appearance of age. It later turned out that the gravel pit contained no fossils. Although the individual roles of the perpetrators were never fully sorted out, science had been dealt one of its biggest blows ever.

The desire to be right is a dangerous thing. The occult is littered with examples of people who have twisted or conveniently ignored facts to shore up their experiences, claims or theories. Fortunately, with the more extreme cases illustrated here, it is relatively easy to see where the facts stop and the fantasy starts.

THE PSYCHIC INVESTIGATORS

INTRODUCTION

INVESTIGATIONS INTO PARANORMAL phenomena are always dogged by controversy but it is often the psychic investigators who end up being more controversial than the cases they study.

The image associated with the paranormal has always rather attracted mavericks. The stigma attached to the subject means that very few scientifically trained people are prepared (or can get a grant) to study paranormal topics objectively. This has led to a void that has been filled by sceptics, amateur pseudo-scientists and fanatics. The accusations, claims and counter-claims put out by these groups mean that very little headway has been made in the study of the paranormal. As it is largely biased sceptics and fanatics who do the majority of popular investigation into the paranormal, it is worth examining their characteristics.

By and large, the sceptics (many of whom are scientifically trained) will not believe in anything that faintly whiffs of the occult. Much of the time there is good reason for this, but rather than researching individual cases in any depth, sceptics prefer to latch on to proven cases of fraud or mistaken identity and use these to explain away any number of phenomena. Many of the sceptical theories used to explain away paranormal occurrences are just as vague, outlandish and non-applicable as the claims they seek to disprove. For example, Arthur C. Clark (in his *Mysterious World*) dismissed ghosts as visual hallucinations, but this would explain only a minute fraction of reported ghost cases.

The reverse of the sceptic is the fanatical occultist. These people will generally believe everything and anything that is presented to them, no matter how unlikely. It is this desire to believe that led to the photographs of the Cottingley fairies (see page 173) being accepted as genuine for over half a century, despite the unlikeliness of the whole scenario. Even after the perpetrators confessed to faking the photographs, there are still those who believe that the fairies did exist and it was just the photographs that were faked. It is this ability to circumvent facts by altering claims and theories that marks out a true fanatic.

A good example comes from a friend of mine who studies crop circles and is convinced that all the formations are genuine paranormal phenomena. When, after declaring a circle genuine, he was confronted with the video evidence of somebody faking it the previous night, he said, 'It doesn't matter as the person [who faked it] was clearly acting under the instructions of the Earth Goddess.' It is hard to have a constructive debate when faced with such shifting arguments.

Most fanatics do not need evidence or plausibility to shore up their claims. Many theories are based around a single anomalous occurrence or event and become hugely exaggerated in a perverse game of Chinese whispers. The alleged Roswell UFO crash (which may well have occurred) has had more and more claims attached to it over the years. It has escalated from a basic case of the American government covering up a crashed flying saucer, to bodies being found and examined, to alien technology being used (and hidden) in government air bases, to government cover-ups on alien contacts, abductions, invasions, etc. Many of these claims have been made by individuals who are keen to promote their books on the subject – a fact that should always make one sceptical.

The popularity and widespread nature of some of the more dubious paranormal tales is because most people love to read fantastic stories of supernatural or alien happenings but not more down-to-earth explanations. Many books by various fanatics quite cheerfully contradict each other without affecting sales: for example, Richard Hoagland claims that NASA scientists have removed all evidence of alien civilizations from their moon-landing photographs, while David Percy claims that NASA faked all the moon-landing photographs, using a stage set on earth. As people must either have been to the moon and photographed it or have not been there and faked the photographs, then one (or both) of these authors must be wrong. Yet both opinions live comfortably side by side in the minds of conspiracy theorists.

Confrontations between sceptical and fanatical investigators tend to be political affairs consisting of soundbites and violent disagreements with few if any resolutions or conclusions. As in politics, the middle ground is occupied by people who try to be objective but tend to lean one way or the other. Most have areas they firmly believe in and those they do not. It is from the middle that many plausible theories arise about certain phenomena. For example, the association of earth lights with active fault zones has been related to the production of geomagnetic energy. However, many theories, both for and against the existence of paranormal phenomena, are too specific and unscientific to stand up to rigorous testing. A few, however, do become acceptable and manage to get publicized.

As the above demonstrates, it is nearly impossible to be a completely objective researcher into the paranormal. Everybody interested in the subject will have preconceived ideas and opinions, no matter how impartial they think they are. Finding investigators to include in this chapter was difficult, for although many people are working, or have worked, in the field, few have had sufficiently diverse lives to illustrate the points I wanted to make. This is not to say that their work or results are not interesting.

Harry Houdini and Harry Price perfectly mirror each other as examples of how not to investigate the paranormal. Both were self-publicists hell bent on respectively disproving and proving the existence of psychic phenomena, even if they had to cheat to do so. In short, their egos got in the way of their research. This now renders much of what they did suspect.

Most serious investigators have woken up to the fact that there is no quick and easy way to collect evidence. The studying of apparently gifted individuals, such as Uri Geller, Doris Stokes, Daniel Dunglas Home (see page 81), etc., rarely resolves anything and often just serves to heighten the controversy. With some psychic phenomena, such as clairvoyance and telepathy, the painstaking process of gathering statistical evidence from laboratory tests is well under way. Investigators into other more random phenomena, such as cryptozoology, ghosts and UFOs, cannot know when and where their evidence will occur next. This means that investigations into such phenomena are almost entirely reliant upon the testimonies of witnesses. None the less, patterns can still be found in witness testimonies, although the conclusions tend to be more vague.

The Society for Psychical Research

❖

ORGANIZED RESEARCH

EVERY SERIOUS BOOK on the paranormal will at some point refer to the work of the Society of Psychical Research (SPR). The society's foundation marked the start of parapsychology as a science and it is worth examining the social conditions and personalities that led to the formation of this still influential institution.

The roots of the SPR lie in the tremendous upheavals that were taking place in British Victorian society. By the middle of the nineteenth century the scientific community had finally broken the grip of the Church over the education system and the population as a whole. Darwin's *The Origin of Species* (1859) had allowed science to challenge the Church's monopoly over the truth and resulted in the questioning of many religious beliefs and values. In the late 1850s, the arrival of Spiritualism from America brought with it a wave of interest in seances and a whole host of mediums appeared from the woodwork to cater for the new craze of table-turning and communicating with the dead. Spiritualism seemed to offer the population something that the Church never could – physical evidence of a life after death. However, it was not long before some of the mediums were exposed as frauds and opinion was split between those who believed in the reality of Spiritualism and those who did not. The scientific establishment, still euphoric about its victory over the Church, firmly sided with the sceptics and actively encouraged the debunking of mediums by people such as Harry Houdini (see page 210). Despite this, there was a small number of disillusioned scientists who had taken the time to attend seances and who believed that there was something to the new religion of Spiritualism. They were determined to apply the law of scientific investigation to what they felt was an entirely new branch of science.

In the latter half of the nineteenth century some scientists took it upon themselves to investigate individual mediums or phenomena. The most noted of these was Sir William Crookes, an eminent and honoured chemist who had discovered the element thallium. From 1869 to 1875 he undertook investigations of a number of mediums, including the great Daniel Dunglas Home (see page 81). The phenomena he witnessed at these seances firmly convinced him of the existence of a 'psychic force' within the human body that needed immediate scientific study. To this end he tried to publish a paper about Home in the respected *Proceedings of the Royal Society of London*, but it was refused. Instead he used his influence to get it published in the *Quarterly Journal of Science* in the summer of 1871. The publication caused an uproar among the scientific community, who thought that one of their members had turned against them. Both Crookes and his work were widely discredited.

Against this background, many scientists interested in the occult watched with dismay as any individual attempt by scientists or noted personages were conclusively rubbished by the establishment. Two such observers at this time were Professor Henry Sidgwick and Frederick Myers, both of Trinity College, Cambridge University. In 1869 they had resigned their fellowships because they no longer believed themselves to be Christians. It was shortly afterwards, during a night-time walk, that the two of them discussed the possibility that the driving mechanisms of the universe might not lie in the dogma of Christianity or physics but instead in the phenomena being reported from the seances of Victorian Britain. In 1873 Myers attended a seance given by the medium Charles Williams. At this he held the hand of Williams's spirit guide, John King, and gradually felt it melt away to nothing while he was still grasping it. Experiences like this and the attacks on Crookes were the final straw and in 1873 Myers, together with a man called Edmund Gurney and, after some persuasion, Sidgwick founded an informal association of people interested in investigating the paranormal. Among the first members associated with this group were Arthur Balfour (a future British prime minister), his sister Eleanor, Lord Rayleigh and Stanton Moses.

One of their first investigations, in 1876, was of the medium Henry Slade, who had caused a sensation in his seances by getting 'spirits' to write messages on slate tablets. Sidgwick, who had by now married Eleanor Balfour, was not at all impressed with Slade, although Myers seems to have had more faith in him. In the autumn of 1876 Slade and another medium were charged and found guilty of deception and were sentenced to three months' hard labour. During Slade's trial another prominent scientist came out of the woodwork and joined the then socalled 'Sidgwick group'. William Barrett, a professor of physics in Dublin, had a fascination with mesmerism (hypnotism) and some of the psychic powers he had seen displayed by people in hypnotic trances. From 1876 to 1882 the Sidgwick group floundered in its aims, with all or some of its members at different points distracted by other matters. In the meantime, a small number of spiritualist and pseudo-scientific groups had also being trying to investigate and experiment with all aspects of the paranormal. Finally, inspired by the new Victorian parlour game of table-turning, Barrett called a conference on psychic phenomena in early

January 1882. The Sidgwick group were at first reluctant to be on the committee but when Sidgwick himself agreed to be president, the rest joined. A month later, on 20 February 1882, the Society for Psychical Research was founded. Its initial membership was chiefly made up of spiritualists and friends of the Sidgwick group, including Charles Dodgson (Lewis Caroll), Mark Twain and William Gladstone.

Soon afterwards six research committees were established to investigate the following phenomena: hypnotism and clairvoyance; telepathy; sensitives; physical mediumship; ghosts and hauntings; records and archives. The main driving force of the society was its gentleman scientists, those members whose personal fortunes enabled them to devote much of their spare time to researching subjects of their own choice. Chief among them were some of the original members of the Sidgwick group, especially Sidgwick himself, Myers and Gurney. Early on Myers and Gurney teamed up with Frank Podmore, a post office worker, and by 1886 had produced the colossal *Phantasms of the Living*. This 2,000-page book sought to establish the reality of *doppelgängers* and the phenomenon of ghosts of the living (see Emilie Sagée, page 31) by presenting such an overwhelming amount of researched first-hand evidence that no one would be left in any doubt that the phenomenon was real.

This painstaking and boring approach to the paranormal did not endear the SPR to its more sensational-seeking spiritualist members, who gradually began to drift away. Fortunately, it did appeal to scientists and even some sceptics, many of whom joined the society in the 1880s, including Sir Oliver Lodge, Sigmund Freud, Carl Jung, Sir William Crookes and Sir Arthur Conan Doyle. A sister society was founded in America in 1885. Things seemed to be progressing well.

Although there had been a number of very public exposures of mediums caught cheating, including Crookes's medium Florence Cook in 1880, none had adversely affected the SPR in its early days. All this changed in 1888.

When the SPR was first formed, Sir William Barrett was heavily involved in investigating the four daughters of a Derbyshire clergyman called Cheery. The girls appeared to display psychic powers and often played something called 'the willing game', whereby one of them would leave the room and the others would decide what they wanted the missing girl to do on her return: for example, pick up a certain object or sing a specific song. Upon entering the room, the others would will the returning girl, who, in the case of the Cheery sisters, would frequently do what was willed of her in her absence. Barrett and then later Myers were very impressed with the Cheery girls and published an article on them in the July 1882 edition of *Nineteenth Century* magazine. It was heavily criticized, but the SPR stood by the findings, claiming that adequate precautions had been taken against cheating. However, in 1888 the Cheery girls were caught cheating and confessed that, due to failing success in recent years, they had developed a visual and aural code with which to communicate with each other. The SPR accepted defeat gracefully but the critics leapt at the chance to discredit, in their view, the 'spiritualist cranks'. Worse was to come when one of the founders of the SPR, Edmund Gurney, was found dead under strange circumstances (probably suicide) in June 1888. Then, on 21 October 1888, two of the Fox Sisters (see page 122), the very founders of Spiritualism itself, publicly confessed to lifelong fraud. Although there was considerable doubt as to the validity of this confession, it too was used to make the society's members look like gullible fools. By the early 1890s, the SPR's reputation was quite badly dented, although its members still carried on regardless, producing thousands of pages of results, much of which remains valuable today.

Still more problems loomed on the horizon. In 1898 Myers was involved in a minor sex scandal with a woman psychic investigator, Ada Goodrich-Freer, who turned out to be a fraud and a liar. Sidgwick died in 1900 and was followed soon after by Myers, who died on 17 January 1901. The book he was working on at the time, *Human Personality and the Survival of Bodily Death*, was published in 1903 and has since been recognized as a masterpiece in parapsychology. Within a few years the craze for Spiritualism had declined and, with its main (and controversial) investigators now all retired or dead, the SPR carried on at a more sedate pace and, if anything, seemed to concentrate on the debunking of mediums, perhaps in order to increase its standing within the scientific community.

The two world wars and the Great Depression caused inevitable disruption to the SPR, but after World War II it made a conscious effort to follow the American Society for Psychical Research in trying to concentrate more on laboratory research rather than just investigating public cases.

The SPR continues its work today with a dedicated membership. Feelings against it no longer run as high as they did in the nineteenth century, partly because most modern scientists (excepting some psychologists) do not seem to need to disprove the paranormal as a matter of principle as they did in the last century, although the mid-1990s upsurge in interest in the paranormal has put the scientific establishment on the defensive again. Even so, the SPR should still be the first port of call for any researchers wishing to investigate paranormal phenomena. Some of its members, including modern pragmatic researchers, are continuing to help the cause of parapsychology.

There is an interesting postscript to the Sidgwick group of the SPR – one that has been interpreted as evidence for their continual survival beyond death. Out of the original Sidgwick group it was Myers who was particularly fascinated by the prospect of life after death. He was convinced that evidence for the survival of personality would one day be found and after his death in 1901, he seemed to have developed a system from beyond the grave to give that proof. The people who became involved in what followed included not only Myers's 'spirit', but also those of Edmund Gurney and Henry Sidgwick. The mediums they communicated through were called Mrs Holland (Alice Fleming, sister of Rudyard Kipling, who resided in India), Mrs Willett (Winifred Coombe-Tenant, who lived in London), Margaret Verrall and her daughter Helen, who lived in Cambridge, and the powerful Boston medium Leonora Piper.

The first indication that Myers was trying to communicate came shortly after his death, when Mrs Verrall, while doing some automatic writing, received a Latin message signed by Myers. The message referred to a sealed envelope that Myers had given to Sir Oliver Lodge before his death, stating that it should be opened only if he managed to posthumously describe the contents. Myers's message contained quotes about love from Plato's *Symposium* and instructions that the envelope should be opened. However, when the envelope was opened it contained the following message: 'If I can revisit any earthly scene, I should choose the valley in the grounds of Hallsteads, Cumberland.'

People were disappointed until it was remembered that Myers had written about the *Symposium* in his book *Fragments of an Inner Life*. The whole book was written about Annie Marshall, a woman friend who had lived in Hallsteads, Cumberland. The group thought that they had found the link that Myers was hinting at.

Better was to come. In retrospect, it would appear that after their death, the Sidgwick group reunited to devise a system whereby fragments of messages would be given to independent mediums so that none of the fragments made sense unless put together with the others. As Myers said in one of his first communications to Mrs Verrall, 'Record the bits and when fitted they will make the whole. I will give the words between you neither alone can read but together they will give the clue he wants.'

Not long after this, in 1903, Mrs Fleming was practising automatic writing when Myers apparently came through. He asked her to pass on his regards to some of his friends and then gave a description of Dr Arthur Verrall, the husband of Mrs Verrall. He asked Mrs Fleming to send the correspondence to the Verralls and even gave her their correct address in Cambridge. Mrs Fleming had no idea who the Verralls were, let alone what their address was. He later accurately described the Verralls' living room to Mrs Fleming. As proof that Myers had survived death, this looked conclusive.

Some of the codes and cross-referencing that ensued between various mediums, using messages reportedly coming from Myers, Gurney and Sidgwick, are horrendously complicated and very tedious for the mediums concerned. The system came be known as cross-correspondence and was eventually to continue for nearly 30 years and to produce over 2,000 automatic-writing transcripts. The highbrow nature of some of the messages and discussions that the 'spirits' delivered also severely tested the patience of at least one of the mediums.

A good but comparatively simple example of cross-correspondence comes again from Myers. On 7 March 1906 Mrs Verrall received a message from him containing a quote from Roden Noel's poem called 'Tintagel'. On 11 March Mrs Fleming received a message from Myers saying, 'This is for A.W. [Dr Verrall]. Ask him what the date May 26th 1894 meant to him.' This again referred to Roden Noel, who had died on the date given. However, on 14 March, before Verrall had received the message from Mrs Fleming and therefore could not know its meaning, she received another cryptic message from Myers. This said, '18, 15, 4, 5, 14. 14, 15, 5, 12. Not to be taken as they stand. See Revelations 13, 18, but only the central eight words, not the whole passage.'

Mrs Fleming could not make head or tail of it and sent it to the SPR. There, Alice Johnson realized that the message referred to a section in the Book of Revelation that says, 'for it is the number of a man'. She then tried to exchange the numbers given for their corresponding letters in the alphabet. It spelled out the name Roden Noel. As if this were not proof enough, Myers referred again to Noel through Mrs Fleming on 21 march and finally referred to him by name in a transcript done through Mrs Verrall on 28 March. As I mentioned previously, this was one of the more simplified examples; other cross-correspondences took years to fully understand. In addition to the Sidgwick group, other cross-correspondences came from the sweetheart and brother of Arthur Balfour, in what became known as 'the Palm Sunday Case', and from Dr Verrall (who died in 1912) himself. With the death of the mediums and the original founders of the SPR, the messages stopped coming through in the early 1930s. Myers still produces the odd communication, including one sent to the psychic healer Matthew Manning in April 1972, warning him that no one alive will ever find out the secrets of the afterlife and that even if they did they would not be believed!

❖

The SPR was the first large organization devoted entirely to the study of the paranormal and as such it was the forerunner of modern parapsychology. The original founders felt that by applying established scientific techniques to psychic phenomena they would be able to produce absolute evidence of their existence within a few years. Over a century later we are not that much closer to producing such proof. The early SPR got itself rather bogged down with the controversy of spiritualism and was tarred with some of the frauds that it produced (see Blackburn and Smith, page 181). It was also at the receiving end of a smear campaign organized by scientists angry that the SPR had been formed in the first place. As a result, the SPR went through a phase of debunking mediums which caused it to fall out with the spiritualist movement as well as the scientific community. This was perhaps not such a bad thing. The SPR, or any similar organization, could never seriously hope to gain respect from a hostile scientific community and the sensational nature of Spiritualism seemed to cause more problems than it solved.

Post-war parapsychology has learned much from the experience of these early societies and little time is now devoted to research on apparently 'gifted' individuals such as Uri Geller and Matthew Manning. Instead there has been a concerted effort to use strict laboratory procedures to try and come up with statistical evidence for the existence of psychic phenomena among everyday people. Unfortunately, this involves a lot of time, money and equipment, which few parapsychology organizations have access to. It also needs a suitably qualified person to oversee the research and this is even more difficult, as the scientific community is still very hostile to parapsychology. A number of universities have set up parapsychology departments, most of which have, at any one time, a small number of postgraduate students working on specific topics. Much of the research done in these institutions focuses on rather mundane but more socially acceptable topics, such as telepathy and precognition, in the hope that repeated testing of individuals will produce statistically significant results. This has so far produced positive results that have been published in major scientific journals. However, judging by the letters they occasion, it would appear that people are still a long way from accepting any results produced by parapsychologists.

Tom Lethbridge

❖

DOWSING

TOM LETHBRIDGE DISCOVERED the occult late in life. Despite this, in the few years that he was able to put his mind to thinking about the subject, he managed to come up with some thought-provoking and coherent theories as to the mechanisms behind certain aspects of the paranormal. His interest was inspired and driven by experiments he undertook using a pendulum.

Lethbridge was born in 1901 and spent the majority of his life working as an academic archaeologist based at Cambridge University. His interest in the paranormal, although always there, only blossomed after he and his wife, Mina, retired to South Devon in 1957. Although he later philosophized on many aspects of the occult, his first experiences were with dowsing.

He had played around with pendulums during his archaeological career and had been convinced that there was more to it than just pure chance. He had previously been able to identify volcanic dikes on the Island of Lundy by using a water diviner's hazel twig. He had also seen pendulums used to identify the sex of fossil skulls and unborn babies. Always a keen thinker, he wondered whether the pendulum was worked by the human brain picking up electrical vibrations from objects and then translating them into subconscious muscle actions that would move the pendulum. This thought was not a new one, but Lethbridge took it a stage further and wondered if different lengths of pendulum could tune into the different 'wavelengths of vibration' given off by various objects.

To test this he attached a pendulum bob (weight) to a long length of string and wound it around a pencil. He held the pendulum above a pure silver dish and slowly unwound the string. At a length of 24 inches the pendulum started to react by swinging in a gentle circle. Wondering if this was the pendulum length for silver, he walked around his garden with the pendulum until it reacted as it had before. At this spot he carefully dug down but instead of finding silver he found a fragment of stoneware pottery which seemed to react to the same way. Aware that the pottery was probably lead-glazed, Lethbridge held the pendulum over a lump of lead and found that it reacted at the same length as the silver and pottery. He then wandered around his garden until the pendulum reacted again. Digging down, he found an old piece of window lead. It appeared that the pendulum length for silver and lead was the same. Lethbridge then set about testing everything he could conceivably get his hands on in order to find out their pendulum lengths. As a result of this he determined that, among other things, sulphur reacts at seven inches, silica at 14 inches, diamond at 24 inches, alcohol at 25½ inches and iron at 32 inches. He also discovered that it was possible to distinguish between objects that react to the same length by the number of times the pendulum swung in a circle: for example, lead swings 16 times, silver 22 times.

Something that puzzled Lethbridge was the fact that nothing would react below 40 inches for the first time, yet all the objects would react again at their normal length plus 40 inches: for example, silver reacts at 22 and 62 inches (40 + 22). Lethbridge later used this to speculate that the pendulum was reacting to similar objects in another dimension that existed on another vibration rate to ours. Lethbridge made another interesting discovery. While experimenting with his pendulum, he observed that as well as reacting to physical objects the pendulum seemed to react to emotions.

He discovered this by testing some ancient slingshot stones that were likely to have been used in battle. He found that they reacted at 24 and 40 inches. Assuming these were emotions, Lethbridge gathered some beach pebbles and tested them; they showed no reaction at all. He and his wife then hurled the stones against a wall and tested them again. This time his wife's stones reacted at 29 and 40 inches and his at 24 and 40 inches. He assumed that 40 inches was the length for anger and aggression, 24 inches for male qualities and 29 inches for female qualities. Further tests also suggested that 40 inches was the length for sleep and death, 27 for thought and 20 for life.

Lethbridge's experiments soon led him to think about other areas of the occult in which he was interested, particularly ghosts and hauntings. Throughout his life Lethbridge had had ghostly experiences, some of which he reflected upon while trying to find a common link between them. Some of his more bizarre encounters involved what he called 'ghouls', which he described as well-defined areas of unpleasantness attached to a location. To illustrate this, he recounted an incident that happened to him in 1924. While at a choristers' school in 1924, he encountered an area on some stairs that, when he entered it, produced an instant feeling of depression and sadness; this was the ghoul. He and a friend discovered that they could move the ghoul ahead of them by walking towards it. After experiencing other ghouls and seeing a ghost in a neighbour's garden, Lethbridge became convinced that it was possible for emotions to be recorded in objects in the same way that his stones had recorded his anger. He thought that this could be responsible for the phenomenon of psychometry (see Gerard Croiset, page 10) and some kinds of hauntings. He linked ghost apparitions with running water and became convinced that water was a good store of electrical and psychic energy. He also had some rather unusual theories, including the possibility that cats used their whiskers to 'dowse' for certain requirements: for example, the long whiskers reacted to sex, the small ones to food.

All these theories were put forward in a series of thought-provoking books, some of which are occult classics, including *Ghost and Ghoul* (1961), *Ghost and Divining Rod* (1963) and *ESP: Beyond Time and Distance* (1965). Unfortunately, Lethbridge was not physically fit and on 30 September 1970 he died of a heart attack, leaving an unrevised manuscript entitled *The Power of the Pendulum*. This was later published in 1976.

❖

Using a pendulum for dowsing is fairly straightforward, so it is one of the few areas of the occult that people can engage in with a degree of success. The movement of pendulums and divining rods can easily be explained by minute muscle movements. However, some of the results cannot be explained away so easily. To give a personal example, I used to ask my brother to throw a tennis ball into a field full of potato plants so that it could not be seen. I would not watch him throw the ball, but would walk along the side of the field until the divining rods I was using reacted. I would then walk along the nearest furrow into the field and, far more often than not, find the ball. I have also dowsed for other hidden objects with success, but must admit that I have not been able to replicate Lethbridge's pendulum-length experiments.

Lethbridge clearly took a scientific approach, but many of his theories have no real evidence to back them up. It is true that most people who believe in dowsing accept that the mind is probably responsible for subconsciously moving the divining tool. There is, however, no evidence that these reactions come from information stored within the mind, the object or some other unquantifiable area, such as Madame Blavaksky's Akasaic Record (see page 128). Using comparisons with psychometry, the evidence does suggest that the information is stored within the objects themselves. However, this leaves a number of unanswered problems. When a pendulum reacts to an impure object, what in the object is it reacting to? Is it reacting to the emotions of the last person to hold it or the blend of minerals/materials within it? Lethbridge managed to get a bottle of wine to react to the lengths for alcohol, paper and glass, but none of these are pure materials and the combination of all three would vary between bottles, so why would such objects have a specific length on the pendulum? Each object should act like a fingerprint, with its chemical make-up being almost unique, so it would appear to me that the pendulum is actually reacting to the mental definition of a bottle of wine rather than the physical properties of the bottle itself. This suggests that the mind is crucial in the location of such objects when using a pendulum. Most dowsers recommend that sustaining a mental image of an object greatly increases the chances of locating it.

It is worrying that the pendulum can be so sensitive to mental images. As such, it is possible that Lethbridge's pendulum confirmed his theories only after he had thought about them, suggesting that his results might simply have been a reflection of what was in his mind beforehand. In this case, anybody trying to repeat the experiments would have success if they believed in his theories or not if they did not.

Even allowing for the uncertainty about its workings, dowsing does appear to work and there has been some success in scientific experiments involving tracing the courses of underground caverns from above ground. Between 1987 and 1988 the German government funded research into dowsing, known as the Scheunen experiments, in which over 10,000 tests were conducted. The report on these tests concluded that a real dowsing phenomenon does exist and that certain individuals could produce extraordinary results. However, the scientist J. Enright re-evaluated the report and found no significant statistical results.

The greatest commercial application for dowsing has been in the field of water-divining. In these days of climate change, increased water consumption and intensive farming, water is a valuable commodity and finding it is big business.

Based on their ability to locate the position and direction of underground water streams, water-diviners claim to be able to pinpoint the best spots to sink boreholes. Their success rate is often remarkably high, even when compared with that of more conventional engineering firms. In 1993 the Channel Island of Jersey preferred to believe the word of a local water-diviner about the health of its water supply than the report of the three-year hydrogeological survey it had commissioned from the British Geological Survey (although this probably had more to do with the water-diviner's optimism about Jersey's water supply in comparison with the hydrogeological survey's rather pessimistic one).

In terms of hydrogeology it is easy to explain the high success rate of water-diviners. Water travels in sheets, sometimes miles wide, within rock types underground (not in thin 'streams', as is assumed), therefore drilling anywhere above a sheet of water will produce a strike.

It is not as easy to explain the success of those people who successfully divine for gold, minerals or, as in one recent American case, dead bodies.

Harry Houdini

❖

SCEPTIC AND DEBUNKER

HOUDINI IS STILL revered today as the greatest escapologist and conjuror of all time. Apart from his stage feats and publicity stunts, he also became notorious among the spiritualist movement for his consistent debunking of mediums. After his death some people speculated that he might have used dubious debunking methods and could even have been psychic himself.

Houdini was born on 6 April 1874 in Appleton, Wisconsin, as Ehrich Weiss, the son of Jewish Hungarian immigrants Dr Mayer Samuel and Cecilia Weiss. He was a lively and active child who was fascinated by conjuring from a very early age. He is reported to have mastered a number of tricks by the age of seven and was capable of picking all the locks in his house.

He continued to practise his conjuring and, aged 11, was allowed to perform in a travelling circus that was visiting town. As a teenager he did numerous odd jobs (including working for a locksmith), but still aspired to be a stage conjuror. He read a copy of the memoirs of the great French magician Robert-Houdin and became determined to better him. To this end he chose the stage name Harry Houdini and started to tour with an act he performed with a friend of his called Charles Hayman. In 1894 he married Bess Rahner and soon incorporated her into his act in place of Hayman.

Houdini developed an interest in escapology after reading a book entitled *Revelations of a Medium*, which detailed many of the parlour-room seance tricks. This book was such an embarrassment to mediums that they actually tried to buy up and destroy all copies, making it a collector's item today.

The couple travelled widely, performing false telepathy acts, escapology and conjuring tricks. Houdini's reputation grew and a series of well-timed publicity stunts drew him to the public's attention. By the turn of the twentieth century, he was well known and by the 1920s he was a household name for his escapalogical feats, having escaped from every attempt at confinement imaginable.

Houdini had been completely devoted to his mother and after her death he consulted a number of mediums in an attempt to speak to her again. After each seance, he came away unimpressed and grew very angry with the mediums he was visiting. Although his mother claimed to come through at a number of seances, she seemed to know only fairly obvious things about him. He was particularly unimpressed when, through one medium, his mother addressed him as 'Harry' – something she had never done in her life.

In 1920, during a tour of England, he finally got to meet one of his heroes, Sir Arthur Conan Doyle. The two became firm friends, although Doyle's fascination with Spiritualism and the occult was a matter of concern to Houdini.

Houdini and Doyle met up again in America, in Atlantic City, in June 1922. Here Houdini witnessed Lady Doyle, a noted medium, go into a trance and write him a highly emotional letter from his dead mother. Houdini was initially amazed, and even had some success when trying automatic writing for himself, but soon dismissed the communication as false. The Doyles were hurt by Houdini's attitude and a rift developed between them.

Houdini became fascinated with Spiritualism and began studying the methods many mediums used to fake their seances. Perhaps sensing the publicity value of the subject, he started to debunk mediums by the truckload. He was convinced that they were all frauds and that he could unmask every one of them. After visiting many seances, he began giving public demonstrations during which he would perform many of the supposedly 'unfakable' seance phenomena, including spirit manifestations, the production of ectoplasm and the unaided movement of objects. Very soon he was universally loathed by the entire spiritualist movement.

Houdini wrote a series of articles for the *Scientific American* magazine, the January 1923 issue of which offered $2,500 to anybody who could conclusively prove that they had mediumistic powers under scientific conditions. Houdini was to be part of the examining panel. A Boston housewife and medium, Mrs Mina Crandon (who would become famous as the medium known as 'Margery'), stepped forward and took up the challenge.

Houdini couldn't make the initial seances, when the panel consisted of Dr Daniel Comstock (a physicist), Dr William McDougall (a Harvard psychologist), Dr Walter Franklin Prince (a psychologist), Hereward Carrington (an eminent psychic researcher) and Malcolm Bird (assistant editor of the *Scientific American*). Houdini was shocked when, in June 1924, the panel announced that Mrs Crandon was genuine and said they were prepared to give her the money and publish an article to that effect in the July 1924 issue. He immediately travelled to Boston to witness a seance for himself.

What happened next is still a contentious issue. It is clear that Mrs Crandon and her husband did not trust Houdini at all and that Houdini was equally determined to prove her a fraud. He even said, 'I will forfeit a thousand dollars if I do not detect her if she resorts to trickery.'

During some initial seances, Houdini is alleged to have caught Mrs Crandon performing a number of tricks, including making noises with her feet, throwing objects herself and physically lifting tables rather than levitating them on their own. Despite privately claiming to have seen her cheating, Houdini did not publicly expose Mrs Crandon but curiously asked for a more stringent test to be performed. Rumours grew that she had defeated Houdini.

The following month Houdini placed Mrs Crandon inside a wooden box with a hole in the top for her head and holes in the side for her arms so that her hands could be held at all times. Mrs Crandon's spirit control, who was her dead brother Walter, had apparently taken quite a dislike to Houdini and after Mrs Crandon had been placed in the box, the lid was ripped off by an invisible force.

The seance was resumed the next night and Mrs Crandon was reinstalled in the box. She was asked by the committee to ring a bell placed inside a box. 'Walter' immediately accused Houdini of having tampered with the bell so that it couldn't ring. An examination of the bell revealed a piece of rubber wedged against the clapper to prevent it from ringing. Next Walter started screaming abuse at Houdini, saying that he had secretly hidden a ruler in the box with Mrs Crandon so that he could later accuse her of cheating. The ruler too was found and Houdini's assistant later admitted that Houdini had instructed him to place it there in case there was no other way of proving the medium fraudulent. There was no question that in this case it was Houdini who had been caught cheating and he was widely discredited for his ungentlemanly behaviour. An attempt was made at another seance but Houdini messed the committee around so much that the event was eventually cancelled. The committee was eventually split over whether Mrs Crandon was genuine and the money was therefore not awarded.

In common with many mediums of the day, Mrs Crandon was eventually caught cheating after a wax thumbprint attributed to her spirit guide was found to match that of her dentist. Significantly, the case of 'Margery' persuaded many psychic investigators to move away from the study of individual spiritualist mediums and into the more controlled conditions of the laboratory.

In 1924 Houdini published a book entitled *A Magician Among the Spirits*, which was largely based upon his debunking experiences during the early 1920s. As could have been anticipated, the book was gratefully received by sceptics and universally dismissed by spiritualists.

In the summer of 1926 Conan Doyle received a message at a seance that said, 'Houdini is doomed, doomed, doomed!' On 22 October a student tried to catch Houdini out on his claim that his stomach muscles could withstand any impact by thumping him when he wasn't expecting it. The blow caused Houdini's appendix to rupture and nine days later, on Hallowe'en 1926, he died.

In the years following his death, many claimed to have contacted his departed spirit, but Bess Houdini refused to believe any of them until she was contacted by a well-known spiritualist medium, Arthur Ford, in early January 1929. Ford claimed to have received a message from Houdini's mother and, after hearing it, Mrs Houdini was sufficiently impressed to attend a full seance a few days later.

At the seance Ford entered a trance and through his control contacted Houdini, who said, 'Rosabelle, answer, tell, pray, answer, look, tell, answer, answer, tell!' There was confusion until Mrs Houdini remembered that her wedding ring contained the inscription of a song that she and Houdini used to sing on stage. It went, 'Rosabelle, sweet Rosabelle, I love you more than I can tell. Over me you cast a spell, I love you my sweet Rosabelle.' Mrs Houdini was totally convinced, particularly when Ford's spirit control explained that Houdini was trying to reveal one of the secret passwords that the couple used in a false mind-reading act. The passwords were 'Rosabelle, believe'. Mrs Houdini was so convinced of the genuineness of the seance that she wrote to the newspapers about the affair. She was, however, to retract her testimonies a few years later when she found that the Rosabelle story was readily available at the time of the seance in a 1927 biography about her husband. Yet again another spiritualist victory had turned into defeat.

As well as Houdini's supposed appearances at seances, after his death rumours started to circulate implying that, while alive, he had used psychic powers to accomplish many of his seemingly impossible tricks.

During his life there had been some suggestion, probably secretly encouraged by Houdini to gain publicity, that he possessed supernatural powers. Hewart Mackenzie (in *Spirit Intercourse*, 1916) claimed to have 'felt' Houdini dematerialize from a padlocked, water-filled container and to have watched him walk on stage from elsewhere about 90 seconds later. Other stories about his supposed paranormal powers were more plausible. For example, while in Britain in the 1920s Houdini went to visit the grave of a magician friend of his, the Great Lafayette. After placing a vase of flowers on his grave, Houdini cried out, 'Lafayette! Give us a sign if you are here!' The pot promptly fell over. Houdini righted it, only to see it fall over again. He attributed the incident to the high winds that day.

Sir Arthur Conan Doyle was convinced that Houdini was a natural medium. In one book and a number of articles, he gave many examples of Houdini's apparent powers. A lot of these, in common with many rumours about Houdini, were based on stage stunts that were seemingly impossible, including remaining under water for over an hour, his one-to-one mind-reading and escapology feats. Doyle said that Houdini had confided to him that he had an 'inner voice' that would tell him when a stunt was safe to do and when it wasn't. A number of mediums who came into contact with him also reportedly felt that Houdini himself had hidden powers. If this was so, then his fanaticism for debunking mediums seems very odd indeed.

❖

Houdini's legend has been much added to since his death. It is likely that most of the talk about his psychic powers can be attributed to spiritualists eager to explain the actions of their arch enemy or to people unable to find the secrets behind many of his stunts. It might also have suited many spiritualists to try and make it appear that Houdini was in fact a rebellious member of their ranks who was trying to deny his own psychic identity by debunking other mediums. It is true that some of his finest stunts have never been repeated since, although this is probably due to his skill as a conjuror/escapologist rather than his psychic powers.

As for his reputation as a debunker of mediums, Houdini comes across as being less than perfect. It now seems to be unquestionable that Houdini was prepared to frame at least one medium (Mrs Crandon) in an effort to debunk her and keep his image intact. This demonstrates a degree of obsessional behaviour regarding his public reputation as the world's greatest escapologist and debunker of mediums. He did, after all, claim to be able to expose any medium as a fraud and was clearly prepared to do anything to uphold his reputation.

In Houdini's favour, it is also possible that Mrs Crandon fixed the bell herself to discredit him. Even so, the public confession from Houdini's assistant leaves little doubt about who planted the ruler in the box.

Fortunately for Houdini, the fact that he was caught cheating once has not been taken to mean that he had always cheated in his efforts to expose mediums. The reverse is true with mediums who have been caught cheating themselves, even if only once. Perhaps all of Houdini's past exposés should now be examined with caution. There is little doubt that he did genuinely find many fraudulent mediums, but we will never know if he ruined the careers of some by using fraudulent means himself.

Houdini illustrates one extreme of a problem that pervades and hampers psychic research: how to overcome the entrenched positions of sceptics and believers. It is hard to know which category of person is worse. A conversation with a sceptic can be a nightmare, because any personal experiences, evidence or theories are dismissed out of hand – often with poor explanations about hallucinations or people's gullibility. Total believers are equally bad. They too will not listen to reasonable evidence or discussion, but instead prefer to string together a number of different aspects of the paranormal to produce rather fantastic stories: for example, the linking of crop circles/cattle mutations/government secrecy to the UFO phenomenon. As with many subjects in the world today, including politics and certain fields of science, by and large the extreme points of view need to be ignored, for they rarely contribute much of use to the debate. Sadly, it is usually the extreme points of view within the paranormal that get the publicity today.

Harry Price

❖

GHOST-HUNTER

Aに THOUGH THE WORLD of the paranormal is accustomed to flamboyant and controversial psychics such as Daniel Dunglas Home, Uri Geller and Doris Stokes, the investigators of such matters are normally more down to earth. However, this was not the case with Harry Price. He was a highly charismatic figure whose energy and enthusiasm for the paranormal made him a minor household celebrity. Despite this, controversy still exists over the validity of many of his investigations and even about aspects of his life.

Harry Price was born in London on 17 January 1881. He was the son of a grocer and part-time travelling salesman. His interest in the paranormal began in 1889 when, aged eight, he saw a public performance by the stage magician the Great Sequah. From then on he practised stage magic himself and collected many manuals on conjuring. He claimed that his first psychic experience took place when he was 15. He and a friend locked themselves into a haunted house one night with an old-fashioned powder-flash camera. After hearing noises in an upstairs room, they set up the camera at the foot of the stairs. About an hour later they heard footsteps descending the staircase and fired the camera. When developed, the plate showed only an empty staircase.

After school, he spent a decade doing a whole variety of jobs, including such things as journalism and patenting medicines. In 1908 he met and married a wealthy Brockley heiress, Constance Mary Knight, and settled down to become a man of means. Always keenly interested in the occult, by the time he joined the Society for Psychical Research (SPR) in 1920 Price had already investigated a number of mediums and haunted houses. He was also an expert conjuror and soon made a name for himself by using this talent within the society to unmask fraudulent mediums – in line with the then sceptical mood of the SPR.

His first effort unmasked the spirit photographer William Hope, whose portraits of people would always include images of the sitter's dead relatives. Price was sent to investigate and published his findings in the 1922 SPR journal. He claimed that Hope had been placing pre-exposed plates into the camera before taking the photographs. It was later alleged that in fact Price, in his keenness to impress the SPR, had tampered with the plates. No satisfactory conclusion was ever reached regarding this.

In the spring of 1922 Price was asked to accompany E. J. Dingwall to Munich to witness the then famous medium brothers Willi and Rudi Schneider in the laboratory of Baron Albert von Schrenck-Notzing. Price was impressed enough with the demonstrations of psychical mediumship he saw to make a public statement to this effect. What he witnessed in Munich seems to have got him thinking about the possibility that not all mediums were frauds after all. Also, according to some sources, Price seems to have been impressed by the unabashed publicity-seeking methods of von Schrenck-Notzing and decided to follow his example in an attempt to make himself famous.

In 1923 Price was to find a medium of his own after talking to a shy young woman, Dorothy Stella Cranshaw, on a train. She claimed to have telekinetic powers and volunteered to be tested by Price. The first few seances were spectacular, with Cranshaw discovering that she had a control spirit, called Palma, who would communicate using raps and would also move objects, including on one occasion a heavy oak table. In front of various observers and under red-light conditions, Cranshaw could make caged musical instruments play and turn on switches which were placed inside a soap bubble.

Price set about trying to measure aspects of the seances scientifically. He did manage to record consistent temperature drops and experienced other phenomena that seem to have finally convinced him of the reality of at least some psychic activity. From this time on he devoted much more energy to pursuing genuine phenomena rather than debunking mediums. This immediately put him at odds with the SPR and their relationship from then on became very strained indeed.

Dorothy Cranshaw (or Stella C., as she is referred to in much of Price's published work) refused to do seances after autumn 1923 and her powers faded soon after her marriage in 1928.

After problems with the SPR, Price formed his own National Laboratory for Psychical Research, which, although initially set up in 1923, did not really get under way until 1926. Its location in the London Spiritualist Alliance was the final outrage to the SPR, which returned Price's previously donated collection of books in 1927. From 1925 to 1931 he was also the foreign research officer for the American Society for Psychical Research.

In April 1926 he came across an amazing 13-year-old Romanian peasant girl, Eleonora Zugun, who was experiencing terrible poltergeist phenomena, including flying objects, slapping, biting and pinching, apports and disappearances and even communication through speech. The girl had been rescued from a lunatic asylum (where she had been placed for being a witch) by a psychical investigator and met Price in Vienna. Price returned with Zugun to London and began a series of laboratory tests which were only partially successful. However, he appeared to have more success when he again tested the younger Schneider brother, Rudi, whom he invited to the laboratory to be studied in 1929. In front of many distinguished witnesses, including committee members of the SPR and noted scientists, Rudi produced many different types of anomalous phenomena, such as violent rappings, the materialization of limbs and moving objects. The experiments took place under very strict conditions: for example, Price made all the sitters at a seance wear electrified gloves so that anybody breaking hand contact would light a bulb. Witnesses still reported the movement and levitation of objects. Price seems to have been initially impressed with all these results and tested Rudi in 1929, 1930 and 1932.

However, in April 1932, Price discovered that one of the SPR committee, Lord Charles Hope, was also running tests on Rudi. This seems to have enraged him and, just before the Hope report was due to be published, Price declared that he had found Rudi cheating and produced some rather dubious photographs to prove it. This statement almost certainly seems to have been made out of malice towards Lord Hope, whose report was in favour of Rudi. It is still widely believed that Price faked the photographs and that Rudi Schneider could have been a genuine physical medium. It is certainly true that in the months before his 'unmasking', Price built up Rudi's public image and stature by allowing many friends and colleagues to devote their time, money and reputations to testing him. In the world of science, a person's reputation needs to be doubted only once to call into question everything that they have achieved, and people on both sides of the paranormal camp were starting to doubt Price.

To add to this doubt, Price's publicity-seeking antics led him to travel to Germany to test a spell that could apparently convert a mountain goat into a man. The spell failed and Price was the subject of much public ridicule for the escapade. He also participated in the enigmatic case of Gef the Talking Mongoose (see page 16) and although it is possible that 'Gef' was in fact a poltergeist, the idea seemed humorous to the public, so his involvement did nothing to further his image as a paranormal investigator. He did, however, also make some serious contributions at this time, including, in 1933, persuading the University of London to open a library and set up a University Council for Psychical Investigation. The library still exists in the university's Senate House building and consists largely of Price's enormous collection.

From 1929 onwards Price became increasingly involved in a case that would gradually take over his life and for which he would become most famous. It involved a rather ordinary but gloomy Essex building called Borley Rectory. The case came to light when the *Daily Mirror* carried a story about a phantom nun there in June 1929. Asked by the newspaper to investigate, Price arrived at the rectory on 12 June. He was told of a number of different types of ghostly phenomena that had recently occurred there, including footsteps, lights, the phantom nun, the ghost of the rectory's founder, Henry Bull, and ghostly whispers. Price claimed to have witnessed many of these phenomena and also wrote of seeing objects move, hearing bells and hearing rapping noises during a seance there. The residents of Borley Rectory, the Smiths, moved out on 15 July 1930 and were replaced by the Reverend Lionel Foyster and his wife, Marianne, on 16 October of that year. Their arrival saw a massive increase in the intensity of the activity.

Many of the phenomena were typical of a poltergeist case, and it seems that Marianne may have been the focus of much of the activity. Foyster kept a diary of the happenings, some which were actually becoming quite violent and malicious. Others were more mysterious, such as the scrawling of messages addressed to Marianne on the corridor walls. Not surprisingly, the Foysters were not overly fond of Borley and left in 1935.

As the building was now empty, Price moved in with 40 recruited investigators and much scientific equipment. Between 1935 and 1939 he documented a wide range of phenomena but it was the communications that he undertook with the poltergeist that are most interesting. One message, on 27 March 1938, stated that the building would be destroyed by fire that night. It in fact burned to the ground in February 1939. Another communication advised that the phantom nun had been strangled in 1667 and her remains were buried in the cellar. Price dug in the cellar in August 1943 and did indeed find fragments of a human skull.

Price wrote up the Borley investigations in two books entitled *The Most Haunted House in England* (1940) and *The End of Borley Rectory* (1946). These were very popular and were hailed either as a landmark in psychic investigation or as works of sheer fantasy. It does seem that Price's investigation methods were not as thorough and precise as he would have us believe. Some of his original investigators have been less than complimentary about his operational procedures, but it was not until after his death, on 29 March 1948, that the real slurs against his character started.

The first major blow came with the publication of 'The Haunting of Borley Rectory', written by three leading members of the SPR. This report accused Price of shoddy investigation techniques and even of causing some of the phenomena himself. It concluded, perhaps not unusually for the SPR, that no psychic phenomena had ever occurred at Borley Rectory.

The final blow to his reputation came with the well-researched biography *In Search of Harry Price*, written in 1978 by Trevor Hall. This book found that Price had lied about his origins, having claimed to be born in Shrewsbury as a member of the establishment. It also revealed his appetite for fame. Apparently one of his ambitions was to be listed in *Who's Who* – something he did achieve.

❖

So what are we to make of Harry Price? His reputation is now in shreds and it is difficult to know whether to take his research efforts seriously or not. There is no doubt that he did cheat in some of his investigations, but we also know that many of his early studies of psychical mediums were corroborated by other investigators at the time. There is some doubt concerning his judgement of Rudi Schneider as a fake and, perhaps, many aspects of the Borley case.

Perhaps his greatest contribution was the accessibility he brought to paranormal research. He seemed, for a while, to have given the public a human face in an area of research traditionally associated with hard-headed sceptics and gullible spiritualists. In attempting to unravel some of the enigmas of the paranormal, though, he ended up creating an enigma about himself and his research.

BIBLIOGRAPHY

Adare, Lord *Experiences with D. D. Home* (Routledge and Sons; London, 1869).

Baigent, M., Leigh, R. and Lincoln, H. *The Holy Blood and the Holy Grail* (Corgi; London, 1982).

— *The Messianic Legacy* (Corgi; London, 1986).

Barrett, Sir William, *Psychical Research* (Home University Library Series; London, 1911).

Blackmore, S. *Beyond the Body* (Paladin; London, 1982).

Crowe, C. *The Night Side of Nature* (Routledge and Sons; London, 1848).

Crowley, A. *Magical and Philosophical Commentaries on the Book of Law* (93 Publishing; Canada, 1974)

Cummins, G. *The Fate of Colonel Fawcett* (Aquarius Press; London, 1955).

Doyle, C. *The Coming of the Fairies* (Samuel Weiser; New York, 1921).

Dunne, J. *An Experiment with Time* (Faber Books; London, 1927).

Edge, H., Morris, R., Palmer, J. and Rush, J. *Foundations of Parapsychology* (Routledge and Kegan Paul; London, 1986).

Eisenbud, J. *The World of Ted Serios* (Paperback Library; New York, 1969).

Fortean Times, magazine (John Brown)

Godley, J. *Dreams of Winners*. (Journal of the Society for Psychical Research; London, June 1947).

Grant, J. and Kelsey, D. *Many Lifetimes* (Corgi; London, 1969).

Gregory, A. *Anatomy of a Fraud* (Annals of Science; Issue 34,1977).

Haining, P. *The Legend and Bizarre Crimes of Spring Heeled Jack* (Frederick Muller; London, 1977).

Home, D. D. *Lights and Shadows of Spiritualism* (Routledge and Sons; London, 1877).

Houdini, H. *A Magician amongst the Spirits* (Arnos Press; New York, 1972).

Ingilis, B. *Natural and Supernatural* (Prism Unity; London, 1977).

— *The Paranormal* (Paladin; London, 1986).

Lethbridge, T. *The Power of the Pendulum* (Routledge and Kegan Paul Ltd.; London, 1976).

Lodge, O. *Survival of Man* (Methuen and Co.; London, 1909).

Machen, A. *The Bowmen and other Legends of War* (Simpkin, Marshall, Hamilton, Kent and Co.; London, 1915).

Mercer, J. *Alchemy* (London, 1921).

Monroe, R. *Journeys Out of the Body* (Doubleday; New York, 1971).

Moore, S. (Editor) *Fortean Studies 1-3* (John Brown; London, 1993-96).

Muldoon, S. and Carrington, H. *The Projection of the Astral Body* (Riding and Co.; London, 1929).

Myers, F. *Human Personality and its Survival of Bodily Death* (Arnos Press; London, 1975).

Myers, F., Gurney, E. and Podmore, F. *Phantasms of the Living* (Trubner and Co.; London, 1886).

Owen, I. *Conjuring up Philip* (Harper and Row; New York, 1976).

Owen, R. *Footfalls on the Boundary of Another World* (Trubner and Co.; London, 1861).

Playfair, G. *This House is Haunted!* (Souvenir Press; London, 1980).

Pollack, J. *Croiset the Clairvoyant* (Doubleday; New York, 1964).

Price, H. *Fifty Years of Psychical Research* (Longmans, Green and Co.; London, 1939).

Prince, M. *The Dissociation of A Personality. A Biographical Study in Abnormal Psychology* (Longmans, Green and Co.; London, 1905).

Randi, J. *The Supernatural A-Z* (Headline; London, 1995).

Steiner, R. *Reincarnation and Immortality* (Rudolf Steiner Publications; New York, 1970).

Stevenson, I. *Twenty Cases Suggestive of Reincarnation* (American Society for Psychical Research; New York, 1966).

Swedenborg, E. *Divine Providence* (The Swedenborg Foundation; New York, 1976).

The Unexplained, part-work (Orbis; London, 1981)

Wilson, C. *The Occult* (Granada; London, 1973).

— *Mysteries* (Granada; London, 1978).

— *Poltergeist - A study of destructive haunting* (New English Library; London, 1981).

— *Afterlife* (Grafton; London, 1987).

White, T. *The Sceptical Occultist* (Century; London, 1994).

Zohar, D. *Through the Time Barrier* (Paladin; London, 1983).

INDEX